THE DIASPORA SPICE Co. COOKBOOK

SEASONAL HOME COOKING FROM
SOUTH ASIA'S BEST SPICE FARMS

SANA JAVERI KADRI & ASHA LOUPY

PHOTOGRAPHS BY MELATI CITRAWIREJA
ILLUSTRATIONS BY ALEESHA NANDHRA

HARVEST
An Imprint of WILLIAM MORROW

To the thirty-five incredible women across India and Sri Lanka who patiently and generously shared hundreds of heirloom family recipes with us. Women's work in the kitchen, especially in South Asia, is rarely validated, compensated, or studied with the gravitas and adoration that it deserves. May we change that forever.

Contents

Introduction vii

Pantry 1

Spice Blends 21

Chutneys and Pickles 35

Snacks 57

Veggies 73

Beans and Lentils 107

From the Sea 131

From the Land 149

Rice, Breads, and Scoopers 177

Drinks 209

Desserts 229

Acknowledgments 247
Universal Conversion Chart 250
Index 251

Introduction

As a modern-day spice trader trying to build a business deeply rooted in equity and culture, I'm often confronted with the reality that folks don't know that the original intent of colonization of South Asia was the domination of the spice trade. Most folks don't realize that the spices in our cabinets have shaped and grown empires, and that our understanding of these spices and how to use them has largely been molded by those who knew the least about them!

The colonial history of the spice trade means that when we think of cardamom, we might think of a Scandinavian cardamom bun, but not Chachu Lukose's delicately seasoned white fish curry from the cardamom hills of Kerala (Meen Moilee, page 138). Or, when we think of pepper, we naturally jump to steak au poivre or cacio e pepe, but not Shirley Parameswaran's Kodava pork curry (Pepper Pork, page 154) from the Coorgi hills, where pepper has grown wild and abundantly for thousands of years.

The British, Dutch, and Portuguese colonizations of India, Pakistan, and Sri Lanka robbed South Asia of a cumulative $50 trillion (!!) over the course of two centuries. The economic impacts of colonialism were and are devastating, but in my line of work, I'm reminded every day just how much colonization also deprived the region culturally and culinarily. The aim of this cookbook is to reveal the depth and complexity of South Asian cuisine, and perhaps for the first time in recent history, to center South Asia in our understanding of how to cook with spices.

Diaspora Spice Co. was born from the longing for flavors of home in their full force, for culinary storytelling that embraces nuance, gristle, and hard truths. We persist now to carve out a piece of the world where our stories of migration, freedom, belonging, and home can finally stretch out and take a deep breath.

The greatest joy of my job is harvest season. Getting to spend the weeks from January through March visiting the fields, the homes, and, most importantly, the kitchens of Diaspora Spice Co.'s growing roster of farm partners, is pure delight for my cook's heart and perpetually eager stomach. After each visit, I leave with a newfound appreciation for the labor and rigor that goes into growing and processing spices and come home energized to recreate the fresh, bright, and beautiful meals I ate in each farm kitchen.

I will always remember visiting our Byadgi Chilli farm partner, Malleshappa Bisirotti, in the black earth plains of Hiregunjal, Karnataka, in 2019—his wife unwrapping a tiffin lunch for us on a cotton sheet in the middle of their field under the shade of a banyan tree, surrounded by ripening chilli plants and the drying millet harvest. She'd made a chutney of wild tomatoes, chilli, and coconut, to be scooped up with light millet rotis dripping with hot ghee (clarified butter). For dessert, she'd ground sesame seeds with jaggery and stuffed the sweet paste into small, thick parathas. And, finally, she'd picked fresh guavas and sprinkled them with their Byadgi chillies and salt. Every single ingredient in our meal was grown and processed on the farm. It was a simple, affordable meal made with beautiful ingredients, and it gave me context for the flavors the Byadgi chillies were grown to be paired with. It was then that I first started to piece together the idea for this cookbook that would take another six years and over forty collaborators to bring to life.

The shape of what would become this book grew little by little with each spice harvest as I ate my breakfast of silky cardamom-and-pepper-laced coconut stew with steamed string hoppers (page 198) in the rainy hills of Kerala during the Aranya Black Pepper harvest. As I had my first sip of saffron and licorice kehwa (page 218) in snowy Pampore, Kashmir, curled up next to the coal-powered samovar in our saffron farm partner's home. As I went foraging for fiddlehead ferns and nettles to turn into a simple Himalayan spring dinner with Amitha, one of our Pahadi Pink Garlic partners high up in the Tons Valley.

But the project really only came into sharp focus when I met Asha. If you are already a Diaspora customer, you know Asha's cooking and gentle, guiding voice well—her gift for developing highly cookable, big flavor recipes has become the backbone of how we connect with our global community of home cooks. I'm incredibly lucky that she's been our recipe developer for five years and counting, and even luckier that she agreed to write this book with me.

Between October 2023 and March 2024, Asha and I, along with our long-time photographer, Melati, spent nearly four months crisscrossing the subcontinent, compiling over 175 recipes from twenty-two of our spice farm partners. Then, we tasted and tested—and re-tested!—in our Berkeley test kitchen until we landed on eighty-five regional, highly cookable, incredibly delicious recipes spanning ten states across India and Sri Lanka. The recipes that lie ahead are our California-ish adaptations of the family heirlooms of thirty-five women from Kandy to Kotgaon, from Ukhrul to Udumbanchola.

Our hope is for this book to act as an accessible introduction and a highly personal guide to cooking with spices and incorporating South Asian techniques and flavors into your home cooking. It is in no way exhaustive or definitive, but we're hoping to bring the sunshine, the forest canopy, the sizzle of curry leaves in coconut oil, the mouth-puckering tang of tamarind, and the incredible hospitality of our spice farm partners into your kitchens, one satisfying, seasonal recipe at a time.

While Diaspora Spice Co. is an Indian incorporated business, and I was born and raised in Mumbai, it's been uncomfortable and important to name that in certain places where we work, we're the occupiers. We work in several regions where I can relate easily to our partners, often speaking the same language as them, where our ancestors might have shared the same struggles. But in regions like Kashmir and Manipur—heavily militarized areas where the Indian government has systematically stripped indigenous populations of their rights—it makes sense that these communities would be mistrustful of an outsider like me. I keep coming back to this quote from my friend and art historian Donna Honarpisheh: "To promote ethical consumption while showing a gaping neglect towards geopolitics is failing to grapple with the very real consequences that these politics have towards economically crippling or nurturing a region." So, no matter how trendy our packaging, or how sexy our sourcing trips look, I find myself constantly asking: Does our work perpetuate erasure of culture and cuisine, or does it hold the promise of undoing some of that harm? It's a simple enough litmus test, and one that constantly drives me to refine, and course correct, our mission. We've been lucky to work with incredible partners in both Kashmir and Manipur, folks whose trust I feel lucky to have won over years of collaboration, and it's their lead we follow in the stories we tell in this book and, ultimately, in the spices we sell.

With this cookbook, we are sharing the culinary heirlooms of our farm partner families, and it is our job to act as equitable translators. The soft wizardry of developing a dish with the bits and bobs left over in a kitchen, feeding a family every day, teaching the next generation how something should taste—in our patriarchal capitalist world, this is considered women's work and is routinely devalued. So, the very first line item in our budget was to pay every single one of our contributors, all women, as close to US recipe development rates as possible. We paid the women directly to ensure they had agency over the money. The compensation sparked many complicated and meaningful conversations about what their knowledge and experience is truly worth—as you can imagine, far more than they'd been led to believe.

On the surface, we just sell spices, and this book is just some recipes, but if you look closely, it's always been so much more than that. Through this book, and in our everyday life of building Diaspora Spice Co., we will continue to take difficult positions that are rooted in our core values of equity, community, and queerness. Please know that it comes from a place of wild hope. It is borne out of a radically tender desire for everyone to be truly okay and for our community of kindred spirits to grow. We will continue to expand this circle of care, so that the number of people for whom integrity, accountability, and deliciousness matter can vastly outweigh those for whom it does not. I don't have all the answers, but I am so thankful for the privilege of telling this story. Thank you for letting us bring you these spices and recipes from South Asia's best farms. It is the honor of my every day.

With love and in community,

Sana Javeri Kadri
CEO and founder, Diaspora Spice Co.

Pantry

For both Asha and me, our pantries are a glorious mix of South Asian and California-inspired ingredients, all in service of making fresh, seasonal home cooking the most delicious it can be. Obviously, the backbone of our larder is spices (duh!), so that's where we'll begin, but it also relies heavily on varying levels of heat and smokiness via chillies, using different fats for flavor, leaning on a full spectrum of sour things from tamarind to sumac for brightness and layered acid, and, as always, hella fresh and dried herbs.

We tried to keep as many of these recipes as accessible as possible by using ingredients you can find in your local grocery store, but until the big grocery chains can catch up to the life-changing flavor of tamarind paste or short-grain jeera samba rice, you might need to make a trip to your local South Asian grocery store for things like split white urad dal or banana leaves! My other rec would be finding good organic online purveyors (we do our best to provide substitutions throughout the book, if applicable) that will deliver straight to your doorstep and save you a trip.

Spices

GROUND TURMERIC
One of the most popular rhizomes for cooking, after its friend ginger, turmeric is a staple in masala dabbas across the majority of our farm partners. You can find turmeric both fresh and dried or ground, but the latter is the spice used most prevalently in this book. Good turmeric isn't just for its bold color; it has a bright, sunshine-y flavor that marries rich earthiness with vibrant notes of citrus and marigolds.

CORIANDER SEEDS
These seeds from the cilantro plant are another integral part of masala dabbas across South Asia, spanning different states and regions. They have a floral, lemony flavor and a subtle sweet nuttiness. They can be ground and added to dishes, or left whole or lightly crushed and toasted or bloomed in a tadka for both flavor and texture.

CUMIN SEEDS
Part of the Apiaceae family—which also includes parsley, celery, and carrots—cumin seeds may be tiny in size, but they are big on earthy, savory flavor with a heady aroma. Like coriander, cumin seeds can also be ground or used whole. In this book, you'll find these seeds in recipes from a variety of regions, from the Kandyan Forest in Sri Lanka to Andhra Pradesh to Rajasthan.

FENNEL SEEDS
We're quite picky when it comes to fennel seeds (it took years to find the perfect ones for Diaspora Spice Co.!). The ideal fennel seed is plump, sweet, and fragrant, with a round anise flavor. Fennel is featured prominently in a lot of recipes from Kerala but also used in other regions we visited like Gujarat, Rajasthan, and Kashmir, and is a key ingredient in Sri Lankan roasted curry powder.

MUSTARD SEEDS
There are a couple of different types of mustard seeds that you'll find in the supermarket: yellow, brown, and black. The level of heat depends on the type of mustard seed, with yellow being on the milder end and black being on the punchier, spicier end of the spectrum. The latter are the ones found in South Asian cooking. These powerful little seeds are activated when bloomed in fat, becoming even more pungent and nutty. If you can't find black mustard seeds, you can substitute brown mustard seeds.

BLACK PEPPER
Poor black pepper has gotten such a bad rep thanks to the dusty pre-ground stuff, but good black pepper—bright, fruity, punchy, floral!—is such a revelation. Ours is a blend of a couple different pepper varieties indigenous to Kerala, which bring even more depth and potency to this everyday spice. Like all spices, essential oils are where the flavor is, so skip the powdered stuff and always go for whole peppercorns.

CARDAMOM
There are two types of cardamom: green and black. Both are intensely aromatic and essential to many dishes in this book, but each has its own flavor profile. Green cardamom, which is harvested on the younger side, is herbal, bright, and lemony with notes of eucalyptus. Black cardamom—a different plant from green—is left to mature on the plant, then dried near wood fires, giving it a deeper, earthier flavor with a subtle smokiness and round menthol taste. Each is unique in flavor, so one cannot be substituted for the other!

Spices Dos & Don'ts

Spices are flavor—tiny, potent vessels of volatile oils locked inside seeds, roots, and fruits. If this book could leave you with one truth, it's this: *Your cooking will taste noticeably better with higher quality spices.* So, here's your spice 101 from your friendly neighborhood spice dealer:

1. Fresh Spices Change Everything

Most grocery store spices are *five to seven years old* by the time they hit your kitchen, and they'll likely sit in your pantry for at least a few years more. Even the supposedly better organic stuff is usually blended from multiple sources with zero traceability. It's like settling for a $5, hangover-inducing red wine when, for not much more, you could have a glass of juicy, single-origin natural wine. You *will* taste the difference. So, if you're buying spices, buy fresh and buy well, whether it's from us or another source that prioritizes quality.

2. Fat and Heat Unlock Flavor

Freshly dried spices are bursting with flavorful, volatile oils, ready to infuse your food. But to unlock them, you need *fat* and *heat*. Sizzle cumin seeds in oil before adding vegetables, toast whole spices before grinding 'em into a podi, or bloom turmeric in ghee for a golden hit of flavor. Sprinkle raw spices on top of your food? No. Heat awakens them.

3. Whole Spices > Pre-Ground

Turmeric and ginger are the exceptions—they hold on to their oils even when powdered—but for everything else, whole spices reign supreme. Pre-ground spices lose their volatile oils within days, if not hours. Grinding fresh peppercorns or nutmeg might seem like a small detail, but it's one that transforms your cooking from *fine* to *flavorful as hell*.

4. Small Batches, No Hoarding

Unless you're cooking for twenty-plus people daily, you don't need a Costco-sized bag of cinnamon. Buy what you'll use in three to four months and replenish. Small quantities keep your spices—and your food—fresh and delicious.

5. Even Dried Herbs Can Surprise You

Ever seen that internet meme about how no one knows what bay leaves are for? The truth is, the bay leaves you've been using probably *smell like nothing*. A freshly dried bay leaf—or its cousin, tejpatta, a cinnamon leaf used across India—smells piney, herbal, and unmistakable when gently bent or torn. Proof that dried herbs *can* still hold their oils when sourced well.

6. Toast, Sizzle, Simmer–and Layer

Spices can be used like the base and top notes of a perfume: opening to your senses in stages. Start by *toasting* whole spices or *blooming* ground spices in fat to unlock their deep, savory base notes, and let them simmer into your stews or curries. Then, finish with a final flourish—Microplane nutmeg onto mashed potatoes, crack black pepper on pasta, or sprinkle toasted cumin seeds over yogurt—so the brighter, aromatic top notes can sing. By layering your spices, you can create a fuller, more intentional experience with every bite.

WHOLE CLOVES

Cloves are the aromatic flower buds of the clove tree, which need to be harvested before blooming. They have a deep, fragrant warmth and delicate menthol quality. Cloves are often associated with holiday baking but are used in a variety of dishes in South Asian cooking, both sweet and savory, like biryani, dal, and Sri Lankan date cake.

CINNAMON

There are two main categories of cinnamon that you'll find readily available: *Cinnamomum verum* (referred to as "Ceylon" or "True Cinnamon" on some packaging) and cassia. The latter is what is probably in the jars on most standard supermarket shelves, but it's worth seeking out the former for its deep, layered cinnamon flavor. Our ground cinnamon, Peni Miris, is a blend from both younger and older verum trees, which creates a powder with the perfect balance of sweet and spicy (*peni*, meaning "honey" and *miris*, meaning "spicy"). You'll also find whole cinnamon quills (or sticks) used in this book, so if you can find cinnamon verum sticks, the flavor payoff will be well worth it!

TEJPATTA LEAVES

While tejpatta are often referred to as "Indian bay leaves," these fragrant leaves aren't the same as the bay laurel leaves you'll find in the spice aisle at larger grocery stores. Tejpatta are from

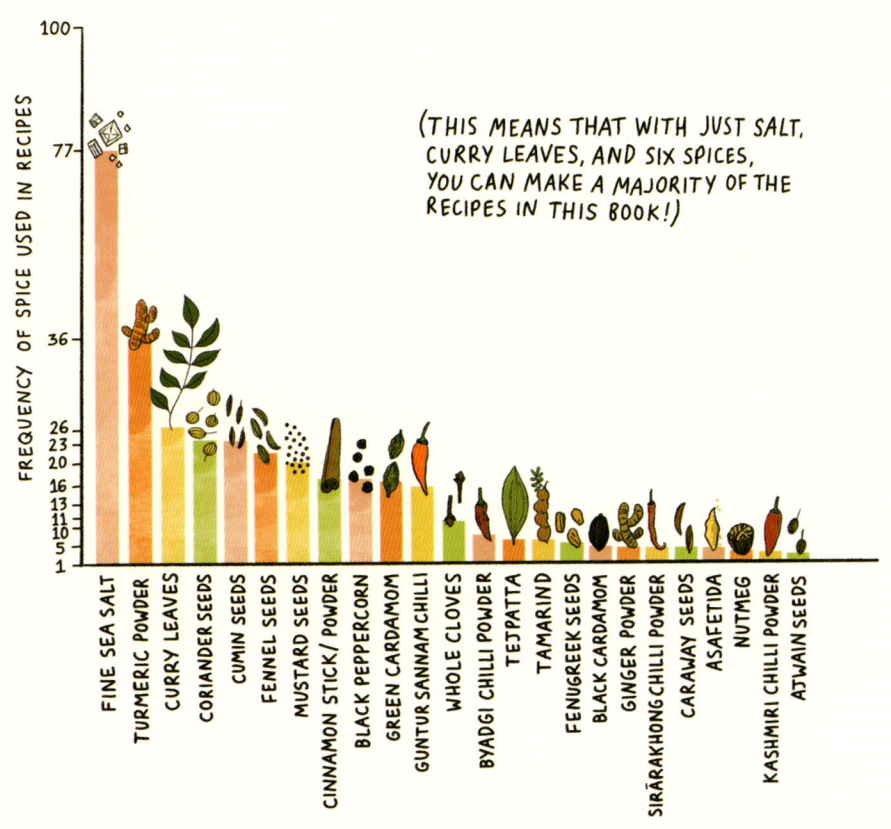

Building Your Masala Dabba

When I left India to finish high school abroad, I couldn't cook to save my life. Still, one of the things my mother packed into my boarding school trunk was a masala dabba: a cheap, stainless steel box stocked with the seven core spices of my mostly Gujarati upbringing: turmeric, cumin, coriander, red chilli powder, salt, mustard seeds, and a little vial of hing (asafetida).

I had no idea what I was doing with that first dabba, but I used it relentlessly, desperate to recreate the familiar flavors of home. Over six years, through bouts of homesickness and sheer trial and error, that masala dabba taught me how to feed myself. Corny as it sounds, it really was more than a box of spice; it was a connection to my family and to flavors I didn't yet know how to wield but loved so fiercely.

Years later, I was gifted my nani's engraved brass masala dabba—the family heirloom that still matters most to me. My nani fondly recalled buying it as a newlywed, a young gynecologist starting her married life in Mumbai. She had her new name, "Dr. Sumitra Javeri," engraved into the side in wobbly Gujarati script, and nearly seventy years later, I cherish that scrawled engraving.

So, What Is a Masala Dabba?

At first glance, a masala dabba is just a round container, usually made from stainless steel, holding seven smaller tins filled with spices. But it really is *so much more* than that. It's a handy tool to make your cooking easier and more intuitive.

Imagine you're making dal: instead of fumbling around the pantry, unscrewing jars, and cursing as you spill cumin all over the counter, you just *pop* open your masala dabba. There, laid out like a palette, are the spices you reach for most often. In seconds, you're heating oil, adding your spices in perfect order, and *boom*—flavor magic.

Think of it as your flavor *toolbox*, perfectly tailored and adaptable to the way *you* cook and holding the spices that *you* use most often—be it everything bagel seasoning or a podi. It's also a visual cue—seeing a rainbow of vibrant seeds and powders every time you cook keeps your ingredients in rotation—no more forgotten chilli powder shoved to the back of the pantry!

the *Cinnamomum tamala* tree that is indigenous to India, Nepal, and China. It brings a gentle, sweet warmth and more floral flavor that really can't be replicated, but in a pinch, you could use a regular ol' bay leaf plus a ½-inch piece of cinnamon stick or omit the tejpatta completely.

FENUGREEK SEEDS

Different from kasuri methi, or fenugreek leaves, fenugreek (or methi) seeds are beloved across many regions of South Asia for their pleasing sweet bitterness and maple-like flavor. They're used in fish curries, masalas, and even roasted to make a Gujarati coffee substitute (page 216). They are popular in Eritrean and Ethiopian cooking, so you may also find them in East African grocery stores.

SAFFRON

One of the most expensive spices in the world (it's said to cost more per pound than gold!), saffron is a prized ingredient in many South Asian kitchens, especially in Kashmir, where our saffron is grown. Each thread is one stamen of the purple crocus flower, which is hand plucked before careful processing to retain as much essential oil as possible. When bloomed in a liquid or fat, it imparts not only a golden hue, but also a fragrant, floral flavor that is unmatched.

ASAFETIDA

Asafetida, aka *hing* in Hindi, is the dried and ground gum resin from the ferula plant. Big, funky, and rich in allium-like flavor, there are two types of asafetida: whole or pure and compounded. Whole hing—which is what we use in this book—isn't cut with anything, so it's very potent (a little goes a long way!). Compounded, which is more readily available, is blended with rice flour and gum arabic, taming its wildness a touch. Our go-to is Pure Indian Foods Best Hing Ever. If you're using a brand that blends with rice or other flours, you may need to use a little extra than what the recipe calls for.

NUTMEG

Just like black pepper, whole nutmeg versus the pre-powdered stuff is like night and day. Our Anamalai Nutmeg, sourced from Tamil Nadu, is sold with its outer shell intact to preserve its essential oils. Use the side of a knife, rolling pin, or meat mallet to gently crack and remove the outer shell. Then, use a Microplane to finely grate the nutmeg for whatever recipe you're cooking.

A Saffron Farmer's Guide to Real Saffron

1. The Bleed Test

Place a strand in warm water or milk. Genuine saffron will release a deep golden hue slowly, while maintaining its structure. Adulterated saffron will bleed color immediately and may disintegrate.

2. Visual Inspection

Look for dark red stigmas with a satin-like finish—slightly glossy but not overly shiny. Fresh, hand-processed saffron feels slightly oily to the touch, while older or machine-processed saffron will appear dry and brittle.

3. Weight and Oiliness

Genuine strands are thicker and denser. For the same weight, Kashmiri saffron will have fewer threads than its counterparts due to its higher oil content.

Fats

COCONUT OIL
Coconut oil is used in many regions across South India and Sri Lanka. Use virgin or unrefined coconut oil—the first pressing and ideally cold-pressed—which actually tastes like coconut and imparts that flavor into the final dish. Skip anything labeled as "refined"—these types of coconut oil are second and third pressings; use heat, chemicals, and additives to extract the oil; and generally lack coconut flavor altogether.

EXTRA VIRGIN OLIVE OIL
While extra virgin olive oil wasn't an oil we found in any of the households we visited, it's essential to our California pantries. Just like spices, harvest dates are important—olives are harvested and crushed in October and November in the Northern Hemisphere, so look on the label for a harvest date of the most recent fall. For this book, we recommend a medium-bodied oil that can be used for both cooking and finishing, like Arbequina Extra Virgin Olive Oil from Séka Hills, made by the Yocha Dehe Wintun Nation in California.

GHEE
If there was an ingredient that was the definition of liquid gold, it would be ghee—a clarified butter that is essential to dishes across South Asia. You can make your own ghee, or there are also great store-bought options, like Ancient Organics and Pure Indian Foods. To make ghee, butter is slowly cooked until the milk solids separate and are just starting to caramelize (not as far as brown butter, though). Then, the toasted solids are strained out, leaving golden butterfat goodness, packed with nutty, almost butterscotch-y flavor. And, because the milk solids have been removed, ghee has a higher smoke point and can be used in high-heat cooking.

MUSTARD SEED OIL
Punchy with a horseradish-y heat, this oil—extracted from mustard seeds—is favored in kitchens across regions in North India, like Uttarakhand and Rajasthan, as well as Kashmir, Bangladesh, and Pakistan. In the United States, the sale of mustard seed oil for edible purposes is severely limited. But our go-to is Yandilla Mustard Seed Oil, which is one of the only US FDA-approved oils of its type. This Australian, cold-pressed mustard oil is made with mustard seeds that have been bred to reduce their levels of erucic acid while preserving the overall vibrant, wasabi-like taste. You can find this oil online and in some specialty stores.

UNTOASTED SESAME OIL
When you say sesame oil in America, most cooks' minds immediately go to dark, deeply nutty roasted sesame oil. But, across South Asia, sesame oil generally refers to untoasted sesame oil. Also known as gingelly oil, this oil is the neutral oil of choice in many of the kitchens we visited. Made from raw, cold-pressed sesame seeds, it's mild with the tiniest whisper of nuttiness that doesn't infringe on other flavors. You can find this in most supermarkets and in South Asian grocery stores (just make sure the label says "untoasted"). Outside of untoasted sesame, our go-to neutral oil is canola.

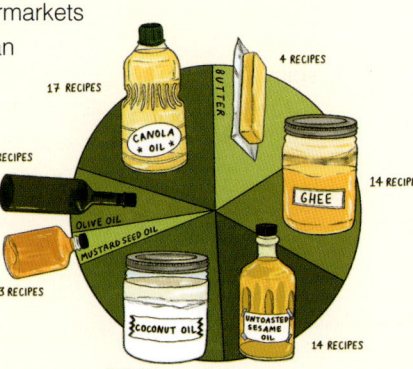

Chillies and Peppers

BYADGI
Byadgi chilli powder is a great beginner's chilli powder if you're new to South Asian chillies. Primarily grown in the Haveri district of Karnataka in South India—where their namesake city, Byadgi, is located—these chillies are just as prized for their cardinal red hue as their sweet, bell pepper–like taste and mild heat.

One of the reasons that these chillies are lesser known in America is the rise of Kashmiri chilli powder, which many South Asian cookbooks and recipes categorize as a "mild, sweet chilli powder." This couldn't be further from the truth. Real Kashmiri chillies—grown in the lush vale of Kashmir—pack a punch with a spicier, cayenne pepper–like heat. But, both in India and abroad, what is being grown and labeled as Kashmiri chilli powder is often actually Byadgi, red bell pepper, and other very mild chillies, which are easier—and, often, commercially cheaper—to grow. If you can't find Byadgi chilli powder, you could use something labeled as "Kashmiri chilli powder," but we recommend substituting sweet or hot Hungarian paprika. Or, if you like things a little spicier, you can use Guntur Sannam chilli powder.

GUNTUR SANNAM
These chillies—grown in Guntur, Andhra Pradesh, the chilli trading capital of the world—are the pride and joy of the region's sour and spicy cuisine. They have a lively, tomato-like fruitiness, building mild-to-medium heat, and find their way into just about every Andhra dish.

Instead of grinding them, whole, dried Sannam chillies are traditionally pounded with salt and a little bit of untoasted sesame oil, creating a coarser final powder that is great for both cooking and finishing. It's our ultimate all-purpose chilli, and definitely the workhorse of my kitchen. Unfortunately, the flavor and fruitiness of Sannam chillies are pretty one-of-a-kind, so it doesn't have a commodity counterpart. For a milder end result, you can substitute Byadgi chillies, both whole and powdered.

SIRĀRAKHONG HĀTHEI
Grown in the hills of Sirārakhong, Manipur, up in the northeastern corner of India, these long, slender red chillies are smoked on bamboo mats after harvest, imbuing them with layered wood-fired flavor that complements their rich, umami-forward taste. They're a staple in Manipuri cooking, from the iconic hoksa—pork braised with just these chillies and salt!—to chicken soups and chutneys. So much of the cooking we experienced across our travels was on open flames, lending a subtle smoky taste to whatever was being cooked. Adding one or two of these whole dried chillies to a pot of beans mimics that flavor even on a gas or electric range. Other smoked chillies don't quite measure up, but in a pinch, you can swap in Spanish smoked paprika or chipotle powder.

SIVATHEI
Also hailing from Manipur, these wildly spicy peppers—we're talkin' ghost pepper hot!—are a staple in this region's fiery cooking. Known by many different names across Northeast India—bhut jholokia, naga mirch, king chilli, Umorok, and Sivathei, which is the Tangkhul name—both the fresh and the dried whole chillies are at every single market. They are also smoked on bamboo mats after harvest, resulting in a flavor that lands somewhere between chipotle and Scotch bonnet. They're most commonly rehydrated, then pounded and combined with seasonal herbs and veggies to create mouthwatering chutneys.

Pantry

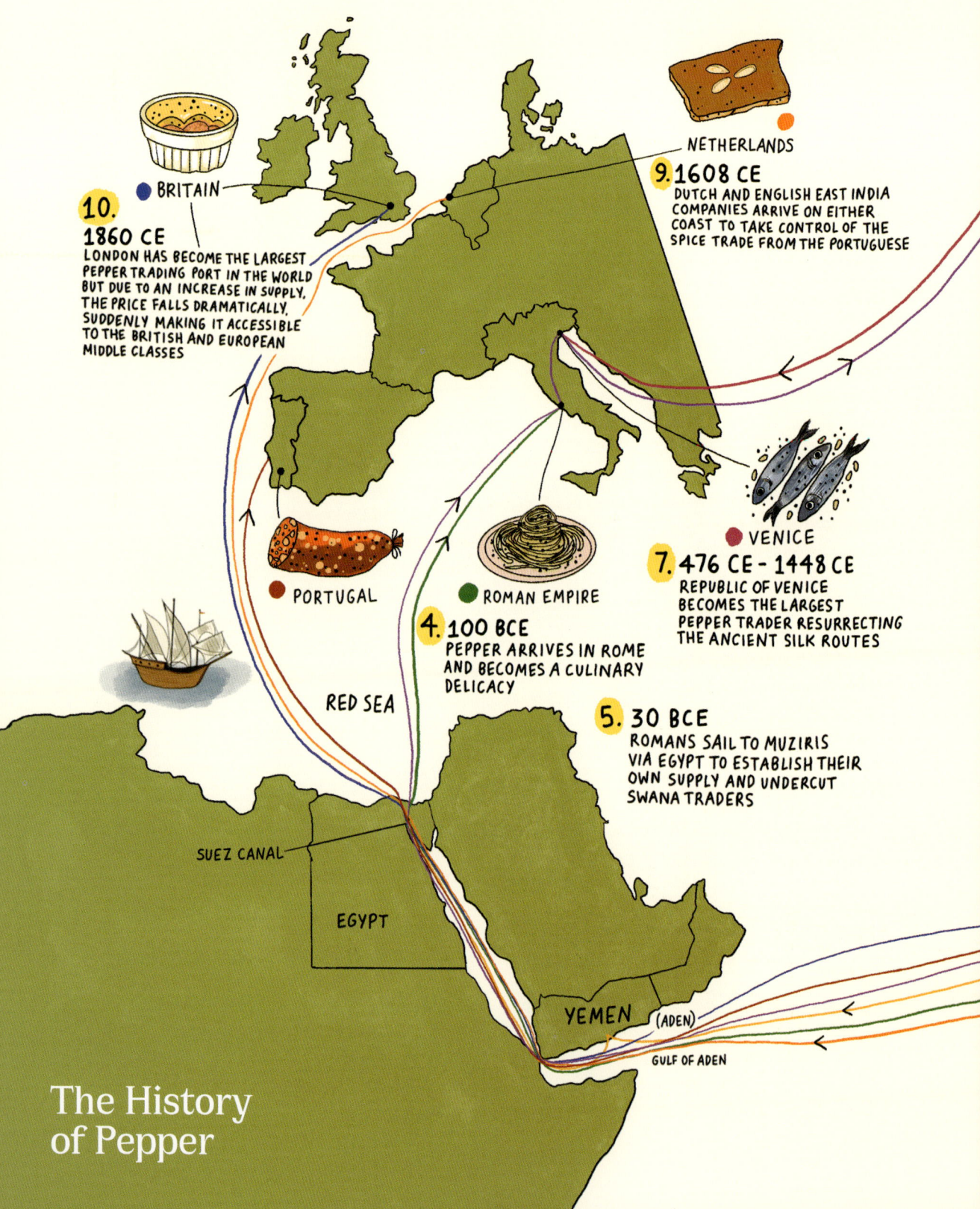

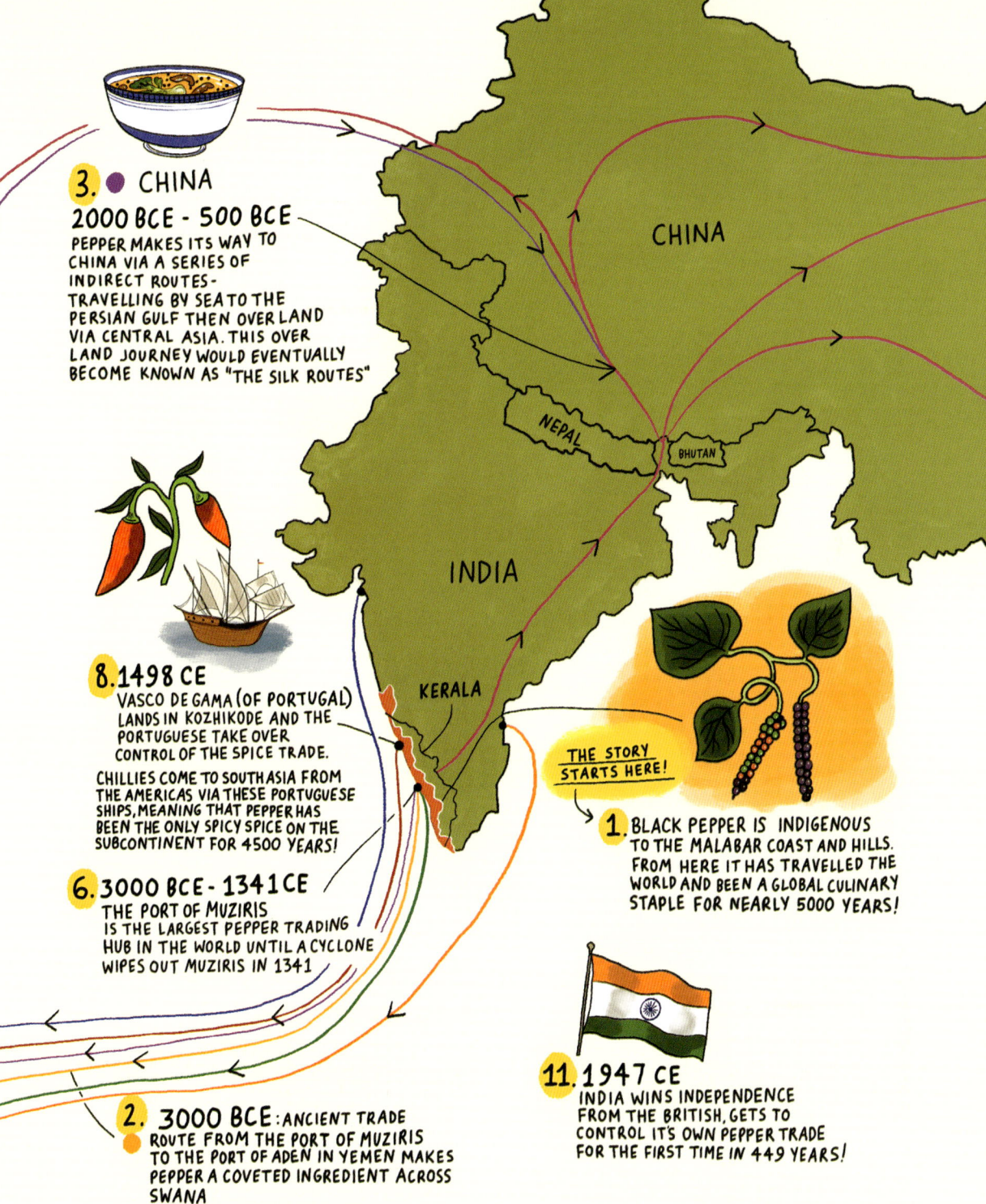

FRESH PEPPERS

Throughout our travels, the main fresh source of heat that was used was green peppers, ranging from long, slim ones to short, fat, incredibly fiery ones. In the US, the most accessible and closest flavor substitute are serrano peppers—bright, sharp, with a biting heat that can range from medium to very spicy. Because of this spice spectrum, I like tasting a little bit of one before I add it to a recipe—that way I know if I want to add one or two.

Other hot peppers you'll find in this book are green Thai bird's-eye chillies, habanero peppers, and Fresno peppers. With any of these peppers, if you're after a little less fire, you can remove the seeds and ribs.

Salty Things

SALTS

We developed the recipes for this book using fine sea salt—both Diaspora Spice Co.'s Surya Salt and regular ol' fine sea salt from the supermarket. For the former, we partnered with the Agariya community, a tribe that has been harvesting and processing salt in the famous desert salt pans of the Wild Ass Sanctuary and Little Rann of Kutch in Gujarat for generations. The salt's high-mineral content is preserved through a slow-filtration process and hand-pounding, resulting in a salt with a clean, bright flavor, subtle brininess, and layered salinity. In our opinion, it just makes whatever you add tastier, but at the end of the day, kosher salt works too.

Just keep in mind, if you are using Diamond Crystal kosher salt, which is lighter and fluffier in texture, use 1½ teaspoons per 1 teaspoon fine sea salt. And, if you prefer Morton's kosher, which is denser and saltier, use ¾ teaspoon per 1 teaspoon fine sea salt. Whatever salt you use, remember to season and taste along the way! You'll also find flaky sea salt, like Maldon or fleur de sel, for finishing dishes in this book.

FISHY THINGS

Preserved and salted fish are key flavoring agents in Sri Lankan and Manipuri cooking. In Sri Lanka, Maldive fish flakes (similar to Japanese bonito flakes) bring umami-packed briny and sweet funky flavor to a variety of dishes, including their famed sambols (Sri Lankan chutneys), while both salted and smoked fish of all sizes pack the markets in Manipur, ready to be used in braises and chutneys.

To mimic those flavors, we reached for two ingredients that are more readily available stateside: fish sauce and tinned anchovies. For the former, our fave is Red Boat Fish Sauce. And for tinned anchovies, look for ones in oil like IASA, Fish Wife, Conservas Ortiz, and Agostino Recca.

Sour Things

LEMON

Asha and I joked that the tagline for this cookbook should be "More acid, please!" because whenever she was developing something, she'd ask, "Does it need more acid?" and the answer was always YES. Lemon is the easiest way to add brightness and vibrancy, lifting the flavors of whatever it's squeezed over or into. For the most part, we used conventional or Lisbon lemons for their sharp, brisk zing, but there are a couple cases where the floral notes of Meyer lemon are key, like Kanthari Chilli Squid (page 146).

TAMARIND

After lemon, tamarind is one of the most frequently used tart and tangy ingredients in this book. This pod-like fruit has a sticky, brown flesh when ripe with a bright sourness, notes of citrus, and rich, molasses-like undertones.

The two that you'll find in our pantries are seedless tamarind blocks—though labeled seedless, the fibrous pulp will still have to be strained after soaking—and tamarind concentrate. In recipes that need tamarind water—like chaaru, sambar, and some chutneys—the soaked, strained pulp and concentrate can be used interchangeably. Just follow the directions on the jar of tamarind concentrate on how much to dilute per cup of water. There are other recipes, such as Andhra-style pachadis, that require the viscosity of the strained tamarind pulp, so concentrate is not a good substitute.

You can find blocks of seedless tamarind pulp in a variety of supermarkets: Latin American, Asian, Southeast Asian, and, of course, South Asian. Tamarind concentrate can also be found on these shelves, as well as in some larger grocery stores in their "international" aisles.

SUMAC

Made from the crushed, dried berries from the sumac plant, sumac isn't often associated with South Asian cooking, but in Manipur, it's a prized ingredient. Also known as Heimang there, they grow a Chinese variety that differs from the ones grown in SWANA (Southwest Asia and North Africa). The latter are fruity, floral, with citrus notes, while the former is still quite lemony with deeper notes of cranberries and a subtle tannic finish akin to black tea. You can use either type for this book.

KOKUM

Kokum—a small mouth-puckering fruit similar to the mangosteen popular in Maharashtrian and Konkani dishes, like Goan fish- and seafood-based curries—has a flavor somewhere between tamarind and sumac with a refreshing tartness, red fruit depth, and soft tannic finish. A similar ingredient is kudampuli, or Malabar tamarind, which is more often used in Kerala, but harder to find in America. The taste between the two is closer than that of tamarind, so kokum is what we reach for when cooking Keralan fish curries. Dried kokum petals or whole dried fruit can be found online and at most South Asian grocery stores.

AMCHUR

Amchur—made from powdered green mangoes—is a form of acid used across India, particularly North India and parts of central South India, like Andra Pradesh. The sour level can vary slightly from jar to jar, depending on the mango varietal that's used and the ripeness they were picked at, but generally amchur has a round tart and tangy taste with a complex, underlying sweetness. It's used in a spectrum of dishes, including dals, marinades, and masalas, like chaat masala.

All Things Coconut

FRESH COCONUT

Fresh coconut meat—both grated and shaved—is essential to dishes from South India and Sri Lanka, making its way into fish curries, sambols, vegetable stir-fries, and flatbread. You could break down your own coconut, but the ease and availability of frozen coconut is hard to beat. Look for "shredded" or "grated" fresh coconut, which you can find at your local South Asian or East Asian grocery stores.

DRIED COCONUT

Desiccated coconut, which is unsweetened and very finely grated, and unsweetened coconut shavings add both texture and coconut flavor to desserts, from cookies to tropical-toasty toppings for puddings and cakes.

COCONUT MILK AND CREAM

Across South India and Sri Lanka, coconut milk is made fresh. Once cracked and finely grated, the coconut meat is mixed with water and squeezed two times. The first pressing yields a thick coconut milk, used mostly for finishing dishes, while the second pressing is added during the cooking process. But don't worry, we're not going to ask you to make your own coconut milk! Canned, full-fat coconut milk is your friend (but, please, please, for flavor's sake, don't use light coconut milk!). And, for desserts, we love canned or boxed coconut cream.

COCONUT OIL

See Fats section (page 6).

Sweeteners

POWDERED JAGGERY

Jaggery is an unrefined sugar—think brown sugar, but with more oomph and caramelly richness—that is made with sugarcane or palm juice. Our Madhur Jaggery—grown in Daund, Maharashtra by the Randive family—is made with sugarcane, which is juiced and prepared using traditional methods, including using okra juice to remove impurities, resulting in jaggery in its purest and most delicious form. Jaggery can come in powdered, liquid, or solid block form. Powdered jaggery is the type you'll need for the recipes in this book.

Herbs and Aromatics

CURRY LEAVES

Across South India and Sri Lanka, curry leaves reign supreme. These fresh, fragrant leaves are probably the most used herb in this book, followed by good ol' cilantro. The complex flavor of curry leaves, also known as *kadipatta*, is hard to capture into words—it hits on so many levels from earthy and herbal to citrusy and savory with a whisper of sulfur-like aroma akin to asafetida. Fat and heat turn these delicate green leaves into the best versions of themselves. Because their flavor mellows with cooking, curry leaves are often added at different stages of cooking—bloomed in oil with whole spices at the beginning of cooking and fried until bright green and translucent in tadka and poured over at the end.

You can find fresh curry leaves at most South Asian grocery stores and some well-stocked specialty produce markets. The delicate leaves don't like moisture or cold, so the best way to store them is folded in a paper towel in a zip-top bag in the crisper of your refrigerator. You can also find frozen and dried curry leaves, but they tend to lose a lot of their flavor in these forms. Frozen leaves can be thawed, patted dry, and added as you would fresh, and the dried can be added with the liquids, but will burn if fried or added to tadkas.

CILANTRO

Cilantro—or fresh coriander—is one of the most used fresh herbs across many regions of India, from Tamil Nadu, Kerala, and Andhra Pradesh in the South to Rajasthan and Uttarakhand in the North. The whole plant holds a lot of flavor, so no need to strip the leaves off the tender stems, just trim ¼ inch off the bottom of the stalks and use everything else.

CULANTRO

Also known as ngo gai, long coriander, recao, and cilantro de hoja ancha, among other names, culantro is used in cooking across the world, from the Caribbean to Latin America and parts of Southeast Asia and India, including the northeastern region of Manipur bordering Myanmar. Part of the Apiaceae family (like its cousin cilantro), culantro's long, saw-toothed

Tadka Technique

If you've ever had a dal, curry, or chutney that seemed to *sing* with flavor—you likely have *tadka* to thank. Known as *tadka* or *chhonk* in Hindi, *vaghar* in Gujarati, or "tempering," this seemingly simple process—spices sizzling in hot fat—lies at the heart of South Asian cooking. Done right, tadka is a technique that transforms ordinary ingredients into deeply layered and aromatic dishes.

1. The Equipment

To perfect your tadka game, I highly recommend investing in a small, high-quality tadka spoon (or butter warmer/saucepan). Designed to handle high heat, they're small enough to fry an egg but just right for blooming spices without burning them. Plus, they make it easy to drizzle that aromatic spiced oil over your final dish without mess or stress.

2. Start with Fat

Tadka begins with a fat—think of it as the foundation for flavor. Use:

- Ghee for richness,
- Coconut oil for nutty sweetness, or
- Neutral oil to let the spices shine.

Heat the fat until it's shimmering but not smoking. The right temperature ensures the spices bloom without burning.

3. Whole Spices–The Flavor Makers

Once the fat is ready, whole spices like mustard seeds, cumin seeds, or fenugreek seeds take center stage. Their essential oils, safely locked away during drying, are coaxed out by the heat.

That unmistakable snap, crackle, and pop as they hit the fat is the sound of transformation—and for many of us, it's the soundtrack to dinner being nearly ready.

4. Add Layers–Dals, Aromatics, and Spices

The final note is a deliberate sequence of additions to build flavor:

- Dals: Split urad or chana dals for texture and nuttiness.
- Aromatics: Fresh curry leaves, slivers of garlic, or ginger join the party.
- Ground Spices (optional): A pinch of turmeric or chilli powder for added color and depth—added *just* at the end and off the heat to avoid burning.
- Asafetida (Hing): A small pinch for a final layer of allium-y complexity.

The result? A golden, spiced oil that amplifies the taste of everything it touches.

5. When to Use a Tadka

- The Starting Point: Used at the beginning of a dish like *sambar* (page 114) or vegetable curries. Think of this as a *reverse tadka*.
- The Finishing Touch: The crowning glory drizzled over dal (page 15), khichdi (page 187), or a coconut chutney (page 39).

Each family builds their own signature roster of tadkas—customizing the sequence of spices, textures, and additions to suit their tastes and available ingredients. It's not just cooking; it's regional food culture at its best.

leaves pack a wallop of herby, vegetal, concentrated cilantro-like flavor with sharper, more peppery notes. You can find it at some well-stocked produce markets and Southeast Asian supermarkets.

PANDAN LEAVES

A tropical plant from the *Pandanus* genus of the screw pine family—the same one that kewra essence for biryani comes from—pandan is intensely aromatic and delicately floral with a grassy sweetness. Often associated with Southeast Asian cooking, it's also popular in parts of South India, like Kerala, and Sri Lanka where it's used in savory preparations, like Sri Lankan Cucumber Coconut Milk Curry (page 91) and Jaffna-Style Crab Curry (page 132). Pandan leaves can be found fresh and frozen in some Southeast Asian supermarkets and South Asian grocery stores. Pandan extract is also more widely available but is better saved for desserts and isn't an adequate swap in savory recipes. If you can't find fresh or frozen leaves, you can skip it and your curry will be just fine!

LEMONGRASS

Beloved for its zingy, citrus, herbal flavor, this stalky perennial herb is an essential ingredient in Sri Lankan cooking, imparting layered lemony flavor to dishes like Parippu (Sri Lankan dal, page 118). In this book, we also use lemongrass in some of our Manipuri recipes as a replacement for Vietnamese balm—an herb with a sharp, citrusy taste somewhere between lemongrass and lemon balm—but it isn't readily available stateside.

DRIED FENUGREEK LEAVES

Commonly labeled as *kasoori methi*, these are the dried leaves from the fenugreek plant. They have a sweet, herbal taste with a subtle maple-like aroma and delicate bitterness. To get the most out of its fragrant intensity, rub the leaves between your palms to awaken their essential oils before adding them to whatever you're cooking. Just like curry leaves, kasoori methi's flavor is so unique there really isn't a substitute. You can find these at South Asian grocery stores and online.

Dal (Lentils, Pulses, and Beans)

The word *dal* refers to both the ingredient and the dish made with said ingredient. Region to region, the dish goes by different names—*dhal*, *pappu*, *parippu*, just to name a few. There are many types of dal (lentils), each bringing their own unique flavor and texture. And, even within varieties of these pulses, they can take four forms: whole, hulled, split, and hulled and split.

CHANA DAL

One of the most well-known dals in and outside of India, these golden pulses—also known as split Bengal gram—aren't lentils at all. A small variety of husked, split chickpea, chana dal has a nutty, earthy flavor and thick, hearty texture. It is used in dals, fillings, tadkas, and to add heft and roasty-toasty flavor to podis (see page 26). In their ground form, chana dal is known as besan (chickpea flour).

SPLIT MASOOR DAL

Along with chana dal, split masoor dal—or split red lentils—are one of the most common types of lentils stateside. High in protein, these are sweeter and milder in flavor with a smaller, flatter shape, making them a great quick-cooking pulse (no soaking required!).

URAD GOTA

Whole white urad dal, or urad gota, is the husked version of urad dal. When soaked and blended, these chubby, round little pulses are known for their rich, creamy flavor and super silky texture, making them the ideal dal for batters like idli, dosa, and vada.

SPLIT WHITE URAD DAL

This split, hulled version of urad dal is buttery with a luscious, velvety mouthfeel. On their own, these tiny, cream-colored lentils would be overpoweringly rich, but mixed with other lentils like moong and chana, like in Rajasthani Dal (page 120), they add just enough satiny texture. These are also a go-to choice to add crunch and bite to tadka.

WHOLE MOONG DAL

Whole moong dal—mung beans—is earthy, vegetal, and more savory in flavor compared to some of the sweeter, nuttier varieties like masoor and toor. Typically, whole moong dal are sprouted and tossed in salads or cooked and used in snacks, while their skinned and split counterparts are used in dishes like dal and khichdi. However, Asha and I are texture girlies and love how whole moong dal softens yet retains its shape, so you'll find it in our renditions of Rajasthani Dal (page 120) and Gujarati Khichdi (page 187).

SPLIT TOOR DAL

Split toor dal—or split yellow pigeon peas—have a rich, sweet, nutty taste and buttery

Eating with Your Hands

I grew up eating with my hands, only really learning how to use a fork and knife with any skill when I moved abroad at sixteen!

Fifteen years later, I know my way around fancy cutlery, but I still can't bring myself to eat a good lamb biryani (page 185) or a plate of tangy fish curry (page 138) with anything but my hands. It just doesn't taste as good. There is something deeply satisfying about using your fingers to mix the perfect bite of rice, curry, yogurt, and achaar—my mouth waters just thinking about it!

As a young adult, I had a lot of shame about eating with my hands, which is why it was SO gratifying to later learn that our culture of eating with our hands is rooted in SCIENCE! When you touch your food with your fingers, you're activating sensory receptors. Your fingers are feeding your brain tactile information about the texture, temperature, and composition of the food, which then enhances the food's effect when it hits your palate. This quite literally makes it taste more delicious. Eating with your hands also slows you down—you focus on the food, take only finger-sized bites, and give your brain time to register satisfaction and fullness. So, as you cook your way through this book, try skipping the cutlery. Instead, scoop with your fingers, and use your thumb to guide the food into your mouth. If you need a place to start, the Sri Lankan Moringa String Hoppers (page 198) are a textural dream—have fun using your hands to saturate them in dal before taking a bite. Or try making perfect morsels of Palak Rista (page 170) meatballs and practice mixing the saffron-rich gravy with just enough steamed long-grain rice!

texture when boiled. They are essential to chaaru, rasam, khichdi, sambar, and Gujarati dal. Quite hefty and delicious on their own, they also are a beautiful choice for dal blends.

RAJMA

Similar to the word *dal*, rajma refers to both beans and the dish the beans are used in. Often the word *rajma* is synonymous with red kidney beans (lal rajma), but just as there are different types of dal, there is a wide array of rajma in different shapes, sizes, flavors, and textures. Other notable types include Jammu rajma (smaller, fatter, and more aromatic) and chitra rajma (brown, speckled, with a milder flavor). South Asian heirloom rajma varieties are harder to find in America, so I reach for comparable picks from California-based purveyor Rancho Gordo, like ayocote morado, cranberry, and Jacob's cattle for lal, Jammu, and chitra rajma, respectively.

Rice

BASMATI

Basmati is by far the most widely known type of South Asian rice, and for good reason. Beloved for its intense, fragrant aroma and long, slender grains, it cooks up into perfectly fluffy, separated grains. It's commonly used in parts of North India and Kashmir.

JEERA SAMBA

Also known as *seeraga samba*, this short-grain rice is popular across South India, including Kerala, Tamil Nadu, and parts of Andhra Pradesh. The size of the grains is akin to cumin seeds—*jeera* meaning cumin—about one-third of the length of basmati. While less aromatic than basmati, jeera samba has a pleasing sweetness and is super absorbent, making it the perfect choice for Thalassery-style fish biryani, coconut lamb biryani, and Andhra lemon rice.

SONA MASOORI

A staple of thalis across South India, this aromatic, medium-grain rice is a cross between two varieties of rice: sona and Mahsuri. Just like basmati, it has a sweet, fragrant smell and flavor, and cooks up light and fluffy with separated grains. It can also be soaked, blended, and fermented in batters for idli, dosa, and appam.

MATTA

Popular in Kerala, coastal parts of Karnataka, and some regions of North Sri Lanka, like Jaffna, matta or red rice still has its bran intact—this is as close as you'll get to brown rice in this book! The bran gives matta rice its brownish, red-flecked hue when cooked. It's fluffy yet toothsome with an earthy taste and subtle minerality. It's exemplary with all things fish and seafood, as well as dishes like ripe mango curry.

IDLI

Idli rice is a short-grain rice that has been parboiled and dried. It's very mild in flavor and blends into a silken texture after soaking, making it ideal for idli—duh!—dosa, and appam batter. If you can't find idli rice, you can also use other short- to medium-grain varieties, like sona masoori.

THICK POHA

To make poha, grains of rice are parboiled, flattened, and dried. There are two varieties of poha: thick and thin. The latter is fried and used in snacks, while the former can be used in sweet and savory porridges and stir-fries, as well as being an integral ingredient in idli, dosa, and appam batters.

Where to Begin

Most Beginner Friendly

Edamame and Cherry Tomato Salad   83

Rajasthani or Gujarati Green Chutney   36 to 38

Spiced Maple-Roasted Carrots with Carrot Top Sambol   92

Turmeric-Banana Snacking Cake   230

Jammy Egg Curry   156

Jaggery Chai   213

45 Minutes and Under

Kadhi and Khichdi   123 and 187

Kerala-Style Grilled Prawns   134

Nimmakaya Pulihora   180

Daikon and Orange Salad with Sesame-Cumin Dressing   78

"Some Like It Mild"

Meen Moilee   138

Parippu Curry   118

Nadru Yakhni or Aab Gosht   102 or 165

Pazha Manga Curry   94

Pahadi Rajma   124

Freezer Friendly

Chaaru (really the entire lentil section)   112

Country Chicken Curry   150

Kashmiri Stock   175

Hoksa   162

Haakh   99

Spiced Chocolate-Coconut Cookies   233

Ultimate Dinner Party

Doud Alle Dip   59

Bitter Melon and Heirloom Tomato Salad   74

Kakuluwo Curry   132

Apricot-Saffron Frangipane Galette   234

Hyun Mezcalita   225

Eid Dinner

Aab Gosht   165

Kashmiri Pulao   178

Blistered Asparagus with Pisyun Loon   76

Spiced Date Cake with Coconut Caramel   237

Fennel Soda   220

Diwali Feast

Coconut Lamb Biryani   185

Zucchini Na Muthiya   67

Bhindi Masala   88

Watalappam-ish Crème Caramel   244

CSA Overflow

Zucchini Na Muthiya   67

Pakora Party   64

Ringan no Oro   96

Burst Tomato Chutney   48

Pipinna Kiri Hodi   91

Pantry Building Blocks

Andhra Chilli Powder   23

Kalu Kudu   22

Lahsun Mirchi Chutney   42

Tomato Pachadi   50

Spice Blends

Kalu Kudu 22

Andhra Chilli Powder 23

**Karam Podi,
aka Gunpowder Podi** 26

Karivepaku Podi 27

Pisyun Loon 28

Kalu Kudu
Sri Lankan Roasted Curry Powder

Recipe by Amitha Dissanayake | Origin: Kandy, Sri Lanka | Makes ¾ cup

Every Sri Lankan family has a slightly different roasted curry powder recipe. This variation comes from Amitha Dissanayake, one of the incredible women who blends, sorts, and processes our Peni Miris Cinnamon and Kandyan Cloves at the Eko Land Estate, spices that she surprisingly omits in this recipe.

Asha and I very nervously watched her toast each spice to the very edge of what one would consider "roasted," convinced that the result would be too bitter. But the final blend was an intensely nutty, rich curry powder that is an ingenious shortcut to adding big flavor to simple food. It's distinctly earthier and more savory than an Indian garam masala and its simplicity complements rather than overpowers dishes.

I'd recommend making one batch and using it across these five recipes: Parippu Curry (page 118), Jaffna-Style Crab Curry (page 132), Sri Lankan Cucumber Coconut Milk Curry (page 91), Fish Puffs (page 61), and Spiced Maple-Roasted Carrots (page 92). Once you've got a feel for the warm, deeply savory flavor it lends to your cooking, you'll be adding a spoon or two to everything you can!

½ cup (6 g) lightly packed fresh curry leaves

½ cup (40 g) coriander seeds

1½ tablespoons (13½ g) fennel seeds

1 tablespoon plus 1 teaspoon (10 g) cumin seeds

Heat a large skillet over medium heat. Add the curry leaves and toast, stirring occasionally, until the leaves are dry and start to brown around the edges, 2 to 4 minutes. Transfer to a medium bowl. Add the coriander seeds and toast, stirring frequently, until they turn deep golden brown, 3 to 5 minutes, and transfer to the bowl with the curry leaves.

Repeat the toasting process with the fennel seeds, toasting until golden brown, 90 seconds to 3 minutes. Repeat the toasting process again with the cumin seeds, toasting until golden brown, 1 to 2 minutes. Transfer the toasted spices to the bowl with the curry leaves and coriander and let cool completely.

Using a spice grinder, grind the cooled curry leaves and spices, in batches, if necessary, into a medium-fine powder. Transfer to an airtight container, shake well to make sure everything is evenly mixed, and store in a cool, dry place for up to 3 months.

Andhra Chilli Powder

Recipe by Venkata Narasamma Kasaraneni | Origin: Kankipadu, Andhra Pradesh | Makes ½ cup

In both the Kasaraneni and Narne family homes (that grow our Pragati Turmeric and Guntur Sannam chillies, respectively), we encountered an unassuming jar of chilli powder that was being used to season absolutely everything. It was more aromatic, full bodied, and savory than just regular ol' chilli powder. After some serious interrogation, we learned what each family was blending into their "house chilli powder." Make a full batch and use it in Gongura Pappu (page 108), Seasonal Sambar (page 114), and Country Chicken Curry (page 150).

- 1½ tablespoons (7½ g) coriander seeds
- 1½ teaspoons (4 g) cumin seeds
- 1 teaspoon (4 g) fenugreek seeds
- ¼ cup (30 g) Guntur Sannam chilli powder
- 1 garlic clove, quartered

Heat a tadka spoon or small skillet over medium heat. Add the coriander seeds and cumin seeds and toast, stirring frequently, until the coriander seeds turn a couple shades darker, 45 to 90 seconds. Transfer to a spice grinder and let cool completely.

Add the fenugreek seeds and grind into a medium-fine powder. Add the Guntur Sannam chilli powder and garlic and pulse in 10-second intervals, scraping down between each interval, until the garlic is completely ground into the powder, 20 to 40 seconds total. Transfer to an airtight container and store in a cool, dry place for up to 3 months.

KALU KUDU, page 22

ANDHRA CHILLI POWDER, page 23

KARAM PODI, AKA GUNPOWDER PODI, page 26   KARIVEPAKU PODI, page 27

Karam Podi, aka Gunpowder Podi
Chilli Coconut Spice Blend

Recipe by Padmavathi Narne | Origin: Vinjanampadu, Andhra Pradesh | Makes 1 cup

Growing up, I only knew gunpowder as the fiery umami spice blend I dipped my Sunday morning idlis into, not the explosive chemical substance it's nicknamed after because it's such a flavor bomb. This blend could be considered Andhra Pradesh's greatest culinary export, found in the kitchens of homesick South Indians and flavor-loving cooks all over the world!

The magic of podi is unlocked with fat. Sprinkle over ghee roast dosa when cooking, slather it with ghee on an idli, or serve with hot rice or khichdi drizzled with ghee + plain yogurt. It's also pretty great on generously buttered popcorn!

⅓ cup (67 g) chana dal

⅓ cup (40 g) Guntur Sannam chilli powder

¼ cup (18 g) desiccated unsweetened coconut

4 garlic cloves, quartered

2 teaspoons (5 g) cumin seeds

1¼ teaspoons (6¼ g) fine sea salt, plus more if needed

1 tablespoon ghee, melted

Heat a large skillet over medium-low heat. Add the chana dal and toast, stirring frequently, until the dal turns golden and smells nutty, 6 to 9 minutes. Transfer to a bowl and let cool completely.

Mix the cooled dal with the Guntur Sannam chilli powder, desiccated coconut, garlic, cumin seeds, and salt. Using a spice grinder, work in batches to blend the dal mixture into a fine powder, transferring each batch to another bowl. Drizzle the blended podi with the melted ghee and, using your fingertips, rub the ghee into the dry ingredients to make sure all the ingredients are evenly distributed. Taste, and season with more salt, if necessary. Store in an airtight container in a cool, dry place for up to 3 months.

What Is a Podi?

Podis have been made across South India for nearly seven hundred years, with each home stocking a few varieties year-round to bring big flavor to any meal. Made from roasted lentils, seeds, and spices, a podi is nutty, savory, and just the right amount of spicy—an ancient powerhouse of flavor and nutrition.

Here's the magic: You spoon a small mound onto your plate, shape it into a little volcano, and pour hot ghee into the crater. The milk fat unlocks the podi's deeper, nutty notes—expanding the spices' flavors into something richer, smoother, and downright luxurious. The traditional way is to dip hot, freshly steamed Idli (page 195) into the ghee-podi, but it is also yummy on toast, atop fried eggs, or sprinkled on roasted veggies. Because the spices have been toasted before being ground, they work beautifully as a garnish to just about any savory dish! Podi atop creamy pasta? I'm there.

Karivepaku Podi
Curry Leaf Spice Blend

Recipe by Venkata Narasamma Kasaraneni | Origin: Kankipadu, Andhra Pradesh | Makes ½ cup

Umami, herbaceous, and oh-so-nutty—I first tried this blend during the 2018 Pragati Turmeric harvest and knew in my bones that the recipe would make its way into the cookbook that I was going to write someday. Many years later, here we are! Extracting the specifics of the recipe out of the Kasaraneni family that grow our turmeric was a highly comical process. The family matriarch Venkata Narasamma's recipe differed greatly from her two daughters-in-laws' versions and since they are all phenomenal cooks, we truly had no idea whose version to go with. It took a few tries of our own without a Kasaraneni family member looking over our shoulder, but I think we landed on one that they'd all be proud of.

This is a great way to use up extra curry leaves and preserve all that vibrant flavor, especially in the US, where we must trek to buy fresh curry leaves from the grocery store only to use five to ten for a recipe. No longer shall the rest of the bunch slowly wither away in the fridge or on our counters!

Enjoy with Idli (page 195) and a generous pour of ghee—hot fat unlocks podis!—sprinkle over Ghee Roast Dosa (page 192), or toss with buttered popcorn. It's also amazing sprinkled over grilled corn slathered in salted butter.

3½ cups lightly packed (36 g) fresh curry leaves

½ teaspoon untoasted sesame oil or other neutral oil

2 teaspoons chana dal

2 teaspoons urad dal

2 garlic cloves, peeled

1½ teaspoons coriander seeds

¾ teaspoon cumin seeds

1¼ teaspoons Guntur Sannam chilli powder

¾ teaspoon fine sea salt, plus more if needed

½ teaspoon amchur powder

Heat a large skillet over medium heat. Add the curry leaves and toast, stirring frequently, until they turn bright green and brittle, 3 to 6 minutes. Transfer to a rimmed sheet pan and let cool completely.

Return the skillet to medium-low heat, add the sesame oil, chana dal, urad dal, and garlic and toast, stirring frequently, until the dals start to turn light golden, 2 to 5 minutes. Add the coriander and cumin seeds and continue to toast until the spices turn golden and the dals turn a shade darker, 30 to 60 seconds more. Transfer to the sheet pan with the curry leaves and let cool completely.

In batches, grind the curry leaf mixture in a spice grinder into a medium-fine powder, transferring each batch to a bowl. Add the chilli powder, salt, and amchur powder to the last batch of grinding. Once all the batches are in the bowl, mix well to make sure all the ingredients are evenly distributed, taste, and season with more salt, if necessary. Store in an airtight container at room temperature, in a cool, dry place for up to 3 months.

Pisyun Loon
Herb Spiced Salt

Recipe by Jaiveer Singh Rana | Origin: Kotgaon, Uttarakhand | Makes ¾ cup

Up high in the Himalayas, salt used to be a very precious commodity. Traveling traders would bring in big blocks of salt from the coast in the summer months, during the short periods that the roads were accessible. Grinding the salt with fresh herbs and spices became a way to stretch it further while preserving a taste of fresh ingredients like citrus or cilantro ahead of the long winter. Balveer Mamaji, our local fountain of knowledge and village lore, says that the spiced salt also plays an important role in keeping folks hydrated. In such a cold climate, it's common to go long stretches without feeling the need to drink water and so pisyun loon, herb spiced salt, sprinkled on fruits and vegetables literally makes people thirsty and reminds them to stay hydrated.

Our version comes from the Singh family, who are one of the high-altitude Pahadi Garlic farm partners that we work with. Gyan Singh and Veera Devi's pisyun loon is bright, herbaceous, and subtly nutty, with a gentle kiss of green chilli heat. It's perfect served over raw vegetables, for finishing grilled things—try it on Blistered Asparagus (page 76)—and as a seasoning for fish and seafood. One of our fave ways to use it is inspired by the French: served with really good butter and an array of small, tender radishes.

1½ tablespoons (13 g) perilla or black sesame seeds

1 teaspoon (2½ g) cumin seeds

2 teaspoons (3½ g) coriander seeds

¼ cup (13 g) roughly chopped cilantro, leaves and tender stems

½ serrano pepper, finely chopped

2 garlic cloves, finely chopped

½ cup (120 g) fine sea salt

Place the perilla or black sesame seeds, cumin seeds, and coriander seeds in a mortar and pound into a medium-coarse powder.

Add the cilantro, serrano pepper, and garlic and pound into a medium-fine paste. Add the salt and, using your fingers, gently mix the paste and salt together until evenly combined (don't worry if the mixture is a little wet).

Spread the seasoned salt out in an even layer on a rimmed sheet pan, place in a bright, sunny place, and dry, mixing and re-spreading the salt a few times, until completely dry to the touch, 4 to 6 hours. Alternatively, you can dry this at the lowest temperature setting in the oven (150°F to 170°F), using the same method and timings. Place the dried salt back in the mortar and gently pound to break apart the clumps, being careful not to pulverize the salt. Transfer to an airtight container and store in a cool, dry place for up to 3 months.

The Kasaraneni Family
Pragati Turmeric

VIJAYWADA, ANDHRA PRADESH

The story of how I met Prabhu Kasaraneni, our Pragati Turmeric farmer, is really the origin story of Diaspora Spice Co. In 2016, I was a fresh college grad in San Francisco, where I kept seeing golden milk lattes on cafe menus. I had spent my childhood in Mumbai being forced by my nani (maternal grandmother) to drink Haldi Doodh (page 219, tastes delicious), warm turmeric milk with anti-inflammatory properties and an infamously god-awful flavor. I just couldn't understand why it was now being sold in America for $8. I also couldn't shake an intense curiosity about who was growing the turmeric to keep up with this Western wellness boom. Maybe I could tell the story of the South Asian turmeric farmers fueling this trend?

So, in February 2017, I quit my job, bought a one-way ticket back to Mumbai, and moved back home to research . . . turmeric?! I spent the next four and a half months emailing, calling, and WhatsApping every lead I could find for organic, high-quality turmeric. Nobody ever got back to me. Finally, I showed up unannounced at the Indian Institute of Spices Research in Kozhikode, Kerala—a government research center I'd found via Google. There, I met Dr. Prasath, who introduced me to the heirloom, high curcumin cultivar that he had developed over the last decade, Pragati Turmeric.

Having tried turmeric from across South Asia, I could see that this was the most beautiful, potent, and delicious variety I was ever going to find. The only problem was that in a commodity market built to prioritize yield, size, and color, there was no premium market for this variety that explicitly prioritized flavor and aroma, so very few farmers were willing to grow it.

I asked Dr. Prasath to connect me with the few farmers he knew that were growing Pragati Turmeric, which is how I found myself on a tiny airplane to meet a certain Mr. Prabhu Kasaraneni in a sleepy riverside village in central Andhra Pradesh. Prabhu is a fourth-generation farmer who had single-handedly transitioned his family farm to regenerative practices and had taken the initiative to buy Pragati rhizomes. The next two and a half days that I spent with his family completely changed the trajectory of my life, and led me to found Diaspora Spice Co.

I have two core memories of that first visit—one is walking through chest-high fields of rustling turmeric plants with the scent of intercropped marigolds flooding my senses, Prabhu showing me his homemade natural fertilizers and explaining how he'd adapted regenerative agriculture techniques specifically for his climate, soil, and this variety of turmeric. I was so struck by his focus, scientific method, and sheer passion. The second memory is of my first lunch in the Kasaraneni family's veranda overlooking their leafy vegetable garden. I'd never eaten Andhra food before, and the mouthwatering punches of sour! spicy! seasoned! were so new and exhilarating. It was like my palate was tasting in three dimensions for the first time! I went back home with a suitcase full of turmeric and a new understanding of how to layer acids (Dried mango! Tamarind! Kokum! Sorrel! Lemon!) with spices to transform even the simplest of meals.

Recipes from the Kasaraneni Family

Andhra Chilli Powder 23

Karivepaku Podi 27

Tomato Pachadi 50

Gongura Pappu 108

Chaaru 112

Nimmakaya Pulihora 180

Haldi Doodh 219

Turmeric-Banana Snacking Cake 230

The Eko Land Community

DIGANA, SRI LANKA

Peni Miris Cinnamon and Kandyan Cloves

Cinnamomum verum is indigenous only to the island of Sri Lanka. Since as far back as the tenth century, sea-faring traders have come to Sri Lankan shores to investigate tales of a spicy, sweet tree bark that could transform their cuisines. For centuries, ships from across Southwest Asia and North Africa traded the spices throughout the world, keeping their source secret. But in the sixteenth century, the Portuguese, Dutch, and British, all keen to cut off their reliance on Arab trading powers, started landing on Sri Lankan shores with the intent of establishing cinnamon monopolies and colonizing the land and its people. They built a supply chain for cinnamon, like many other spices (see our pepper story on page 8), that prioritized size, color, and volume over what matters—flavor, aroma, and oil content.

Sri Lanka finally won independence from the British in 1972, leaving a nation that reflected an interwoven tapestry of Sinhalese, Tamil, Moorish, Malay, and European culture after nearly five hundred years of occupation. Our farm partners, Nihal and his son Remon Elegalla, who run Eko Land, are part of one such mixed Sri Lankan family—Nihal is Sinhalese, his wife, Nel, is Dutch Burgher, and their team of nine incredible women are Sinhalese and Tamil from the local Digana community. It took two years of prototyping with them to arrive at our beloved Peni Miris Cinnamon. We blended sweet, honey-tasting cinnamon from young trees with extra spicy cinnamon from old-growth wild trees. The women of the Eko Land facility taste-test and grade every single lot of bark. When a lot is "Diaspora-grade," aka sweet or spicy enough, it is set aside for our small-batch grinding

The Diaspora Spice Co. Cookbook

schedule. It's a little mad, but it means that your cinnamon smells like roasted figs and orange blossoms, which seems pretty worth it, right?!

Meanwhile, cloves are indigenous to the North Molucca Islands of Indonesia but were brought to Sri Lanka alongside nutmeg by the Dutch, who committed unspeakable atrocities in the name of greater supply, control, and profit from the spice trade. Today, the best Kandyan farmers grow cloves alongside several layers of produce—herbs and medicinal plants at the base; a middle canopy of fruiting shrubs, spice trees, and vines; and an overstory layer of hardwood trees like jackfruit, breadfruit, and durian. This biodiversity is the secret to what makes Eko Land's hand-sorted, peak season cloves the tastiest lil gems I've ever encountered!

The recipes from the Eko Land community come from a few different kitchens—first is the Elegalla family's own favorites—creamy Parippu Coconut Dal, and fragrant Moringa String Hoppers. But the biggest inspiration for these recipes comes from Amitha Dissanayake and Sumithra Attanayake—two of the women who run the Eko Land spice processing facility. We got to spend two days in their leafy farmhouse kitchens overlooking vegetable gardens cooking sumptuous feasts of seasonal Sri Lankan farm fare: fresh, crunchy, and bright veggie-forward sambols and salads and silky, coconut milk–enriched curries and dals!

Recipes from the Eko Land Community

Kalu Kudu 22

Pol Sambol 39

Bitter Melon and Heirloom Tomato Salad 74

Sri Lankan Cucumber Coconut Milk Curry 91

Spiced Maple-Roasted Carrots with Carrot Top Sambol 92

Parippu Curry 118

Kakuluwo Curry 132

Sri Lankan Moringa String Hoppers 198

Pol Roti 203

Watalappam-ish Crème Caramel 244

Chutneys and Pickles

Green Chutney 36

Pol Sambol 39

Carrot Top Sambol 41

Lahsun Mirchi Chutney 42

Palli Chutney 45

Fava Bean Chutney 46

Burst Tomato Chutney 48

Vengaya Thayir Pachadi 49

Tomato Pachadi 50

Green Chutney

I would classify green chutney as one of India's mother sauces. If you are my mum, you use muthiyas (page 67), pakoras (pages 64 and 66), or idlis (page 195) as an excuse to shovel in as much green chutney as physically possible—it is the main event. And Mom's not wrong—it is the perfect bright, herbal, acidic, punchy complement to so much of South Asian cuisine. Green chutney grilled cheeses are iconic, slathering black cod in green chutney and steaming it is the easiest blender-to-stovetop dinner, and folding together labneh and green chutney is the yummiest dip for crudités or simple roast potatoes. If I have a tub of green chutney in my fridge, it's guaranteed that it's gone in less than two days.

We're particularly fond of two variations. The first is a simple, punchy Rajasthani version from the Bishnoi family farm, which grows our Jodhana Cumin, while its Gujarati, southern counterpart, made on the Sakariya family farm, is nuttier, sweeter, and a bit richer.

Rajasthani Green Chutney

Recipe by Mohani Devi Bishno | Origin: Osian, Rajasthan | Makes ½ cup

3 cups (150 g) roughly chopped cilantro, leaves and stems

1 to 2 serrano peppers, roughly chopped

Juice of 1 lemon (2 to 4 tablespoons)

1 teaspoon cumin seeds

1 teaspoon fine sea salt, plus more if needed

2 to 4 tablespoons ice water

Combine the cilantro, serrano peppers, lemon juice, cumin seeds, salt, and 2 tablespoons ice water in a blender and blend on high speed until smooth (if you are having trouble blending everything, add 1 tablespoon ice water at a time until a smooth chutney forms). Taste and season with more salt, if necessary. Serve immediately.

RAJASTHANI GREEN CHUTNEY (at left), page 36, and GUJARATI GREEN CHUTNEY, page 38

Gujarati Green Chutney

Recipe by Nayna Sakariya | Origin: Shedubhar, Gujarat | Makes 1 cup

1 teaspoon plus
1 tablespoon untoasted sesame oil or other neutral oil

2 tablespoons raw peanuts

1 tablespoon plus
1 teaspoon split urad dal

3 cups (150 g) roughly chopped cilantro, leaves and stems

½ cup (10 g) roughly chopped mint leaves

1 serrano pepper, roughly chopped

Juice of 1 lemon
(2 to 4 tablespoons)

1 teaspoon finely chopped fresh ginger

1 teaspoon fine sea salt

½ to 1 teaspoon powdered jaggery

¼ cup (60 ml) ice water, plus more as needed

½ teaspoon black mustard seeds

½ teaspoon coriander seeds

12 fresh curry leaves

Heat 1 teaspoon of the sesame oil in a small skillet over medium-low heat. Add the peanuts and 1 tablespoon of the urad dal and toast, stirring frequently, until the dal turn light golden and the peanuts start to brown in spots, 2 to 4 minutes. Transfer to a blender and let cool completely.

Add the cilantro, mint, serrano pepper, the juice of ½ lemon, the ginger, salt, jaggery, and ice water to the blender and blend on high speed until smooth. You're aiming for a thick, dippable texture, so if the chutney is a little too thick, add 1 tablespoon ice water at a time until you reach the right consistency. Taste and season with more salt or the remaining lemon juice, if necessary. Transfer to a bowl.

To make the tadka, heat the remaining 1 tablespoon sesame oil in a tadka spoon or small saucepan. When shimmering, add the mustard seeds, coriander seeds, and remaining 1 teaspoon urad dal and cook, swirling the pan frequently, until the urad dal turns light golden, 30 seconds to 1 minute. Add the curry leaves—be careful, these will crackle and pop!—and cook until bright green and translucent, 10 to 30 seconds. Pour the tadka over the chutney and serve immediately.

Pol Sambol

Sri Lankan Coconut and Shallot Chutney

Recipe by Amitha Dissanayake | Origin: Kandy, Sri Lanka | Makes 1½ cups

Pol means coconut, and Sri Lanka is an island that knows how to use its coconuts in every form. A countertop coconut grinder was a fixture in every farm kitchen we visited—which meant that freshly grated coconut or first-press coconut milk were both always just an arm workout away. Like any staple, pol sambols differ from home to home, but Asha and I quickly figured out that we liked ours heavy on the chilli, lemon, and salt. Serve as a condiment with Parippu Curry (page 118), Sri Lankan Cucumber Coconut Milk Curry (page 91), or Sri Lankan Fish Puffs (page 61).

Some versions of pol sambol will use Maldive fish, which is a dried and cured skipjack tuna used in small quantities across Sri Lankan food for pungency and layered salinity. I often sub in a couple oil-packed anchovies or ¼ teaspoon shrimp paste for the same effect.

2 tablespoons virgin coconut oil

24 fresh curry leaves

2 large shallots (about ⅓ pound/151 g), finely diced

1 teaspoon fine sea salt, plus more if needed

1¼ cups (106 g) lightly packed fresh or thawed, frozen grated coconut, lightly packed

1 tablespoon plus 1 teaspoon Guntur Sannam chilli powder

1 tablespoon fresh lemon juice

Heat the coconut oil in a large skillet over medium heat. Add 12 of the curry leaves and cook until bright and translucent—be careful, they crackle and pop!—10 to 30 seconds. Add the shallots and ½ teaspoon of the salt. Cook, stirring occasionally, until just softened, 3 to 5 minutes.

Add the coconut and chilli powder to the skillet. Cook, stirring frequently, until heated through and the chilli powder blooms, 1 to 3 minutes.

Turn off the heat. Tear the remaining 12 curry leaves into the skillet and add the lemon juice and the remaining ½ teaspoon salt. Mix well, taste, and season with more salt or lemon juice, if necessary.

Transfer the mixture to a bowl and let sit for 30 minutes to let the flavors marry. Serve at room temperature.

POL SAMBOL (bottom), page 39, and CARROT TOP SAMBOL (top), page 41

Carrot Top Sambol

Recipe by Amitha Dissanayake | Origin: Kandy, Sri Lanka | Makes 1½ cups

This sambol is traditionally made with gotu kola (*Centella asiatica*, or Indian pennywort), a dark green traditional medicinal plant used across South and Southeast Asia and considered a superfood by every all-knowing Sri Lankan aunty.

At cinnamon farmers' homes across Kandy, Asha and I ate a spread of this gotu kola sambol, pol sambol (coconutty and spicy, page 39), and katta sambol (spicy, fishy) as side dishes to add a punch of acidity and bright, spicy flavor to gentle, creamy, coconut-forward dishes like dal, rice, and vegetable curries. Asha and I have a shared love of salads and dark leafy greens, so I remember at least two occasions of making eye contact right as we were both reaching for seconds of the gotu kola sambol. Clearly, we had a favorite.

The challenge was finding an accessible, appropriate substitute for gotu kola in our Californian kitchens, and, of course, Asha in her infinite wisdom narrowed in on good ol' carrot tops. Once we knew we were using carrot tops, we had to also develop a companion recipe to actually use the darn carrots, and not just their tops. You'll find the fruits of that necessity on page 92—it's a sweet and spicy revelation on a sheet pan.

1 large shallot (about 3 ounces/85 g), finely chopped

1 habanero pepper, finely chopped (see Recipe Notes)

1¼ teaspoons fine sea salt, plus more if needed

2 cups (50 g) carrot top leaves, tough stems removed

1 cup (85 g) fresh or thawed, frozen grated coconut, lightly packed

1½ teaspoons fish sauce

Juice of 1 lime (1½ to 2 tablespoons)

Put the shallot, habanero pepper, and salt in a mortar and pound into a very coarse paste.

Roughly chop the carrot top leaves, add to the shallot mixture, and pound until bruised and starting to break down, 2 to 5 minutes. (Alternatively, you can finely chop the shallot, habanero, and carrot tops together on a cutting board, transfer to a bowl, season with the salt, and then move on with the recipe.)

Stir in the coconut, fish sauce, and lime juice. Taste and add more salt or lime juice, if necessary. Let sit for 30 minutes at room temperature to let the flavors marry.

RECIPE NOTES: You can remove the seeds if you want a milder sambol.

Like with the pol sambol, this sambol often has Maldive fish flakes in it, so if you're looking for an extra burst of umami, you can add a couple chopped tinned anchovies.

Lahsun Mirchi Chutney

Rajasthani Garlic-Chilli Chutney

Recipe by Saroj Rathore, Jyoti Rathore, and Poonam Rathore | Origin: Osian, Rajasthan | Makes 1 cup

On the Bishnoi family farm, in Inana, Rajasthan, where our Jodhana Cumin grows, the meals are simple, hearty, and packed with seasonal produce. What pulls every meal together is this garlic-chilli chutney, adding fiery-allium deliciousness into every bite. Enjoy with Rajasthani Dal (page 120), alongside Bajra Na Rotla (page 204) drenched in ghee with jaggery and a vegetable sabzi like Bhindi Masala (page 88), or dollop on top of a simple bowl of yogurt rice.

18 to 22 dried Kashmiri chillies (40 g)

⅓ cup (80 ml) untoasted sesame oil or other neutral oil, plus more for topping the jars

20 garlic cloves (100 g), peeled

2 teaspoons fine sea salt, plus more if needed

¾ teaspoon powdered jaggery or light brown sugar, plus more if needed

2 teaspoons cumin seeds

Juice of 1 lemon (2 to 4 tablespoons)

Remove and discard the stems of the chillies (if you want a milder chutney, you can empty out and discard the seeds), place in a large bowl, cover with boiling water, cover the bowl with a plate or plastic wrap, and let soak until the chillies are soft and pliable, at least 45 minutes, up to 4 hours. Reserve 1 cup (240 ml) of the soaking liquid, drain the soaked chillies, and transfer to a blender. (Alternatively, you can use a food processor.)

Place the sesame oil and garlic in a large skillet over medium heat. Cook, stirring occasionally, until the garlic turns light golden, 7 to 10 minutes. Using a slotted spoon, transfer the garlic to the blender with the chillies, and reserve the skillet with the oil for later use.

Add the salt, jaggery, and ½ cup (120 ml) chilli soaking liquid to the blender and blend on low speed, increasing the speed to high, until it forms a medium-coarse paste, adding a splash more soaking liquid if too thick, 15 to 30 seconds.

Return the skillet with the reserved garlic oil over medium heat. When shimmering, add the cumin seeds and cook, stirring frequently, until fragrant, 15 to 30 seconds. Add the blended chilli-garlic mixture, stirring to combine with the oil, and fry until the paste turns from bright red to brick red, 5 to 8 minutes. Turn off the heat and stir in the lemon juice. Taste and season with more salt and jaggery, if necessary.

Let cool completely and transfer to a clean jar, making sure there is a layer of oil covering the top (it may look too oily, but the chillies will continue to rehydrate as it rests). Transfer to the refrigerator and let sit for 1 to 2 days to let the flavors marry, then store for up to 3 months, making sure the top is covered in a thin layer of oil after every use.

Palli Chutney
Peanut Chutney

Recipe by Padmavathi Narne and Sulochana Meiyappan | Origin: Vinjanampadu, Andhra Pradesh, and Pollachi, Tamil Nadu | Makes 1 cup

In our travels, we found that the Andhra peanut chutney was nutty with a tamarind tartness, whereas the Tamil version was silky smooth and spicy. Ours combines the best bits of both! It's traditionally eaten with idli or dosa but is just as good on a thick slice of buttered toast (or with a spoon, straight out of the blender!).

1 golf ball–sized piece (40 g) seedless tamarind pulp

1 cup (240 ml) plus 2 tablespoons boiling water

4 teaspoons untoasted sesame oil or other neutral oil

½ cup (100 g) raw peanuts

1 tablespoon plus ½ teaspoon split urad dal

2½ teaspoons chana dal

2 garlic cloves, peeled

20 fresh curry leaves

½ to 1 serrano pepper, roughly chopped

2 teaspoons powdered jaggery or light brown sugar, plus more if needed

1 teaspoon fine sea salt, plus more if needed

¼ teaspoon cumin seeds

1 dried Byadgi or Guntur Sannam chilli, broken in half

Break the tamarind pulp into a few pieces, place in a bowl, and cover with the boiling water. Let soak for 30 minutes.

Meanwhile, heat 1 teaspoon of the sesame oil in a small skillet over medium-low heat. Add the peanuts and toast, stirring frequently, until they start to turn light brown in spots, 2 to 4 minutes. Transfer to a plate. Return the skillet to medium-low heat, along with 1 teaspoon of the remaining sesame oil, 1 tablespoon of the urad dal, 2 teaspoons of the chana dal, and the garlic, and cook, stirring frequently, until the urad dal turns light golden, 1 to 3 minutes. Add 12 of the curry leaves and cook, stirring frequently, until bright green, 10 to 30 seconds. Transfer to the plate with the toasted peanuts and let cool completely.

Strain the tamarind water through a fine-mesh sieve into a blender, discarding any leftover seeds and pulp. Add the cooled peanut-dal mixture, the serrano pepper, jaggery, salt, and cumin seeds and blend until smooth. If it's too thick, thin with 1 tablespoon water at a time until you reach a dippable consistency that coats the back of a spoon. Taste and season with more salt or jaggery, if necessary. Transfer to a bowl.

To make the tadka, heat the remaining 2 teaspoons sesame oil in a tadka spoon or small saucepan. Add the remaining ½ teaspoon urad dal and ½ teaspoon chana dal and cook, swirling the pan frequently, until the urad dal turns light golden, 30 seconds to 1 minute. Add the dried chilli and remaining 8 curry leaves and cook until bright green and translucent, 10 to 30 seconds. Pour the tadka over the chutney and serve immediately.

Fava Bean Chutney

Recipe by Zeinorin Angkang | Origin: Ukhrul, Manipur | Makes 1 cup

Chutneys are a way of life in Manipur. The base of these fiery condiments is the Sivathei chilli, which is the Tangkhul name for the naga chilli, bhut jolokia, or, more commonly, ghost pepper. These chillies are famous for their million-plus Scoville units of heat—making them one of the hottest chillies in the world!—and are a cornerstone of Manipuri cooking. We source ours from our friends Zeinorin and Leiyolan in Ukhrul, who slowly smoke them over bamboo mats before drying. To make the chutney, one or two Sivathei chillies are rehydrated, pounded with garlic and salt, then combined with seasonal vegetables and herbs, like fava beans, tomatoes, and potatoes. Every Manipuri meal has at least one chutney, scooped up in tiny bites with mountains of piping hot rice and a simply braised meat, vegetable, or smoked fish curry.

Serve alongside Sirārakhong Hāthei Chilli-Lemongrass Chicken and Rice (page 158), grilled pork shoulder or pork chops, or a simple piece of fish (grilled, roasted, pan-fried, you name it!).

½ to 1 dried Sivathei chilli (or any dried/smoked ghost pepper)

1½ pounds (680 g) fava beans in the pod

1 garlic clove, roughly chopped

1 teaspoon fine sea salt, plus more if needed

3 spring onions or 4 green onions

½ cup (10 g) roughly chopped mint leaves

Juice of ½ lemon (1 to 2 tablespoons), plus more if needed

1 teaspoon fish sauce

RECIPE NOTE: Instead of fava beans, you can use 1 cup (170 g) frozen peas or 1 cup (155 g) frozen, shelled edamame.

Place the dried Sivathei chilli in a small bowl, cover with boiling water, and soak for at least 30 minutes.

Shell the fava beans, discarding the outer pods. Prepare an ice bath in a medium bowl. Then, bring a large pot of water to a boil over high heat. Add the shelled fava beans and blanch until they float to the surface and turn bright green, 1½ minutes for smaller beans and 3 minutes for bigger, late-season beans. Drain and transfer the blanched fava beans to the ice bath for 5 minutes, then peel and discard the outer casing, leaving the bright green beans (you should have about 1 cup blanched, peeled fava beans).

Place the soaked chilli, discarding the soaking liquid, in a mortar along with the garlic and salt. Pound into a fine paste.

Thinly slice the white and light green parts of the spring onions and finely chop the dark green parts. Add the light and dark green parts to the chilli-garlic mixture along with the mint and pound into a coarse paste. Add half of the fava beans and pound into a very coarse paste. Add the lemon juice, fish sauce, and the remaining white parts of the spring onion and the other half of the fava beans and gently fold the ingredients together. Taste and season with more salt and lemon juice, if necessary. Let sit for 10 minutes for the flavors to marry.

FAVA BEAN CHUTNEY (bottom), page 46, and BURST TOMATO CHUTNEY (top), page 48

Burst Tomato Chutney

Recipe by Asha Loupy | Makes 1½ cups

½ to 1 dried Sivathei chilli

2 teaspoons canola oil

20 to 25 cherry tomatoes (about ½ pound/227 g)

1 teaspoon salt, plus more if needed

1 garlic clove, roughly chopped

2 spring onions or 3 green onions

⅓ cup (17 g) roughly chopped cilantro, tender leaves and stems

1 tablespoon lemon juice, plus more if needed

1 teaspoon fish sauce

Place the dried Sivathei chilli in a small bowl, cover with boiling water, and soak for at least 30 minutes.

Meanwhile, heat the canola oil in a large skillet over medium-high heat. When shimmering, add the cherry tomatoes, stirring to coat the tomatoes in the oil. Cook, undisturbed, until the bottoms of the tomatoes start to turn deep golden and blister, 2 to 4 minutes. Sprinkle with ¼ teaspoon of the salt, stir, and continue to cook, stirring occasionally, until the tomatoes start to burst and become slumpy, 3 to 6 minutes. Transfer the tomatoes to a small bowl and let cool for 15 minutes.

Meanwhile, place the soaked chilli, discarding the soaking liquid, in a mortar along with the garlic and remaining ¾ teaspoon salt and pound into a fine paste.

Thinly slice the white and light green parts of the spring onions and finely chop the dark green parts. Add the dark green parts to the chilli-garlic mixture along with the cilantro and pound into a coarse paste. Add a quarter of the tomatoes, gently smash, and mix them in until well combined. Add the lemon juice, fish sauce, the remaining light green parts of the spring onion, and the rest of the tomatoes, and gently fold the ingredients together, making sure to keep some of the tomatoes whole. Taste and season with more salt and lemon juice, if necessary. Let sit for 10 minutes for the flavors to marry.

RECIPE NOTES: Many Manipuri chutneys use smoked or salted fish as seasoning, which is why we reached for fish sauce to add that umami salinity. If you want to dial up the brininess even more, you can pound a couple tinned anchovies into the mix when you add the garlic.

Be careful when handling the dried Sivathei chillies—they are hot, hot, hot!—make sure to wash your hands after touching them.

Vengaya Thayir Pachadi
Red Onion Raita

Recipe by Sulochana Meiyappan | Origin: Pollachi, Tamil Nadu | Makes 2 cups

There are so many different types of raitas in the world, but in Tamil Nadu, if you're eating biryani, this one rules them all. The stinging sharpness of the red onion combined with cooling yogurt is the perfect foil to the rich, layered spices of biryani. The pachadi was made to be paired specifically with our Coconut Lamb Biryani (page 185) but is a perfect side to any rice and lentil combo you can imagine!

- 1 red onion, thinly sliced
- 1 cup (227 g) plain, full-fat yogurt (not Greek)
- 1 serrano pepper, halved lengthwise and thinly sliced
- ¼ cup (13 g) roughly chopped cilantro, leaves and tender stems
- ¾ teaspoon fine sea salt, plus more if needed

Place the red onion slices in a bowl and cover with cold water. Let soak for 30 minutes, then drain well and pat the onions dry.

In another bowl, mix the yogurt, serrano pepper, cilantro, and salt. Add the drained, soaked onions and stir to coat the onions in the yogurt mixture. Taste and season with more salt, if necessary. Serve with Coconut Lamb Biryani (page 185) or Thalassery Fish Biryani (page 183).

Tomato Pachadi

Andhra-Style Tomato Pickle

Recipe by Venkata Narasamma Kasaraneni | Origin: Kankipadu, Andhra Pradesh | Makes 3 cups

Roti pachadi refers to a fresh chutney that is stone ground in a mortar and pestle. However, this version is more of a pickle than a fresh chutney, so that it can last for several months. The Kasaraneni family usually sun-dry tomatoes on their sunny farm terrace, but we've opted to use an oven to achieve the same concentration of flavor in a fraction of the time. Enjoy with yogurt rice, Gongura Pappu (page 108), or Idli (page 195), or tucked into a grilled cheese!

14 (850 g) plum tomatoes

4 teaspoons fine sea salt

1 teaspoon ground turmeric

3 golf ball–sized pieces (180 g) seedless tamarind pulp

¾ cup (180 ml) boiling water

20 garlic cloves (100 g)

⅓ cup (40 g) Guntur Sannam chilli powder

¾ cup (180 ml) untoasted sesame or peanut oil, plus more for topping the jars

2 tablespoons chana dal

2 tablespoons split urad dal

2 tablespoons black mustard seeds

1 cup (10½ g) fresh curry leaves

To prepare the tomatoes, cut them into sixths or eighths, depending on their size. Place in a bowl with the salt and turmeric, gently toss, cover, and let sit at room temperature for at least 3 hours or up to overnight (if macerating for more than 4 hours, transfer to the refrigerator).

Preheat the oven to 175°F. Use a slotted spoon to remove the tomatoes and place them on a wire rack–lined sheet pan, reserving any liquid that has accumulated. Bake until semi-dry, 2½ to 4 hours, depending on the ripeness of the tomatoes.

Meanwhile, rip the tamarind into small pieces, add to the reserved liquid along with the boiling water, and toss to coat. Cover and let soak while the tomatoes bake, massaging a few times to break up the pulp. Then, strain through a fine-mesh sieve, pressing with a spatula to extract as much pulp through as possible, into a large bowl.

Finely grate 4 of the garlic cloves into the tamarind mixture and sprinkle the chilli powder over the top of the mixture, but do not stir!

Heat the sesame oil in a medium saucepan over medium heat. Add the remaining 16 garlic cloves, the chana dal, urad dal, and mustard seeds. Cook, stirring occasionally, until the garlic and lentils are starting to turn light golden, 2 to 5 minutes. Add the curry leaves and cook until they are bright green, 15 to 45 seconds. Pour this mixture over the tamarind mixture, making sure to hit the chilli powder.

Mix well and let cool for 30 minutes. Add the semi-dried tomatoes and gently fold them in. Transfer the pachadi to sterilized jars and top with a little bit of oil. Refrigerate for 2 days to let the flavors marry before eating. Store the pachadi in the refrigerator for up to 3 months, making sure a thin layer of oil is covering the surface.

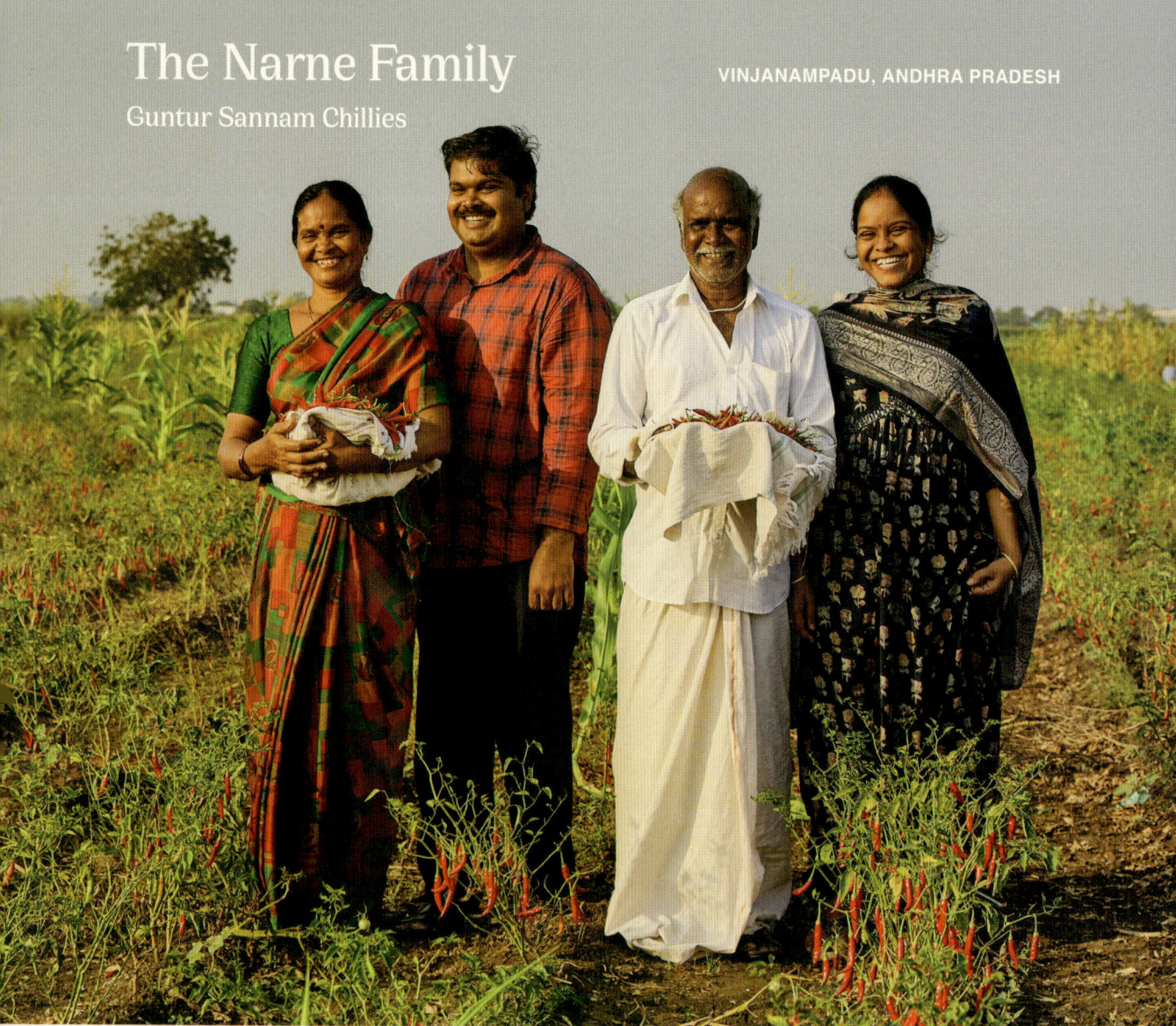

The Narne Family
Guntur Sannam Chillies

VINJANAMPADU, ANDHRA PRADESH

Guntur Sannam Chillies were the very first chillies I sourced back in 2018, and to this day, they're the MVPs of my kitchen. Whether I'm making Korean kimchi stew, Italian arrabbiata, or a classic Andhra chicken curry, their medium heat, bright tomato-y punch, and hint of nuttiness always delivers.

I first heard of the Narne family via Prabhu Kasaraneni, our Pragati Turmeric farm partner (page 30), and that introduction became the first link in an incredible network of regenerative farmers that we work with across South Asia. Today, the cross-pollination of skills, seeds, and camaraderie that exists between our 140+ partners is one of the strongest parts of our supply chain, and it all started with Prabhu's admiration for the Narne family's farming methods.

Brothers Hanumantharao Narne and Satyanarayanarao Narne live and farm alongside each other along with three generations of their families. Their farm is legendary in regenerative agriculture circles for being some of the earliest adopters of zero budget natural farming, an indigenous method that uses hyper-local, natural inputs like cow dung and botanical extracts to build self-sustaining ecosystems. Picture thriving fields buzzing with pollinators, abundant intercropping of lentils, spices, and veggies, and zero synthetic fertilizers or pesticides. Farmers from across India travel to meet the Narne family and learn from them.

To preserve the chillies' vibrant flavor, they're milled on the farm in the traditional way—in small batches, with a touch of rock salt and cold-pressed sesame oil—both natural preservatives and flavor boosters.

Recipes from the Narne Family

Karam Podi, aka Gunpowder Podi 26

Palli Chutney 45

Aloo Masala 105

Seasonal Sambar 114

Ghee Roast Dosa 192

The Sakariya Family
Nandini Coriander, Hariyali Fennel

SHEDUBHAR, GUJARAT

In the early days of Diaspora Spice Co., finding partners who were growing regeneratively, aligned with our values, were truly growing for flavor, AND could scale felt near impossible. It took five years of relentless hunting in rather strange places, including a Gujarati-Maharashtrian natural farming WhatsApp group. That's how I ended up driving down a dusty unpaved road in the winter of 2019 to meet Dharmesh bhai Sakariya—a nursery shop owner, sixth-generation farmer, and, supposedly, coriander grower extraordinaire.

The Sakariya family farm is twenty acres of regeneratively grown, diverse crops like custard apples, millets, heirloom wheat, and, of course, their Nandini Coriander—named after their beloved cow and the farm's undisputed star, Nandini. Where conventional coriander tastes a little nutty but mostly just powdery, this coriander was bright, incredibly lemony, and absolutely what I was looking for.

A couple years later, Dharmesh asked what else we might need as I grew the business, and I mentioned my two-year quest for the perfect fennel: sweet, vibrant, and potent enough to blow away the competition. "Give me two years," he said. I forgot. He absolutely did not. Dharmesh dug into his mom's seed bank, nurtured an heirloom variety, shade-drying the resulting seeds for peak flavor and color, and delivered. Four years and dozens of samples later, the Sakariyas gave us the most licorice-y, parrot-green fennel we've ever tasted—proof that heirloom seeds, low input farming, and sheer determination grow the most delicious spices in the world.

The Sakariyas are not only incredibly self-sufficient, but they're also dedicated to working together as a family. Their stoves run on fuel from cow dung in their shed, and every meal is a celebration of grains, vegetables, and spices they grow themselves; they really are living their values every single day.

Recipes from the Sakariya Family

Gujarati Green Chutney 38

Pakora Party 64

Sakariya Fam Pakora 66

Ringan no Oro 96

Kadhi 123

Khichdi 187

Methi Latte 216

Fennel Soda 220

Snacks

Doud Alle Dip 59
Sri Lankan Fish Puffs 61
Pakora Party 64
Sakariya Fam Pakora 66
Zucchini Na Muthiya 67

Doud Alle Dip
Roasted Squash and Labneh Dip

Recipe inspired by Aaliya Mir | Origin: Pampore, Kashmir | Serves 4 to 6

Aaliya, our saffron farm partner's wife, is one of the best home cooks I've ever encountered, but lucky for us she is an even more gifted teacher. Kashmiri cuisine can take a lifetime to master, but in just a few peaceful days in Aaliya's kitchen, we started to grasp the techniques, the ingredient pairings, and the building of flavors of Kashmiri Valley cuisine.

This dip is inspired by doud alle, a seasonal pumpkin, walnut, and yogurt chutney. Since October is both the time of the walnut harvest in the saffron fields and the heirloom pumpkin harvest in their backyard kitchen garden, Aaliya's pumpkin walnut chutney is a beautiful expression of Kashmiri autumn. We've tweaked it to be a dip instead of a chutney, but the heart of it remains. This recipe uses a traditional Kashmiri spice combination of caraway, fennel, and chilli powder for the tadka, and the result is a very fun, party-ready dip.

½ cup (56 g) raw walnut halves

One 1- to 1½-pound (454 to 680 g) honeynut or butternut squash

4 tablespoons (60 ml) extra virgin olive oil

2 teaspoons fine sea salt, plus more if needed

3 garlic cloves

1 cup (240 g) labneh

1 to 2 teaspoons mild honey, such as acacia, orange blossom, or wildflower, optional

1 teaspoon caraway seeds

1 teaspoon fennel seeds

1 teaspoon Guntur Sannam chilli powder

Flaky sea salt, for finishing

Preheat the oven to 325°F. Spread the walnuts on a sheet pan and roast until lightly toasted, 11 to 14 minutes. Remove from the oven and let cool.

Increase the oven temperature to 400°F. Cut the squash in half lengthwise and scoop out and discard the seeds. Drizzle with 1 tablespoon of the olive oil and sprinkle the cut sides with 1 teaspoon of the sea salt. Place the squash cut-side down on a baking sheet and roast until tender, 25 to 30 minutes for honeynut squash or up to 45 to 55 minutes for butternut squash. Remove from the oven and let cool for 30 minutes.

Place the cooled, roasted walnuts in a mortar and pound, breaking them up into small pieces about the size of pebbly sand, leaving some bigger pieces for texture.

Grate 1 of the garlic cloves.

Scoop the roasted squash flesh into a bowl and add the labneh, the grated garlic clove, two-thirds of the toasted walnuts, and the remaining 1 teaspoon sea salt. Mix with a fork, mashing the squash so that it still has a rustic texture (if you prefer a smoother dip, you can

continues

continue mashing until you reach the desired consistency or blend the squash separately before adding it to the labneh).

Taste and adjust sweetness with the honey, if desired, and salt, if necessary. (With honeynut squash, you might not need any honey, but with out-of-season butternut squash, season with honey to taste.) Set aside.

To prepare the tadka, thinly slice the remaining 2 garlic cloves. Then, heat the remaining 3 tablespoons olive oil in a small skillet over medium heat. Add the sliced garlic, caraway seeds, and fennel seeds and cook, stirring or swirling frequently, until the garlic turns light golden, 1 to 3 minutes. Turn off the heat, add the chilli powder, and mix to combine.

To serve, transfer the dip to a shallow serving bowl and create a swoosh pattern on the surface with the back of a spoon. Spoon the prepared tadka over the dip, sprinkle with the remaining crushed toasted walnuts, and garnish with flaky sea salt.

Sri Lankan Fish Puffs

Recipe inspired by Perera & Sons | Origin: Colombo, Sri Lanka | Makes 16 puffs

Perera & Sons is a century-old (est. 1902!) Colombo institution known for their breakfast buns. While Portuguese colonial rule in the sixteenth century introduced bread to Sri Lanka, Sri Lankans have really made it their own, weaving the flavors of the island into plush rolls stuffed with a variety of fillings, like sambol, spiced fish, and potatoes. These two have become staples in the glass cases of Perera & Sons, and mandatory road trip snacks for the long, winding drive from Colombo to Kandy, where our Peni Miris Cinnamon and Kandyan Cloves are grown.

This recipe is our ode to these famous baked goods. Of course, Asha put the Diaspora spin on the fish bun, brightening the classic tuna-potato filling with tangy bursts of cherry tomatoes, swapping the sweet, fluffy dough for frozen puff pastry and really amping up the spices. Keep in mind, you'll need to thaw the puff pastry overnight in the fridge ahead of time!

2 tablespoons canola oil

24 fresh curry leaves

2 large shallots (about ⅓ pound/151 g), diced

2 garlic cloves, finely chopped

1 serrano pepper, finely chopped

10 to 12 cherry tomatoes, halved (about ¼ pound/113 g)

2 teaspoons Sri Lankan Roasted Curry Powder (page 22)

1¼ teaspoons fine sea salt

½ teaspoon ground turmeric

½ teaspoon Byadgi chilli powder

continues

To prepare the filling, heat the canola oil in a large skillet over medium heat. Add the curry leaves—be careful, they will crack and pop!—and cook until bright green and translucent, 10 to 30 seconds. Add the shallots, garlic, and serrano pepper and cook, stirring occasionally, until the shallots soften and start to turn light golden around the edges, 5 to 8 minutes.

Add the cherry tomatoes, curry powder, salt, turmeric, chilli powder, and cinnamon. Cook, stirring occasionally, until the tomatoes start to soften and become jammy, 4 to 7 minutes. Add the boiled potatoes and mash them into the tomato mixture. Cook until the potatoes have absorbed some of the liquid from the tomatoes, 2 to 4 minutes. Turn off the heat, transfer the mixture to a bowl, and let it cool completely. Add the drained tuna, breaking it up into big chunks when adding to the potato mixture, and gently fold it in, making sure not to fully mash the fish. Keep chilled while you roll out the pastry.

On a lightly floured surface, roll the puff pastry into a 16 x 16-inch square. Using a sharp knife, cut the puff pastry into four equal pieces

continues

Snacks

¼ teaspoon ground cinnamon

⅓ pound (151 g) boiled, peeled Yukon Gold potatoes

One 6- to 8-ounce (170 to 225 g) jar good-quality oil-packed tuna, drained

One 14-ounce (396.9 g) package frozen puff pastry, thawed

All-purpose flour, for rolling the pastry

1 large egg

Freshly cracked black pepper

crosswise, then repeat the same process lengthwise, leaving you with sixteen 4 x 4-inch squares. Whisk the egg well and set aside.

To fill and fold the puffs, take one puff pastry square and place a heaping tablespoon of filling in one corner of the bottom half of the square. Press down on the filling to spread it out, making sure to leave a ¼-inch border around the edges. Brush the bottom two edges with egg wash and fold the top pastry over diagonally. Seal the edges with a fork, dipping it in flour if it starts to stick. Repeat with the rest of the pastry and filling.

Transfer the assembled puffs to a parchment-lined sheet pan, spacing them about 1 inch apart. Reserve the leftover egg wash. Place the puffs in the freezer for 20 minutes.

Meanwhile, preheat the oven to 375°F.

Remove the chilled puffs from the freezer. Brush each with a thin layer of egg wash and garnish each with a couple of cracks of black pepper. Cut a slit in the top of each puff and bake until the puff pastry is cooked through and golden brown, 33 to 38 minutes. Let cool for 10 minutes before serving. Serve warm or at room temperature.

Pakora Party
Diaspora's Pakora

Recipe inspired by the Sakariya Family | Origin: Shedubhar, Gujarat | Serves 4 to 6

Crashing the Sakariya family's pakora party, where they fry an assortment of herby vegetable fritters en masse, was one of the absolute highlights of our cookbook travels. For the party, they pull a gas cylinder out onto their front porch, place a GIANT kadhai onto it, and begin frying. Everything that they can harvest from their garden will be made into a pakora! Herbs! Greens! Root veg! Toss it all in!

We've given you two ways to pakora. First up, the Diaspora take, which is a crunchier vegetable fritter and a great way to use up odds and ends from your CSA box or the sad bits of veggies languishing in the crisper. We're partial to karela (bitter melon), sweet potatoes, spinach, zucchini, Brussels sprouts, or asparagus. But the world is a choose-your-own-pakora adventure. My favorite is a trio of bitter melon, pumpkin, and onions, for the perfect balance of bitter, earthy sweetness and allium-y umami.

The second pakora is the Sakariya family recipe—which is more fluffy and puffy thanks to the addition of some baking soda—with a little California twist of lemon zest and dill. Whatever route you choose, pakoras NEED to be dipped in a tangy or herby sauce/chutney to balance out the fried batter. The kids go wild for ketchup, but I am a sucker for our acidic, bright Green Chutney (pages 36 to 38).

¾ pound (340 g) vegetables of your choice, thinly sliced or cut into matchsticks

1 small red onion, thinly sliced (about 6 ounces/170 g)

1 to 2 serrano peppers, thinly sliced

1 cup (50 g) roughly chopped cilantro, leaves and tender stems

¾ cup (90 g) besan (chickpea flour)

¼ cup (40 g) rice flour

1 teaspoon ground turmeric

½ teaspoon Guntur Sannam chilli powder

Place the vegetables of your choice, the onion, serrano peppers, cilantro, chickpea flour, rice flour, turmeric, chilli powder, the whole spice combo of your choice, and salt in a large bowl and toss to coat the vegetables in the flour mixture. Let sit for at least 15 minutes, up to 1 hour.

Gently massage the vegetable mixture. Then, add 1 tablespoon of water at a time, mixing periodically, until a thick batter forms (you're looking for something a little thicker than pancake batter).

Heat 1½ inches of canola oil in a Dutch oven or other large, heavy-bottomed pot over medium-high heat to 350°F. Gently drop 2-tablespoon portions of the battered vegetables into the hot oil and fry, flipping halfway through, until the vegetables are cooked through and the outside is deep golden and crisp, 4 to 8 minutes depending on the vegetables you're using.

Using a slotted spoon, transfer the fried pakora to a baking rack–lined tray to drain, sprinkling with a little extra salt or chaat masala, if desired. Repeat with the remaining pakora mixture. Serve hot with ketchup or the chutney of your choice.

Whole spice combo of your choice (see below)

1¼ teaspoons fine sea salt, plus more if needed

Canola oil, for frying

Fine sea salt or chaat masala, optional

Ketchup or chutney of choice, for serving

OPTION 1: FRAGRANT, AROMATIC SPICE COMBO

1 teaspoon cumin seeds

½ teaspoon fennel seeds

OPTION 2: PUNCHY, AROMATIC SPICE COMBO

1 teaspoon black mustard seeds

½ teaspoon coriander seeds, lightly crushed

½ teaspoon nigella seeds

OPTION 3: SAVORY, HERBACEOUS SPICE COMBO

½ teaspoon cumin seeds

½ teaspoon coriander seeds, lightly crushed

½ teaspoon fennel seeds

Pinch of ajwain seeds

RECIPE NOTE: If you're using karela (bitter melon), thinly slice it, toss with ½ teaspoon Surya salt, let sit for 30 minutes, and then pat dry before using. This will reduce some of the bitterness.

Sakariya Fam Pakora
Mixed Herb and Onion Fritters

Recipe by Bhanuben Sakariya | Origin: Shedubhar, Gujara | Serves 6 to 8

1 cup (120 g) besan (chickpea flour)

½ cup (80 g) rice flour

1¼ teaspoons fine sea salt

1 teaspoon baking soda

⅛ teaspoon asafetida, optional

1 bunch spring onions, thinly sliced (4 to 5 spring onions)

2 stalks green garlic, thinly sliced

1 cup (50 g) roughly chopped cilantro, leaves and tender stems

½ cup (10 g) roughly chopped fresh mint leaves

¼ cup (8 g) roughly chopped fresh dill fronds

1 serrano pepper, thinly sliced

1 tablespoon finely chopped ginger

1 lemon

2 tablespoons kasoori methi (dried fenugreek leaves), optional

1½ teaspoons coriander seeds

1 teaspoon fennel seeds

½ teaspoon ground turmeric

⅛ teaspoon ajwain seeds

Canola oil, for frying

Green Chutney (pages 36 to 38), for serving

Combine the besan, rice flour, salt, baking soda, and asafetida, if using, in a large bowl.

Add the spring onions, green garlic, cilantro, mint, dill, serrano pepper (if you want a milder heat, remove the seeds and ribs), ginger, the zest of 1 lemon, reserving the juice for later, kasoori methi, if using, coriander seeds, fennel seeds, turmeric, and ajwain seeds, and toss to coat everything in the dry ingredients.

Add 3 tablespoons lemon juice from the zested lemon and, using your hands, gently massage the ingredients, adding 1 tablespoon of water at a time until a thick batter forms that just holds the alliums and herbs together.

Heat 1½ inches of canola oil in a Dutch oven or other large, heavy-bottomed pot over medium-high heat to 350°F. Working in batches, drop 2-tablespoon pieces of the batter into the oil and fry until puffed and golden brown, 2 to 5 minutes, flipping halfway through. Transfer the fried bhajiya to a wire rack–lined baking sheet to drain, and repeat with the remaining batter. Serve hot with Green Chutney alongside.

RECIPE NOTES: If you can't find green garlic or it is out of season, you can substitute 1 medium leek, white and light green parts, thinly sliced, and 2 finely chopped garlic cloves.

If you can't find spring onions, you can substitute 1 bunch green onions (6 to 8).

Zucchini Na Muthiya

Savory Pan-Fried Zucchini Cakes

Recipe inspired by Swati Snacks | Origin: Ahmedabad, Gujarat | Serves 6

Farsan are a category of savory steamed or fried snacks that are consumed across Western India, but we Gujaratis take our farsan hour especially seriously. The favorite farsans of my childhood were all about textural contrast—soft, steamed interior, crunchy browned exterior, and a delicious sesame and mustard tadka on top to pull it all together. One of my faves, doodhi na muthiya, literally means fists of bottle gourd, which is a watery, mild squash that grows year-round on the subcontinent. The muthiyas are rustic, hand-shaped dumplings made from a silky blend of wheat, semolina, and chickpea flours that are then seasoned with hella herbs and layered with savory spices in both the batter and the tadka.

Swati Snacks is an institution that has been specializing in fresh, seasonal Gujarati food since 1963, and their farsan is especially renowned, with most of the ingredients for the cafe coming from their family farm outside Ahmedabad, the capital of Gujarat. Their muthiya are soft and spongy, highlighting the squash and herbs, whereas the Sakariya family's version are deep-fried and compact for maximum crispiness.

Our version is the best of both worlds. We swapped zucchini for doodhi because it's so much more easily available here in the US—and there can never truly be enough zucchini recipes come midsummer!—but we kept all the other seasonings very much the same. And don't forget—farsans are ultimately to West Indians what idlis are to South Indians—a perfect vessel for scooping large volumes of Green Chutney (pages 36 to 38) into your mouth.

1 teaspoon coriander seeds, lightly crushed

¾ teaspoon fennel seeds

½ teaspoon cumin seeds

½ cup (60 g) all-purpose flour

½ cup (60 g) besan (chickpea flour)

½ cup (60 g) semolina flour

1 teaspoon granulated sugar

continues

Heat a tadka spoon or small skillet over medium heat. Add the coriander seeds, fennel seeds, and cumin seeds and toast, swirling the pan occasionally, until the coriander turns a couple of shades darker and the fennel smells fragrant and toasty, 15 to 45 seconds. Transfer to a large bowl along with the all-purpose flour, besan, semolina flour, sugar, sea salt, turmeric, baking soda, and asafetida, if using, and mix well.

Fill a large pot (big enough to fit a bamboo or flat mesh steamer) with 1 inch of water, cover, and bring to a boil over medium-high heat. (Alternatively, you can create a makeshift steamer in a large pot by placing three balled-up pieces of aluminum foil in the pot and then resting an oiled heatproof plate on top of the foil balls.)

continues

1 teaspoon fine sea salt

¾ teaspoon ground turmeric

¾ teaspoon baking soda

⅛ teaspoon asafetida, optional

2 to 3 medium zucchini (about ¾ pound/340 g)

3 green onions, thinly sliced

¼ cup (13 g) roughly chopped cilantro, leaves and tender stems

1 tablespoon finely chopped ginger

1 garlic clove, finely grated

1 tablespoon lemon juice

4 tablespoons (60 ml) untoasted sesame oil, plus more for oiling the steamer

1 tablespoon white sesame seeds

1½ teaspoons black mustard seeds

24 fresh curry leaves

Flaky sea salt, optional

Green Chutney (pages 36 to 38), for serving

EQUIPMENT

10-inch bamboo steamer or fine-mesh flat steamer basket

Meanwhile, remove and discard the fibrous stems from the zucchini and grate on the large side of a box grater. Transfer the grated zucchini to a clean kitchen towel and squeeze over the sink to release as much liquid as possible (there will be a lot!). Add the squeezed, grated zucchini to the dry ingredients along with the green onions, cilantro, ginger, garlic, and lemon juice. Using your hands, mix the ingredients together, gently massaging and squeezing them together to release any residual moisture in the zucchini until a firm dough comes together about the consistency of Play-Doh (if the dough is too dry, add 1 teaspoon water at a time until it comes together).

Divide the dough into two pieces and, using lightly oiled hands, form into two 8-inch-long logs. Line a 10-inch bamboo steamer or fine-mesh flat steamer basket with a piece of parchment paper and place the logs 1½ inches apart in the steamer. Reduce the heat to medium-low and steam, covered, until puffed and cooked through—it should be firm to the touch and a toothpick should come out clean when inserted into the middle—30 to 40 minutes. Remove from the pot and let cool, covered, for 15 minutes (this will make it easier to slice).

Using a serrated knife, cut the steamed muthiya into ½-inch-thick slices. Heat 1 tablespoon of the sesame oil in a large skillet over medium-high heat. When shimmering, add half of the sliced muthiya, cut-side down, and pan-fry until golden on both sides, 2 to 4 minutes per side. Transfer to a serving platter. Heat 1 tablespoon of the remaining oil and repeat the frying process with the other half of the muthiya.

Return the skillet to medium heat and add the remaining 2 tablespoons oil. When shimmering, add the sesame seeds and mustard seeds and cook, stirring frequently, until the sesame seeds start to turn light golden, 1 to 2 minutes. Add the curry leaves—be careful, these will crackle and pop!—and cook, stirring occasionally, until bright green and translucent, 10 to 30 seconds.

To finish, spoon the toasted seed–curry leaf mixture over the muthiya and sprinkle with flaky sea salt, if desired. Serve with Green Chutney.

The Hill Wild Community
Sirārakhong Hāthei Chillies

UKHRUL, MANIPUR

When Zeinorin Angkang talks about her vision for Ukhrul, a hilly rural district in northeastern Manipur nestled right by the Indo-Burmese border, her eyes light up. Along with her husband and business partner Leiyolan (Alan) Vashum, they aren't just bringing the flavors of Ukhrul to the world—they're committed to ensuring that their Tangkhul Naga community (a Tibeto-Burmese ethnic group indigenous to these hills) thrives.

Zeinorin grew up exploring Ukhrul's edible jungles, pockets stuffed with foraged fruits and berries. Those early adventures shaped her appreciation for the flavors of her homeland. This love is woven into her and Alan's current work running Hill Wild, an incredible network of farmers and foragers sharing tools, creating markets, and encouraging sustainable business practices.

Throughout Zeino's and Alan's lives, Manipur has grappled with insurgencies, increased militarization, and a lack of recognition for its hundreds of tribes of its indigenous peoples, leaving communities like theirs—the Tangkhul Naga—constantly caught between resilience and erasure. Despite the constant disruption and conflict taking a heavy toll on their community, Zeino and Alan run Hill Wild to ensure the story of their tribe is not one of survival but one of joy, culture, and abundance.

In my work sourcing spices, it has been important to recognize that some communities have very good reasons to be wary of outsiders like me, an urbanite from Mumbai. I first visited Manipur in 2019, hoping to source the state's famous king chillies. It was the first time that I came back from a trip completely empty-handed, not having had a grasp of the local language and culture. It was a good reminder that to build truly equitable supply chains, sometimes it is more ethical to *not* go straight to the source but to use a trusted local partner instead. Zeino and Alan's intentional and meticulous care for their community has made Hill Wild the perfect sourcing partner to us.

I can safely say that the Sirārakhong Hāthei Chillies and Wild Heimang Sumac sourced by Hill Wild are the most delicious I've ever had. The chillies, grown communally in the Sirārakhong village, are dried on the plant and wood-smoked on bamboo mats right after harvest, giving them an incredible smoky, fruity heat. The Heimang sumac, foraged by the women of the Tangkhul community in winter, is sun-dried and ground into a zesty powder that tastes like black tea and cranberry.

Recipes from the Hill Wild Community

Fava Bean Chutney 46

Burst Tomato Chutney 48

Singju 80

Edamame and Cherry Tomato Salad 83

Sirārakhong Hāthei Chilli-Lemongrass Chicken and Rice 158

Hoksa 162

Heimang Soda 224

Veggies

Bitter Melon and Heirloom Tomato Salad 74

Blistered Asparagus with Pisyun Loon 76

Daikon and Orange Salad with Sesame-Cumin Dressing 78

Singju 80

Edamame and Cherry Tomato Salad 83

Bhindi Masala 88

Pipinna Kiri Hodi 91

Spiced Maple-Roasted Carrots with Carrot Top Sambol 92

Pazha Manga Curry 94

Ringan no Oro 96

Haakh 99

Nadru Yakhni 102

Aloo Masala 105

Bitter Melon and Heirloom Tomato Salad

Recipe by Asha Loupy | Origin: Colombo, Sri Lanka | Serves 4 to 6

Karawila sambol is an iconic Sri Lankan dish that has converted many a bitter melon hater. Our first time trying it was a signature Asha-Sana moment when we made eye contact and knew that it was going to become a California-fied super hit. This salad dazzles on every level—funky, bitter, sweet, salty, textural! Guaranteed to make you do a lil happy dance with each bite.

2 medium Indian bitter melons (about ½ pound/227 g)

2½ teaspoons fine sea salt

1 pound (454 g) heirloom tomatoes

½ small red onion (about 3 ounces/85 g)

2 limes

1 garlic clove, finely grated

1 tablespoon fish sauce

2 teaspoons powdered jaggery or light brown sugar

3 tablespoons extra virgin olive oil

Canola oil, for frying

10 to 12 cherry tomatoes, halved (about ¼ pound/113 g)

1 serrano pepper, thinly sliced

1 cup (50 g) cilantro, torn into big bite-sized pieces

RECIPE NOTE: If you want less heat, you can halve the serrano pepper, remove the seeds and ribs, and thinly slice into half-moons.

To prepare the bitter melons, thinly slice into ⅛-inch rounds, transfer to a bowl, and toss with 1 teaspoon of the salt. Let sit at room temperature for at least 30 minutes (this will draw out some of the bitterness), up to 2 hours.

Cut the tomatoes into different sizes, some thick slices, wedges, and chunks and place in a fine-mesh sieve over a large bowl. Sprinkle with ¾ teaspoon of the remaining salt, very gently toss, and let sit for 30 minutes.

Thinly slice the onion, transfer to a bowl, add a couple handfuls of ice, and cover with cold water. Let sit for 15 to 30 minutes.

Zest and juice the limes (about 2 teaspoons zest and 3 to 4 tablespoons juice) into a jar. Add the garlic, fish sauce, jaggery, and the remaining ¾ teaspoon salt to the bowl and shake until the jaggery is dissolved. Add the olive oil and shake until the dressing is emulsified. Set aside.

Place the salted bitter melon on half of a clean kitchen towel, leaving any water that's accumulated in the bowl, fold the other half of the towel over, and press gently to dry well. Heat ⅛ inch canola oil in a large skillet over medium heat. When shimmering, fry the bitter melon in batches until cooked through and golden brown on both sides, 1 to 3 minutes per side. Transfer the fried bitter melon to a wire rack–lined baking sheet.

To assemble the salad, arrange the salted tomatoes on a serving platter, discarding or saving any liquid that's accumulated for another use, reserving the bowl. Shake the dressing to re-emulsify, then spoon half over the tomatoes. Drain the sliced red onion and add to the bowl along with the cherry tomatoes, serrano pepper, fried bitter melon, and half of the remaining dressing, and gently toss to coat. Arrange the dressed bitter melon mixture around and on top of the dressed tomatoes. Garnish with the cilantro, spoon the remaining dressing on top, and serve immediately.

Blistered Asparagus with Pisyun Loon

Recipe by Amita Rawat | Origin: Kotgaon, Uttarakhand | Serves 4

Come spring, fiddlehead ferns, stinging nettles, and wild asparagus cover the Himalayan mountainside in green while over thirty varieties of pink, red, and orange rhododendrons burst into bloom. It's a deep exhale and a truly beautiful sight after the months of bitter, snowy cold. On one of my first Pahadi garlic sourcing visits, Amita took me on an afternoon foraging hike—I looked on in awe as she deftly scaled the mountains and identified varieties of delicious edible plants where my untrained eyes just saw weeds. We went home with a heaping bunch of tender wild asparagus that we sautéed and seasoned simply with pisyun loon. This is our slightly Californian take on her foraged Pahadi springtime staple—it's simple, seasonal food at its best.

3 tablespoons extra virgin olive oil

¾ pound (340 g) asparagus, woody ends trimmed

1 lemon

Pisyun Loon (page 28), for finishing

Heat a large cast-iron skillet over high heat. Add 2 tablespoons of the olive oil and heat until shimmering, then add the asparagus, tossing in the oil and spreading into an even layer. Cook undisturbed until starting to brown and blister on the side touching the pan, 2 to 4 minutes. Flip and continue to cook until tender but still retaining a bite, 2 to 4 minutes, depending on the thickness of the asparagus.

To serve, transfer to a serving platter, zest the lemon over the spears, squeeze the juice of half of the lemon over top, drizzle with the remaining 1 tablespoon oil, and gently toss to coat. To finish, sprinkle with a couple pinches of pisyun loon.

Daikon and Orange Salad with Sesame-Cumin Dressing

Recipe inspired by Pahadi Khatta Hua Nimbu Mooli | Origin: Kalap, Uttarakhand | Serves 4 to 6

After thirteen hours of travel to Dehradun, Uttarakhand, Asha and I stumbled into Garhwali chef Yojana Khanduri Chaudhary's home, a little worse for wear and with very hungry tummies. The minute we walked in, the most wonderful aromas wrapped around us like a much-needed, warm hug. Everything Yojana cooked that night—from tender lamb curry to her famous achaars—was iconic, but the dish that really stood out was the Khatta Hua Nimbu Mooli, a simple radish and citrus salad, dressed with toasted sesame and cumin seeds, green chillies, yogurt, mustard seed oil, and lemon juice. Each bright, spicy, roasty-toasty, crunchy bite brought us back to life.

½ pound (227 g) daikon

2 medium Cara Cara or navel oranges (about 1 pound/454 g)

1½ tablespoons sesame seeds

½ teaspoon cumin seeds

3 tablespoons extra virgin olive oil

Juice of ½ lemon (1 to 2 tablespoons)

1 teaspoon mild honey or maple syrup

1 teaspoon fine sea salt, plus more if needed

3 cups (60 g) lightly packed arugula

½ cup (25 g) roughly chopped cilantro, leaves and tender stems

1 Fresno chilli, very thinly sliced

½ cup (120 g) labneh

Flaky sea salt, for finishing

To prepare the daikon, peel and thinly slice into ⅛-inch rounds. (If your daikon is larger than 2 inches in diameter, cut in half lengthwise, then thinly slice into half-moons.) Transfer the sliced daikon to a bowl of ice water and let rest for 15 minutes.

To segment the oranges, take one orange at a time and cut ¼ inch off the top and the bottom of the fruit. Place the orange cut-side down and, using a sharp knife, cut the peel and pith off in strips, starting from the top and cutting around the curve of the fruit. Discard the peels. Cut between the membranes to remove each orange wedge and transfer the segments to a bowl. Before discarding the membrane-y center of the orange, squeeze out any juice to the bowl. Set aside.

Heat a tadka spoon or small skillet over medium heat. Add the sesame seeds and cumin seeds and toast, stirring frequently, until the sesame seeds turn light golden, 1 to 3 minutes. Transfer to a mortar and let cool completely. When cooled, grind into a medium-coarse powder. Set aside.

Pour any juice that's accumulated from the oranges into a jar, leaving the segments behind for later use. Add the olive oil, lemon juice, honey, and salt and shake until the dressing is emulsified. Taste and season with more salt, if necessary.

To assemble, drain the daikon, discarding any ice, and pat dry well. Wipe out the bowl and add the daikon back to the bowl along with the orange segments, arugula, cilantro, Fresno pepper, reserved ground

RECIPE NOTES: For a milder heat, remove seeds and ribs from Fresno peppers before slicing. And if you can't find Fresno peppers, swap in serrano or jalapeño peppers.

If you can't find daikon, good ol' Easter radishes work in a pinch!

If preparing ahead, keep all components separate and assemble right before serving.

sesame-cumin mixture, and half of the dressing. Using clean hands, gently toss to coat, taste, and season with more salt, if necessary.

To serve, swoosh the labneh in a thin layer over a serving platter, pile the salad on top, drizzle with more dressing, if desired, and finish with flaky sea salt. Serve immediately.

Singju
Manipuri Cabbage Salad

Inspired by the Ava Women's Market | Origin: Sirārakhong, Manipur | Serves 4 to 6

We first tried singju—a salad that lands between bhel (the Indian tangy, crispy rice snack) and nostalgic Chinese American cabbage salad—at the Ukhrul Ava Women's Market, the largest women-run market in Asia. It's a vital food economy for the Tangkhul community, rooted in wild-foraged, locally farmed, indigenous produce. Ours doubles the crunch with baked, crushed instant ramen and seasoned white beans.

One 15-ounce (439 g) can white beans

6 tablespoons (90 ml) extra virgin olive oil

1 teaspoon Sirārakhong Hāthei chilli powder

1½ teaspoons fine sea salt, plus more if needed

One 3-ounce (85 g) package ramen, preferably Indomie

1 tablespoon perilla or black sesame seeds

3 cups (165 g) lightly packed finely shredded green cabbage

2 cups (50 g) lightly packed pea shoots or sprouts

Juice of ½ lemon (about 2 tablespoons)

1 teaspoon ground sumac

RECIPE NOTE: If you're prepping this salad ahead of time, keep the cabbage, crispy bits, and dressing separate, and toss right before serving to maintain the crunchiness of the bean-ramen mixture.

Preheat the oven to 400°F.

Rinse and drain the white beans and dry well. In a large bowl, toss the beans with 3 tablespoons of the olive oil, the chilli powder, and ¾ teaspoon of the salt. Spread the beans on a baking sheet and roast, stirring halfway through, until they start to turn light golden, 12 to 15 minutes.

Meanwhile, crush the noodles from the package of ramen into big bite-sized pieces and add to the reserved bowl along with the seasoning packet and 2 tablespoons of the olive oil. Discard any sauce packets that come with the ramen, or save for another use. Add this mixture to the par-roasted beans, stir, and spread into an even layer. Roast, stirring occasionally, until the noodles and beans are golden and crisp, another 10 to 15 minutes. Let cool completely.

While the crispy bits are cooling, heat a tadka spoon or small skillet over medium heat. Add the perilla or black sesame seeds and toast, stirring frequently, until fragrant and starting to pop, 1 to 3 minutes. Grind the toasted seeds into a coarse powder using a mortar and pestle.

Add the ground seeds to a bowl with the green cabbage and the remaining ¾ teaspoon salt. Massage to soften the cabbage, 30 seconds to 1 minute. Add the pea shoots, lemon juice, ½ teaspoon of the ground sumac, the remaining 1 tablespoon olive oil, and the cooled crispy bits. Gently toss to combine. Taste and season with more salt, if necessary.

To serve, transfer the mixture to a shallow serving bowl or platter. Sprinkle with the remaining ½ teaspoon ground sumac and serve immediately.

Edamame and Cherry Tomato Salad

Recipe by Asha Loupy | Origin: Ukhrul, Manipur | Serves 4 to 6

Soybeans are such a deeply important ingredient across Manipur's many regional and tribal food cultures. They're most commonly fermented into a condiment similar to Japanese natto that is nutty, pungent, and a great source of year-round umami and good microbes. Zeinorin, our dear friend and sourcing partner for Manipuri wild-foraged and indigenous spices, has fond memories of drinking her mom's homemade roasted soybean milk as a kid (YUM!). The inspiration for this recipe is a soybean tomato salad she came up with as an easy way to add more protein to her diet. Asha chose to swap in edamame and watercress in place of dried soybeans and pennywort, just in the name of what's more easily available in the US, so you don't have to soak and cook the beans. The resulting salad is so fresh, bright, and addictive, pairing superbly with the spicy, rich pork Hoksa (page 162).

1¾ cups (283 g) frozen shelled edamame

1 tablespoon plus ¾ teaspoon fine sea salt, plus more if needed

½ small red onion, thinly sliced (about 3 ounces/85 g)

Juice of ½ lemon (1 to 2 tablespoons)

1½ tablespoons extra virgin olive oil

1½ teaspoons fish sauce

½ to 1 teaspoon Sirārakhong Hāthei chilli powder

12 to 15 cherry tomatoes, halved (about ⅓ pound/151 g)

3 cups (66 g) lightly packed watercress, torn into big bite-sized pieces

½ cup (8 g) lightly packed mint leaves

To prepare the edamame, bring 2 cups water with 1 tablespoon of the salt to a boil in a medium saucepan over high heat. Add the edamame and boil until al dente, 3 to 4 minutes. Drain, rinse with cold water, and set aside.

Meanwhile, macerate the onions. In a large bowl, mix the lemon juice, olive oil, fish sauce, chilli powder, and the remaining ¾ teaspoon salt. Add the onion and let sit until softened and slumpy, 10 to 15 minutes.

Add the blanched edamame and the cherry tomatoes to the bowl with the onions and toss to combine. Add the watercress, tear the mint leaves into the bowl, and gently toss to combine. Taste and season with more salt, if necessary.

To serve, transfer the salad to a shallow serving bowl or platter. Serve immediately.

The Bishnoi Family
Jodhana Cumin

OSIAN, RAJASTHAN

The Bishnoi family, as is tradition in their region, share their last name with their entire community—the Bishnois.

The community's unique values are palpable across our farm partner Mangilal ji Bishnoi's farm, where our Jodhana Cumin thrives in the sandy soil, alongside seasonal crops like bajra (millet), sesame, and mustard. Almost everything they eat is grown and preserved on their land or traded with their neighbors. The family follows traditional water harvesting methods, using every resource hyper efficiently in the arid desert climate.

Deeply rooted in sustainability and a respect for all living beings, the community's philosophy is woven into every aspect of how they live and work. Often called India's original eco-warriors, the Bishnois' commitment to conservation dates to the fifteenth century, when Guru Jambheshwar laid down twenty-nine tenets for living, from protecting trees and wildlife to coexisting harmoniously with nature. The Bishnois have been known to chase down armed poachers, rescue and care for injured animals, save endangered species, and lead heroic reforestation efforts across the Rajasthani desert. In a time of rampant biodiversity loss and climate change, I can't stress how revolutionary their way of life is.

What sets Mangilal ji's cumin apart is not just the terroir of Rajasthan's Thar Desert but the care and ancestral knowledge that goes into cultivating it. Grown without chemical inputs, the seeds capture the essence of the land—warm, earthy, and robust. When I asked Mangilal ji about his farming practices, he spoke with pride about using techniques that are not only sustainable but also deeply tied to their cultural identity as Bishnois.

Their food—simple yet deeply nourishing vegetarian fare—reflects their philosophy. A hot millet roti with fiery chilli-garlic chutney and a glass of freshly churned buttermilk served under the shade of a khejri tree? It's a meal as comforting and rooted in the land as the cumin itself. Mangilal ji and his family don't just grow spices; they're ensuring the flavors of their heritage will endure for generations to come.

Recipes from the Bishnoi Family

Rajasthani Green Chutney 36
Lahsun Mirchi Chutney 42
Bhindi Masala 88
Bajra Na Rotla 204

The Mir Family
Kashmiri Saffron

PAMPORE, KASHMIR

> Agar firdaus bar roo-e zameen ast,
> Hameen ast-o hameen ast-o hameen ast.
> If there is a paradise on earth,
> It is this, it is this, it is this.
>
> —AMIR KHUSRAU IN THIRTEENTH-CENTURY AD
> WHILE VISITING KASHMIR

My friend Sharanya Deepak, an incredible food journalist, introduced me to Raqib Mir in 2020. She'd interviewed him for a story and had been struck enough by his passion and dedication to quality to suspect that we'd have a lot in common! She was very correct. A fourth-generation saffroner, Raqib is an expert in growing and processing Kashmiri Saffron. In fact, when I sent a saffron sample from his farm to a lab in Berlin, they called me back incredulous because the crocin content was so high that it went beyond what their lab had the tools to measure!

Kashmiri Saffron grows in the mineral-rich Karewa plateau of Pampore. This specific terroir amplifies the saffron's crocin (which gives its vivid red color), picrocrocin (its distinctive flavor), and safranal

Recipes from the Mir Family

Doud Alle Dip 59

Haakh 99

Aab Gosht 165

Kashmiri Pulao 178

Noon Chai 214

Kehwa 218

Apricot-Saffron Frangipane Galette 234

(its earthy aroma). Traditional wisdom in Kashmir celebrates snowmelt as the ideal and only source of irrigation—giving the soil balanced, slow moisture, essential for the saffron corms to thrive, without waterlogging. Kashmiri Saffron is an incredibly low-yield crop that is highly labor intensive at every step, but the result is a gorgeous saffron that is unlike any other.

How to spot good quality saffron:

1. Look closely at the shape: Kashmiri Saffron strands are longer, thicker, and uniquely trumpet-shaped with a rounded crown or "taj." This shape not only distinguishes it visually but also holds a higher oil content, amplifying its aroma and weight.
2. Check out the color: Kashmiri Saffron is a rich "bloody red" with golden undertones, due to those high crocin levels, and releases its deep color slowly when infused. Other saffron often appears more orange or pink in comparison and will be quick to bleed in an infusion but won't be as strong.
3. Make sure it is hand-processed: Machine-processed saffron will show faint grill marks—this means it has lost vital oil content during the processing and will turn brittle and stale much faster! Fresh Kashmiri Saffron will never crumble because it is painstakingly hand-processed to preserve its delicate balance of aromatic oils.

Over the years, Raqib and I have become good friends—we're the same age, we're both obsessed with quality, and we're more than a little entrepreneurial. Just when I thought I couldn't like him more, he introduced me to Aaliya, his wife and the best Kashmiri home cook I've met (read about their wedding feast, which inspired so many of our recipes, on page 166). Her Kehwa (page 218), green tea brewed with saffron, cardamom, and licorice, tastes like a hug in a mug. Her Haakh (page 99), slowly stewed with greens freshly harvested from Dal Lake, is the most comforting dish; it's now the first dish I make the minute it gets cold outside. Our time spent cooking in her warm kitchen during the crisp autumn days of the saffron harvests are core memories for Asha, Melati, and me.

Bhindi Masala
Stir-Fried Spiced Okra

Recipe by Pooja Bishnoi and Manju Bishnoi | Origin: Osian, Rajasthan | Serves: 4

Bhindi is the single food I can eat every single day of my life and truly never tire of. This recipe is a mash-up of the bhindi we ate on the Bishnoi family farm and the one I grew up eating.

Our trick to reducing the slime factor is two-fold. First, cut the okra right before you put it in the pan. Second, parcook it in a very hot skillet, undisturbed and unsalted, until it starts to turn deep golden brown in spots. Then, lower the heat and add the salt, spices, and aromatics.

1 pound (454 g) small to medium okra

3 tablespoons untoasted sesame oil or other neutral oil

1 teaspoon fine sea salt, plus more if needed

1 teaspoon coriander seeds, lightly crushed

1 teaspoon cumin seeds

½ teaspoon black mustard seeds

1 large shallot (about 3 ounces/85 g), finely diced

4 garlic cloves, finely chopped

¾ teaspoon ground turmeric

¾ teaspoon Sirārakhong Hāthei chilli powder or smoked paprika

¼ cup (13 g) finely chopped cilantro, leaves and tender stems

Juice of ½ lemon (1 to 2 tablespoons)

Right before cooking, cut and discard the stems off the okra, then slice crosswise into ½-inch pieces. (Doing this right before cooking will help reduce sliminess.)

Heat 2 tablespoons of the sesame oil in a large cast-iron skillet or other heavy-bottomed pan over medium-high heat. Add the okra, stirring to coat in the oil and spreading into an even layer, then cook, undisturbed, until starting to brown in spots, 5 to 8 minutes.

Sprinkle the okra with ½ teaspoon of the salt, then push the okra to one side of the pan and add the remaining 1 tablespoon oil to the open space in the pan. Reduce the heat to medium and add the coriander seeds, cumin seeds, and mustard seeds to the oil and cook, stirring frequently, until fragrant and the coriander has turned a couple shades darker, 15 to 30 seconds.

Add the shallot and garlic on top of the spices, stir to combine, and cook, stirring occasionally, until the shallot just starts to soften, 2 to 3 minutes. Add the turmeric, chilli powder, and the remaining ½ teaspoon salt, stir to combine, and continue to cook until the okra is cooked through and tender with a slight bite, 4 to 8 minutes.

Turn off the heat and stir in the cilantro and lemon juice. Taste and season with more salt, if necessary. Serve warm or at room temperature with steamed rice, curd rice, chapati, or Bajra Na Rotla (page 204).

RECIPE NOTE: While not traditional, the smokiness of Sirārakhong Hāthei chillies is absolutely dreamy when paired with okra. That being said, you can use any non-smoked chilli powder, like Byadgi, Guntur Sannam, or Kashmiri, as well.

Pipinna Kiri Hodi
Sri Lankan Cucumber Coconut Milk Curry

Recipe by Amitha Dissanayake | Origin: Kandy, Sri Lanka | Serves 4 to 6

Yes, this recipe may take some convincing to make because cooking cucumbers may feel foreign and thus "weird." But gently simmered in an aromatic, pandan-laced, coconut gravy, the supple bites of cucumber are revolutionary. Serve with steamed rice or Pol Roti (page 203), plus Pol Sambol (page 39) or Carrot Top Sambol (page 41).

2 English cucumbers (about 1¼ pounds/567 g)

1 teaspoon fine sea salt, plus more if needed

2 tablespoons virgin coconut oil

3 large shallots (about ½ pound/227 g), thinly sliced

4 garlic cloves, finely chopped

Two 6-inch pandan leaves, tied in knots

1 tablespoon Sri Lankan Roasted Curry Powder (page 22)

1¼ teaspoons ground turmeric

¾ teaspoon Byadgi chilli powder

One 14-ounce (398 ml) can full-fat coconut milk

Juice of ½ lemon (1 to 2 tablespoons)

To prepare the cucumbers, peel and halve each cucumber, then scoop out and discard the seeds, and cut each half on the bias into 1½-inch pieces. Transfer to a bowl, toss with ½ teaspoon of the salt, and let sit for 30 minutes. Transfer the cucumbers to a clean kitchen towel, discarding any accumulated liquid, and pat dry.

Heat the coconut oil in a Dutch oven or other large, heavy-bottomed pot over medium heat. Add the shallots, garlic, and pandan leaves and cook, stirring occasionally, until the shallots soften and start to turn light golden, 5 to 8 minutes. Add the curry powder, turmeric, chilli powder, and ¼ cup (60 ml) water and continue to cook, stirring frequently, until most of the water has evaporated, 1 to 3 minutes.

Stir in the coconut milk and the remaining ½ teaspoon salt, bring to a simmer, cover, reduce the heat to medium-low, and cook until the spices lose their rawness, 10 to 15 minutes. Stir in the cucumber, cover again, and cook until the cucumber is tender yet retains a slight bite and easily pierced with a knife, 9 to 14 minutes.

To finish, remove the pandan leaves and stir in the lemon juice. Taste and season with more salt and/or lemon juice, if necessary. Serve immediately.

RECIPE NOTE: If you can't find pandan, you can swap in a 12-inch stalk of fresh lemongrass, cut into 4-inch pieces and bruised with the back of your knife.

If making ahead of time, prepare the gravy up until the point where you'd add the cucumber and stop, then reheat and cook the cucumber before serving.

Spiced Maple-Roasted Carrots with Carrot Top Sambol

Recipe by Asha Loupy | Origin: Kandy, Sri Lanka | Serves 4 to 6

While many of the recipes in this book are deeply rooted in tradition, this one is definitely inspired by our South Asian farm partners but concocted in our Californian home kitchens. The roasted curry powder adds savory depth and balance to the sweet butter that the carrots are tossed in. The delicious contrast of sweet roasted root veggies against bright, punchy carrot top sambol makes this sheet pan dish feel very composed and sophisticated.

It's a very Californian recipe, but the flavors take me right back to an al fresco farm lunch on the cinnamon farms of Kandy, Sri Lanka.

1½ pounds (680 g) bunched baby carrots

3 tablespoons unsalted butter, melted

2 tablespoons maple syrup

2 tablespoons powdered jaggery or light brown sugar

2 teaspoons Sri Lankan Roasted Curry Powder (page 22)

¾ teaspoon fine sea salt

¼ teaspoon ground cinnamon

Half recipe Carrot Top Sambol (page 41)

8 to 10 oil-packed anchovy fillets, optional

1 lemon

Preheat the oven to 425°F. Line a rimmed sheet pan with parchment paper and set aside.

To prepare the carrots, cut the tops off, reserving them for the Carrot Top Sambol, and scrub well (no need to peel). If any of the carrots are larger than 1 inch in diameter, cut them in half lengthwise. Place the carrots on the prepared sheet pan.

Combine the melted butter, maple syrup, jaggery, curry powder, salt, and cinnamon in a bowl, then pour over the carrots, tossing to coat, and spread the dressed carrots into a single layer. Roast until cooked through and caramelized, 30 to 35 minutes, flipping two-thirds of the way through. Let the carrots cool for 5 minutes, then flip around in any leftover glaze on the pan.

To serve, transfer the roasted carrots to a serving plate and sprinkle liberally with the Carrot Top Sambol and anchovy fillets, if using. Cut the lemon into wedges and arrange them on and around the carrots for people to squeeze over their individual servings. Serve warm or at room temperature.

RECIPE NOTE: This dish uses a half recipe of the Carrot Top Sambol (page 41), so you can either cut the recipe in half, or make the full recipe and pair the remaining half of the sambol with another Sri Lankan dish, like Parippu Curry (page 118) or Sri Lankan Cucumber Coconut Milk Curry (page 91), later in the week.

Pazha Manga Curry

Kerala-Style Ripe Mango Curry

Recipe by Chachu Lukose | Origin: Udumbanchola, Kerala | Serves 4 to 6

Come April on the subcontinent, it's oppressively hot, but the one respite is that mango season is in full swing. In Gujarat, where my family is from, and in Kerala, where Chachu, the matriarch of our Baraka Cardamom farm's family is from, there are specific curries to celebrate and experience every stage of a mango's ripeness—from green-skinned and mouth-puckeringly sour to nearly melt-in-your-mouth ripe. While my favorite was always Kerala's chemmeen manga curry (shrimp with raw mango and coconut), I was never convinced of the ripe mango curries until I tried this one. Here, the mango gives a delicate sweetness to the gravy, while a good squeeze of lime juice brings acidity and a chilli-based tadka adds just enough heat to keep things interesting.

Enjoy warm with steamed rice or Skillet Appams (Kerala-Style Lacy Rice Pancakes, page 201). This is also a superb side piece for big, bolder Kerala dishes like Pepper Pork (page 154), Kerala-Style Grilled Prawns (page 134), and Meen Pollichathu (page 140).

FOR THE CURRY

- 2 medium to large underripe mangoes (1⅓ pounds/600 g) (see Recipe Notes)
- 2 tablespoons virgin coconut oil
- 12 fresh curry leaves
- 2 large shallots (about ⅓ pound/151 g), thinly sliced
- 3 garlic cloves, finely chopped
- 1 serrano pepper, roughly chopped
- 1 teaspoon fine sea salt, plus more if needed
- ¾ teaspoon ground turmeric
- One 14-ounce (398 ml) can full-fat coconut milk
- Juice of 1 lime (about 2 tablespoons)

To prepare the mangoes, take one mango at a time, place upright, and cut both cheeks off the mango. Then, cut the two remaining sides off the mango. Cut the larger pieces in half lengthwise, so you're left with 6 pieces. Take each wedge, place it skin-side down, and run your knife between the peel and the flesh to remove the peel. Discard the peels and pit and set the fruit aside.

Heat the coconut oil in a Dutch oven or other large, heavy-bottomed pot over medium heat. When shimmering, add the curry leaves—be careful, these will crackle and pop!—and cook until bright green and translucent, 10 to 30 seconds. Add the shallots, garlic, serrano pepper, and ½ teaspoon of the salt and cook, stirring occasionally, until the shallots soften but aren't taking on any color, 4 to 6 minutes. Add the turmeric and cook, stirring frequently, until fragrant, about 30 seconds.

Stir in the coconut milk, reserved mango pieces, ¼ cup (60 ml) water, and the remaining ½ teaspoon salt and bring to a gentle boil. Cover, reduce the heat to medium-low, and cook, stirring occasionally, until the mango is just cooked through and easily pierced with a paring knife, 10 to 14 minutes. Turn off the heat, stir in the lime juice, taste, and season with more salt, if necessary. Keep warm while you prepare the tadka.

FOR THE TADKA

1 tablespoon virgin coconut oil

¾ teaspoon black mustard seeds

12 fresh curry leaves

1 to 2 dried Guntur Sannam chillies, broken in half

½ teaspoon Guntur Sannam chilli powder

To make the tadka, heat the coconut oil in a tadka spoon or small saucepan over medium heat. When shimmering, add the mustard seeds and cook, swirling occasionally, until they start to sputter, 15 to 30 seconds. Add the curry leaves and chillies and cook until the curry leaves turn bright green and translucent, 10 to 30 seconds. Turn off the heat, add the chilli powder, and swirl to bloom the chilli powder in the residual heat. Pour the tadka over the mango curry and serve hot.

RECIPE NOTES: While the word *ripe* is in the title, you want to look for slightly underripe mangoes that are still firm to the touch. They have just enough sweetness but still retain their shape and texture when cooked (if your mangoes are too ripe, they'll get mushy and start to disintegrate into the gravy).

If you want a milder heat, you can remove the serrano pepper's seeds and ribs before chopping.

Ringan no Oro
Gujarati Charred Eggplant

Recipe by Hetal Sakariya | Origin: Shedubhar, Gujarat | Serves 4 to 6

One of my favorite things to eat when visiting the Sakariya family—who grow our coriander and fennel in Shedubhar, Gujarat—is ringan no oro, a smoky, lush eggplant curry flavored with tomatoes and garlic. On the farm, the eggplants are pierced, studded with garlic, and then buried directly in the coals to cook, imbuing them with the dreamiest, wood-fired flavor. Nearly every culture seems to have figured out the brilliant pairing of eggplant and fire—this is Gujarat's silky, moreish contribution to the smoky eggplant canon.

For our Gujarat meets California version, the eggplant is cooked on the gas stove or under the broiler, then chopped and folded into a simple burst tomato–green garlic sauce. To get that extra garlicky goodness, it's all topped off with a garlic, black mustard, and chilli tadka. Enjoy as a main or side with piping hot short grain rice, plus some curry leaf podi and ghee, or serve as a dip with pita, focaccia, or Bajra Na Rotla (page 204).

FOR THE EGGPLANT

- 2 medium globe eggplants (about 2¼ pounds/1 kg)
- 2 teaspoons coriander seeds
- 1 teaspoon cumin seeds
- 3 tablespoons untoasted sesame oil or other neutral oil
- 2 green garlic stalks, white, light green, and dark green parts, thinly sliced
- 1 serrano pepper, quartered lengthwise
- 1-inch piece ginger, finely chopped
- 1¼ teaspoons fine sea salt
- 20 to 25 cherry tomatoes (about ½ pound/227 g)
- 1 tablespoon fresh lemon juice

continues

To roast the eggplant, place the eggplants on two gas burners, one on each burner, set to medium-high heat. Cook until deeply charred on all sides, starting to slump, and cooked through, 12 to 16 minutes, depending on the size of your eggplant. If you have one big eggplant, you can char it on all sides, then finish cooking it in a 425°F oven until soft. (Alternatively, you can grill the whole eggplant over medium-high heat or broil it about 6 inches from the heat source until charred on all sides and softened all the way through.)

Wrap the charred eggplant in plastic wrap or place in a large zip-top bag, seal, and let the eggplant steam for at least 30 minutes, up to 2 hours. Using your fingers, remove and discard the charred skin and stems of the eggplant, then roughly chop the remaining flesh. Set aside.

Place the coriander seeds and cumin seeds in a mortar and gently pound to lightly crush the spices just enough to break apart the coriander seeds. Set aside.

Heat the sesame oil in a Dutch oven or other large, heavy-bottomed pot over medium heat. When shimmering, add the crushed spices and cook, stirring frequently, until the coriander turns a couple shades darker and the spices smell toasty, 15 to 45 seconds. Add the green

continues

FOR THE TADKA

1½ tablespoons untoasted sesame oil or other neutral oil

4 garlic cloves, thinly sliced

1 teaspoon black mustard seeds

18 fresh curry leaves

1 teaspoon Byadgi chilli powder

garlic, serrano pepper, ginger, and ½ teaspoon of the salt and cook, stirring occasionally, until the green garlic softens but doesn't take on any caramelization, 4 to 7 minutes.

Stir in the cherry tomatoes and ½ cup (120 ml) water, cover, and cook, stirring occasionally, until the tomatoes start to burst open, 5 to 9 minutes. Gently press the tomatoes down with the back of a spoon to crush them, then stir in the reserved chopped eggplant and the remaining ¾ teaspoon salt. Cover, reduce the heat to medium-low, and simmer, stirring occasionally to let the flavors meld, for 10 minutes. Turn off the heat, stir in the lemon juice, taste, and season with more salt, if necessary.

To make the tadka, heat the sesame oil in a tadka spoon or small saucepan over medium heat. When shimmering, add the garlic and mustard seeds and cook, swirling the pan frequently, until the garlic starts to turn light golden around the edges, 1 to 3 minutes. Add the curry leaves—be careful, these will crackle and pop!—and cook until bright green and translucent, 10 to 30 seconds. Turn off the heat, add the chilli powder, and swirl to bloom the chilli powder in the residual heat, 15 to 30 seconds. To serve, transfer the ringan no oro to a shallow serving bowl and pour the tadka over. Serve warm or at room temperature.

RECIPE NOTE: If you are unable to find green garlic, you can use 1 small leek (white and light green parts only) or 3 green onions plus 1 minced garlic clove. If you don't have Byadgi chilli powder, the tadka isn't too discerning—swap in Guntur Sannam chilli powder, Kashmiri chilli powder, or even sweet or hot paprika.

Haakh
Kashmiri Braised Greens

Recipe by Aaliya Mir | Origin: Pampore, Kashmir | Serves 4 to 6

Though Kashmiri cuisine is very mutton-heavy, one of my favorite Kashmiri dishes is a simple, comforting pot of greens, braised with black cardamom, lots of fennel, caraway, turmeric, and Kashmiri Chillies. Haakh can be made with whichever hearty greens you have on hand. In the Kashmir Valley, it's whichever leafy green happens to be growing on Dal Lake at that time of year. For our version, we went with a mix of collard and mustard greens, providing a combination of sumptuous silky bites with a little spicy punch from the latter. Slowly cooked in stock—which creates a warmly spiced pot likker—these greens have similarities to braised, ham-hock fleck pots of greens found in the American South, so we love finishing them with a splash of apple cider vinegar. When it comes to the braising liquid, if you've made any version of our Kashmiri stocks—lamb or our cheat version (page 175)—for another dish like Kashmiri Pulao (page 178) or Palak Rista (page 170), this is a great time to use it. But you can also use your favorite store-bought beef, chicken, or vegetable stock in a pinch, and the result will still be comforting, cozy bliss!

FOR THE GREENS

1 bunch collard greens (about 1¼ pounds/567 g)

1 bunch mustard greens (about 1¼ pounds/567 g)

¼ cup (60 ml) mustard seed oil

1 teaspoon caraway seeds

1 teaspoon fennel seeds

2 dried Kashmiri chillies, torn in half

4 black cardamom pods, lightly crushed

3 large shallots (about ½ pound/227 g), thinly sliced

3 garlic cloves, finely chopped

1¼ teaspoons fine sea salt, plus more if needed

continues

To prepare the collard greens, remove the fibrous stem about three-quarters up each leaf, discarding the stems or saving for another use, and rip the leaves into big bite-sized pieces. Keeping the greens separate (you'll be adding each type at different times), move on to the mustard greens, repeating the process of removing the stems and ripping them into pieces. Set aside.

To make the base for the greens, heat the mustard seed oil in a Dutch oven or other large, heavy-bottomed pot over medium heat. When shimmering, add the caraway seeds, fennel seeds, chillies, and black cardamom and cook until the seeds start to sputter and smell fragrant and the chillies turn a shade darker, 15 to 45 seconds.

Stir in the shallots, garlic, and ½ teaspoon of the salt and cook, stirring occasionally, until the shallots soften and turn light golden around the edges, 7 to 10 minutes. Add the fennel and turmeric and continue to cook until fragrant, 15 to 30 seconds. Add the stock, the reserved collard greens, and the remaining ¾ teaspoon salt, stir to combine, and bring to a simmer. Cover, reduce the heat to low, and cook until the collard greens are halfway cooked (you're looking for tender but still with a bite), 1 hour to 1 hour 15 minutes. Stir in the reserved mustard greens, cover, and continue to cook until the collard greens

continues

- 1½ teaspoons ground fennel seeds
- 1½ teaspoons ground turmeric
- 2 cups Kashmiri Lamb Stock (page 174) or good-quality, store-bought beef or vegetable stock
- 1½ teaspoons apple cider vinegar, plus more if needed, optional

FOR THE TADKA

- 1 tablespoon mustard seed oil
- 2 garlic cloves, thinly sliced
- 1 teaspoon Kashmiri chilli powder

are fully cooked and the mustard greens are cooked through and silky, 40 to 50 minutes more. Stir in the vinegar, if using, taste, and season with more salt or vinegar, if necessary. Cover and keep warm.

To make the tadka, heat the mustard seed oil in a tadka spoon or small saucepan over medium heat. When shimmering, add the garlic and cook, swirling the pan occasionally, until the garlic turns light golden, 1 to 3 minutes. Turn off the heat, add the chilli powder, and swirl to bloom the chilli powder in the residual heat, 15 to 30 seconds. Pour over the greens, stir, and transfer to a serving bowl. Serve hot with steamed basmati rice or Kashmiri Pulao (page 178).

RECIPE NOTES: If you can't find mustard seed oil, you can use a neutral oil, like canola, for cooking the greens, and ghee for making the tadka. Or, for a super lush potful, go with all ghee!

If you want to make this vegetarian, use the cheat version of the Kashmiri Lamb Stock (page 175) and swap in vegetable stock for the lamb or beef stock.

Nadru Yakhni

Kashmiri Lotus Root Yogurt Curry

Recipe by Dilshad Akhtar Digoo | Origin: Pulwama, Kashmir | Serves 4

Nadru, or lotus root, is probably the most prized Kashmiri vegetable. It's grown in abundance on the famous floating farms of Dal Lake—the only true floating gardens in the world! Farmers use two kinds of indigenous water weeds to weave floating mat-like structures called raadhs that are then packed with mud and can be moved throughout the lake for cultivation. The primary crops grown on the lake are lotus stems for this dish, turnips, kohlrabi, sweet spring onions, and collard greens (see Haakh, page 99). This farming technique dates back at least four hundred years when the Mughal emperor Jahangir made Srinagar his summer capital, and the residents of the valley have been relying on the lake's abundant harvest ever since.

For me, the humble lotus root took on a whole new level of importance when I saw farmers harvesting them out of the lake on a crisp fall morning, adeptly weaving through the tangle of floating plots in their slim wooden canoes.

Yakhni is a yogurt and saffron gravy that is tangy, silken, and deeply comforting. Its name comes from the Farsi word *yakhna*, the word for an earthenware pot used to cook a simple daily stew. With several waves of Persian migration through the Kashmir Valley over the centuries, this warming dish is an ode to Persian food culture through the lens of Kashmiri produce and spices. Enjoy hot with steamed long-grain rice or Kashmiri Pulao (page 178).

Pinch of Kashmiri saffron

1 pound (454 g) fresh lotus root (2 to 4, depending on their size)

1½ teaspoons fine sea salt, plus more if needed

¼ cup (60 ml) canola oil or other neutral oil

5 tablespoons (75 g) ghee

8 green cardamom pods, lightly crushed

4 black cardamom pods, lightly crushed

½ teaspoon cumin seeds

¼ teaspoon asafetida

continues

Put the saffron in a medium bowl (big enough to fit the yogurt), top with an ice cube, and allow to steep until the ice melts, 15 to 30 minutes.

Meanwhile, prepare the lotus root. Taking one root at a time, cut off ½ inch from each end of the root and place in a large bowl of lukewarm water with ½ teaspoon of the salt. Let sit for 15 minutes.

Remove the lotus roots from the water and discard the water. Wash out the bowl and fill with fresh cold water. Peel the lotus roots using a vegetable peeler and slice into ¼-inch rounds. Transfer the sliced lotus root to the bowl of cold water, gently swishing them around to loosen any residual grit stuck inside, and allow to soak for another 5 minutes. Lift the sliced lotus root out of the water, transfer to a kitchen towel–lined baking sheet, and pat dry.

Heat the canola oil in a Dutch oven or other large, heavy-bottomed pot over medium-high heat. Fry the lotus root in batches, placing a single

continues

1 teaspoon garam masala

1 teaspoon ground fennel seeds

½ teaspoon ground ginger

2 cups (454 g) full-fat plain yogurt (not Greek)

2 tablespoons besan (chickpea flour)

2 tablespoons dried mint

¾ teaspoon Kashmiri chilli powder

layer of the sliced lotus root in the pan and frying until golden on both sides, 5 to 6 minutes per side. Transfer the fried lotus root to a wire rack–lined sheet pan and set aside.

Turn off the heat, pour out the oil, and wipe out the pan. Return the pan to medium heat and add 3 tablespoons of the ghee. When the ghee is melted, add the green cardamom, black cardamom, cumin seeds, and asafetida to the pan and cook, stirring frequently, until the cumin seeds start to sputter and to turn light golden, 30 seconds to 1 minute. Add the garam masala, fennel, ginger, the reserved fried lotus root, remaining 1 teaspoon salt, and 1 cup (240 ml) water. Stir to combine, cover, and cook for 5 minutes.

While the lotus root is cooking, add the yogurt, besan, and 1 cup (240 ml) water to the bowl with the saffron and whisk well for 3 to 4 minutes.

Uncover the lotus root and slowly add the yogurt and besan mixture, stirring constantly. Continue to stir constantly for 5 minutes to prevent the yogurt from breaking, then cover and cook until the lotus root is tender but still retains a little bit of a bite, 8 to 12 minutes. Taste and season with more salt, if necessary. Turn off the heat, crumble in the dried mint, stir, cover, and keep warm while preparing the tadka.

To make the tadka, heat the remaining 2 tablespoons ghee in a tadka pan or small saucepan over medium heat. When the ghee is melted, turn off the heat, add the chilli powder, and swirl to bloom the chilli powder in the residual heat, 15 to 30 seconds.

To serve, transfer the yakhni to a shallow serving bowl and pour the tadka over the top.

Aloo Masala
Spiced Potatoes

Recipe by Padmavathi Narne | Origin: Vinjanampadu, Andhra Pradesh | Serves 6 to 8 as a dosa filling

The filling of a masala dosa is too often an afterthought. Given the variety of incredible masala dosas that Asha and I were able to enjoy along the length and breadth of South India, doing this right felt like a big responsibility. I like my dosa crispy, laden with ghee, a generous sprinkling of Gunpowder Podi (page 26), and my aloo masala on the side so that I can scoop generous amounts with each bite of dosa without it getting soggy. See the photo on page 193.

1½ pounds (680 g) Yukon Gold potatoes, peeled and halved

3 tablespoons plus 2 teaspoons fine sea salt, plus more if needed

2 tablespoons untoasted sesame oil

1½ teaspoons split, skinned urad dal

1 teaspoon chana dal

1 teaspoon black mustard seeds

½ teaspoon coriander seeds

½ teaspoon cumin seeds

24 fresh curry leaves

1 white onion, quartered and thinly sliced

½-inch piece ginger, finely chopped

1 serrano pepper, roughly chopped

1 teaspoon ground turmeric

½ to 1 teaspoon Guntur Sannam chilli powder

¼ cup (13 g) roughly chopped cilantro

1 tablespoon fresh lemon juice, plus more if needed

Place the potatoes in a large pot, cover with 3 inches of cold water, add 3 tablespoons of the salt, cover, and bring to a boil over high heat. Reduce the heat to medium, keep at a gentle boil, and cook until the potatoes are cooked through and easily pierced with a paring knife, 15 to 25 minutes, depending on the size of the potatoes. Drain well, return to the pot, and let sit for 5 minutes to let the residual heat of the pan steam any excess water off the potatoes.

While the potatoes are boiling, prepare the masala base. Heat the sesame oil in a large skillet over medium heat. When shimmering, add the urad dal, chana dal, mustard seeds, coriander seeds, and cumin seeds. Add the curry leaves and cook until bright green and translucent, 10 to 30 seconds. Stir in the onion, ginger, and 1 teaspoon of the remaining salt and cook, stirring occasionally, until the onions soften and turn light golden around the edges, 11 to 14 minutes. Add the serrano pepper, turmeric, chilli powder, and ¼ cup (60 ml) water. Cook, stirring frequently, until most of the water has evaporated, 2 to 4 minutes.

Add the cooked potatoes and the remaining 1 teaspoon salt and, using a potato masher or the back of a spoon, gently crush the potatoes, incorporating them into the onion mixture and making sure to leave some bigger chunks, and cook until any residual moisture evaporates and the potatoes start to pull away from the pan, 4 to 6 minutes. Turn off the heat and fold in the cilantro and lemon juice. Taste and adjust salt and lemon juice, if necessary.

PAHADI RAJMA, page 124

Beans and Lentils

Gongura Pappu   108
Chaaru   112
Seasonal Sambar   114
Parippu Curry   118

Rajasthani Dal   120
Kadhi   123
Pahadi Rajma   124

Gongura Pappu
Andhra-Style Dal with Sorrel

Recipe by Divya Kasaraneni | Origin: Kankipadu, Andhra Pradesh | Serves 6 to 8

Sorrel leaves are a monsoon staple known by different names across India, but nowhere has sorrel become as synonymous with the cuisine as in Andhra Pradesh. For me, a trip to the Kasaraneni family home during the turmeric harvest is incomplete without a lunch of bright, punchy gongura pappu served over steamed red rice. Without fail, a jar of sorrel pickle is sneakily pressed into my hands to take home with me by Venkata Narasamma, Prabhu's grandmother and the family matriarch.

There are thousands of variations of lentils and beans cooked as a staple across South Asia—endless combinations of chana, toor, moong, masoor, urad, chawli, matki, and rajma (see page 15 for a full glossary in our pantry section). My Gujarati nani favored simple split toor, whereas my Punjabi dadi favored heavy rajma and creamy split urad. The Kasaraneni family make their pappu with chana because it's what they grow (along with almost every single other ingredient in this recipe!), and it gives the dish a silky creaminess that can't really be beat. Where other lentil dishes might be supporting characters in a meal of meat mains or dramatic veggies, this one has flavor-packed main character energy.

FOR THE DAL

2¾ cups (250 g) chana dal

2½ teaspoons fine sea salt, plus more if needed

1½ teaspoons ground turmeric

3 tablespoons untoasted sesame oil or other neutral oil

½ teaspoon cumin seeds

1 white onion, finely diced

4 garlic cloves, finely chopped

1-inch piece ginger, finely chopped

2 to 3 serrano peppers, quartered lengthwise

3 plum tomatoes (about ½ pound/227 g), diced

Place the chana dal in a bowl and rinse with cold water, swishing it around with your fingers, and rinsing several times until the water runs clear. Drain and transfer the dal to an electric pressure cooker (like an Instant Pot) and add 1½ teaspoons of the salt, 1 teaspoon of the turmeric, and 5 cups (1.2 L) water. Cook on high pressure for 18 minutes, then allow to naturally release for 15 minutes. Release the pressure, mash some of the dal with the back of a spoon or a potato masher, and keep warm.

When the pressure cooker is naturally releasing, start the dal base. Heat the sesame oil in a Dutch oven or other large, heavy-bottomed pot over medium heat. When shimmering, add the cumin seeds and cook, stirring occasionally, until they start to sputter and smell toasty, 30 to 45 seconds.

Add the onion and sauté, stirring occasionally, until softened and the edges start to turn light golden, 6 to 9 minutes. Stir in the garlic, ginger, and serrano peppers and continue to cook until the garlic turns light golden and the ginger softens, 3 to 4 minutes more. Add the tomatoes, chilli powder, the remaining ½ teaspoon turmeric, and ¼ cup (60 ml) water and stir to combine. Reduce the heat to medium-low, cover, and

1½ tablespoons Andhra Chilli Powder (page 23)

2 tablespoons amchur powder

1½ cups (65 g) roughly chopped fresh sorrel

⅓ cup (17 g) roughly chopped cilantro, leaves and tender stems

Juice of ½ to 1 lemon (1 to 4 tablespoons)

FOR THE TADKA

1½ tablespoons untoasted sesame oil or other neutral oil

4 garlic cloves, quartered

2 teaspoons split urad dal

1 teaspoon black mustard seeds

1 to 2 whole Guntur Sannam chillies, torn in half

18 fresh curry leaves

cook, stirring occasionally, until the tomatoes break down and become jammy, 5 to 8 minutes, adding more water a tablespoon at a time if it starts to look dry. Add the amchur powder, the cooked chana dal and its cooking liquid, the remaining 1 teaspoon salt, and 1 cup (240 ml) water. Stir to combine, increase the heat to medium, and bring back to a simmer. Cook uncovered, stirring frequently so the dal doesn't stick to the bottom, to let the flavors meld, for 15 minutes. In the last 5 minutes of cooking, add the sorrel to wilt in the dal. (If the dal is too thick, add hot water until you reach the desired consistency. If it is too thin, keep simmering for an extra 5 minutes.)

To make the tadka, heat the sesame oil in a tadka spoon or small saucepan over medium heat. When shimmering, add the garlic, urad dal, mustard seeds, and chillies and fry, stirring or swirling frequently until the garlic is golden and the mustard seeds are popping, 2 to 4 minutes. Add the curry leaves—be careful, these crackle and pop!—and cook until bright green and translucent, 10 to 30 seconds more.

To finish the dal, pour the tadka into the dal, add the cilantro and juice of ½ lemon, and stir to combine. Taste and season with more salt and lemon juice, if necessary. Serve with hot rice and ghee.

RECIPE NOTE: Fresh sorrel lends tangy, tantalizing magic to food from Andhra Pradesh, a region known for its sour-spicy, punchy flavors. If you can't find sorrel, you can use one 5-ounce (142 g) container baby spinach and use the juice from the whole lemon.

GONGURA PAPPU, page 108

CHAARU, page 112

Chaaru
Andhra-Style Spicy Lentil Soup

Recipe by Divya Kasaraneni | Origin: Kankipadu, Andhra Pradesh | Serves 4

Each of the five southern states of India has a version of this light, fiery, tamarind-based soup—called *chaaru* in Telugu, *saaru* in Kannada, and *rasam* in Malayalam and Tamil. Farm lunches on the veranda of the Kasaraneni family home overlooking the rice and turmeric fields involve being served bowl after bowl of chaaru by a rotating cast of aunties and grannies, and marveling at how it can be so impossibly light and yet so deeply flavored.

It is my undisputed favorite of all South Asian lentil preparations—fighting words, I know! A steaming bowl of chaaru eaten with hot ghee rice is a daily ritual and a home remedy for just about every common ailment. When I had COVID in March 2020 and completely lost my sense of smell and taste, piping hot bowls of sour, spicy chaaru, with just a little rice mixed in to round out the meal, were all that could register to my fogged-up palate. The black peppercorns, ginger, and green chillies work overtime to form a sinus-clearing symphony of heat and flavor.

FOR THE CHAARU POWDER

- 2 tablespoons toor dal
- 1½ teaspoons coriander seeds
- 1½ teaspoons black peppercorns
- 1½ teaspoons cumin seeds
- ½ teaspoon fenugreek seeds
- 2 teaspoons Guntur Sannam chilli powder
- 1 teaspoon ground turmeric

FOR THE CHAARU

- 1 golf ball–sized piece (40 g) seedless tamarind pulp
- 5 to 6 plum tomatoes (about 1 pound/454 g), quartered

To make the chaaru powder, heat a tadka spoon or small skillet over medium-low heat. Add the toor dal and toast until the dal just starts to turn golden, 2 to 4 minutes. Transfer the toasted dal to a small bowl. Increase the heat under the skillet to medium, add the coriander seeds and black peppercorns, and toast, swirling the pan occasionally, until the spices are fragrant and the coriander starts to turn golden brown, 1 to 2 minutes. Transfer the toasted spices to the bowl with the dal. Return the skillet to medium heat and toast the cumin seeds and fenugreek seeds, 30 seconds to 1 minute.

Transfer the toasted toor dal and spices to a spice grinder along with the chilli powder and turmeric and blend into a fine powder. (This can be kept in an airtight container in a cool, dark place for up to 3 months.)

To make the chaaru, break the tamarind pulp into several smaller pieces, cover with 1 cup (240 ml) boiling water, and let sit for 15 minutes. Transfer the soaked tamarind and its water to a medium saucepan, add the tomatoes, serrano peppers, ginger, turmeric, and 1 cup (240 ml) water, and stir well. Place over medium-high heat and bring to a boil. Cover, reduce the heat to medium, and simmer until the tomatoes are soft and falling apart, 15 to 20 minutes. Strain through a fine-mesh sieve placed over a large bowl, using the back of a wooden

- 1 to 2 serrano peppers, roughly chopped
- 1-inch piece ginger, thinly sliced
- ½ teaspoon ground turmeric
- 1½ tablespoons Chaaru Powder (recipe above)
- ¾ teaspoon fine sea salt, plus more if needed
- ½ teaspoon powdered jaggery or brown sugar
- 2 tablespoons ghee
- ½ teaspoon cumin seeds
- ½ teaspoon black mustard seeds
- 12 fresh curry leaves
- ¼ cup (13 g) roughly chopped cilantro, leaves and tender stems

spoon to work the mixture through the sieve, leaving the tomato skins and other solids behind.

Transfer the strained mixture, discarding the leftover solids, back to the saucepan and add the chaaru powder, salt, jaggery, and 2½ cups (590 ml) water. Bring to a boil over medium-high heat, reduce to medium, and simmer for 15 minutes to let the flavors meld. If the mixture is looking too thick, add another ½ cup (120 ml) water. (You're looking for a thin, broth-like consistency.)

Melt the ghee in a small skillet over medium heat. Add the cumin seeds and mustard seeds and cook, swirling the pan, until the seeds start to sputter and the cumin seeds turn light golden, 15 to 45 seconds. Add the curry leaves—be careful, these will crackle and pop!—and fry until bright green and translucent, 10 to 30 seconds more.

Pour the tadka over the chaaru and garnish with the cilantro. Taste and add more salt, if necessary. Enjoy on its own as a soup or sip out of a mug. Or serve with steamed rice (short- or long-grain works here!) and an extra dollop of ghee.

RECIPE NOTE: Like almost every recipe in this chapter (Kadhi on page 123 is the exception!), chaaru is an absolute dream to freeze. Make a double or triple batch, portion into pint containers, freeze, and then defrost an individual bowlful in the microwave or on the stove.

Seasonal Sambar
South Indian Lentil Soup

Recipe by Padmavathi Narne | Origin: Vinjanampadu, Andhra Pradesh | Serves 6 to 8

Like Chaaru (page 112), sambar is a daily staple across South India. At the Narne household—the family that grows our Guntur Sannam Chillies—in Andhra Pradesh, the base for this vegetable-heavy lentil soup is rich and hearty. Coriander, cumin, fenugreek, and lots of dried chillies create a spicy, savory backbone, while a hearty dose of tamarind brings that quintessential tang.

For Padmavathi Narne and her daughter Vijayalakshmi, both prolific, passionate home cooks, the veggies for their sambar change from season to season, based on what is growing on the farm. When we were there, it was filled with chunks of pumpkin, potatoes, carrots, moringa seed pods, and meltingly tender pearl onions (the best bites, imo!). But, come summer, they transition to zucchini, eggplant, green beans, and okra (add the sturdier vegetables, like eggplant when you'd add the winter squash, and the more tender ones toward the end during the last 10 to 15 minutes of cooking to preserve their fresh texture)—a sambar for all seasons!

Enjoy sambar as a soup, with hot rice and a big dollop of ghee, or—my two favorite ways—alongside an extra-crispy Ghee Roast Dosa (page 192) with an ample sprinkling of podi, or smothered over plush, freshly steamed Idli (page 195).

FOR THE SAMBAR

- 2 walnut-sized pieces (70 g) seedless tamarind pulp
- 1¼ cups (250 g) toor dal
- 2½ teaspoons fine sea salt, plus more if needed
- 1 teaspoon ground turmeric
- 3 tablespoons untoasted sesame oil or other neutral oil
- 24 fresh curry leaves
- 2 large shallots (about ⅓ pound/151 g), diced
- 10 to 12 red pearl onions (about ⅓ pound/151 g), diced

To make the sambar, break the tamarind pulp into several smaller pieces, cover with 3 cups (710 ml) boiling water, and let sit for at least 30 minutes. Strain through a fine-mesh sieve, gently pressing the pulp to extract all the tamarind, discard the solids, and reserve the tamarind water for later use.

Meanwhile, place the toor dal in a bowl and rinse with cold water, swishing it around with your fingers and rinsing several times until the water runs clear. Drain and transfer the lentils to an electric pressure cooker (like an Instant Pot) and add 1½ teaspoons of the salt, ½ teaspoon of the turmeric, and 5 cups (1.2 L) water. Cook on high pressure for 18 minutes, then allow to naturally release for 15 minutes. Release the pressure, whisk vigorously to break up the lentils, and keep warm.

While the pressure cooker is naturally releasing, start the sambar base. Heat the sesame oil in a Dutch oven or other large, heavy-bottomed pot over medium heat. When shimmering, add the curry leaves—be careful, these crackle and pop!—and cook until bright green and

3 or 4 medium Yukon Gold potatoes, peeled and quartered lengthwise (about ⅓ pound/151 g)

2 plum tomatoes (about ⅓ pound/151 g), diced

2 serrano peppers, quartered lengthwise

1 medium carrot, peeled, cut in half lengthwise, and then sliced on the bias into ½-inch pieces

½ pound (227 g) winter squash, like kabocha, acorn, butternut, or delicata, seeds and guts scraped out and cut into 1¼-inch chunks (see Recipe Notes about peeling vs. not peeling)

¼ pound (113 g) fresh or frozen moringa drumsticks, cut into 1½- to 2-inch pieces

1½ tablespoons Andhra Chilli Powder (page 23)

⅓ cup (17 g) roughly chopped cilantro, leaves and tender stems

Juice of 1 lemon (2 to 4 tablespoons), plus more if needed

FOR THE TADKA

1½ tablespoons untoasted sesame oil or other neutral oil

1½ tablespoons chana dal

1 teaspoon black mustard seeds

1 to 2 whole Guntur Sannam chillies, torn in half

12 fresh curry leaves

translucent, 10 to 30 seconds. Add the shallots and cook, stirring occasionally, until they soften and start to turn light golden around the edges, 4 to 7 minutes.

Add the pearl onions, potatoes, tomatoes, serrano peppers, carrot, winter squash, moringa drumstick pieces, chilli powder, ½ teaspoon of the remaining salt, the remaining ½ teaspoon turmeric, and ¼ cup (60 ml) water and stir to coat everything in the spices. Cook, stirring frequently, until the tomatoes start to break down and the vegetables soften, 6 to 10 minutes. (If it starts looking too dry, add a tablespoon of water at a time to make sure the spices don't burn.)

Add the cooked lentils, reserved tamarind water, and the remaining ½ teaspoon salt. Stir, bring back to a simmer, cover, and cook, stirring occasionally to make sure the lentils aren't sticking to the bottom of the pot, until all the vegetables are cooked through, making sure to check the sturdier vegetables like the potatoes and squash, 25 to 35 minutes. (If the sambar is looking a little too thick, you can add more water ½ cup (120 ml) at a time, or if it is too thin, you can simmer it uncovered during the last 10 minutes of cooking or until you reach the desired consistency.)

To make the tadka, heat the sesame oil in a tadka spoon or small saucepan over medium heat. When shimmering, add the chana dal, mustard seeds, and chillies and fry, stirring or swirling frequently until the lentils turn a few shades darker and the mustard seeds start sputtering, 30 seconds to 1½ minutes. Add the curry leaves and cook until bright green and translucent, 10 to 30 seconds more.

To finish the sambar, pour the tadka into the dal, add the cilantro and lemon juice, and stir to combine. Taste and season with more salt and lemon juice, if necessary. Serve with hot rice and ghee.

RECIPE NOTES: Squash varieties like kabocha, delicata, and acorn do not need peeling and soak up the gravy beautifully. If you use a squash variety with a thicker skin, you may want to peel it before cutting and cleaning it.

If you want a milder heat, you can remove the seeds and ribs from the serrano peppers.

SEASONAL SAMBAR, page 114

PARIPPU CURRY, page 118

Parippu Curry

Sri Lankan Lentils with Coconut and Lemongrass

Recipe by Sumithra Attanayake | Origin: Kandy, Sri Lanka | Serves 4 to 6

"Life without love is like a restaurant without dal" is a corny Sinhalese line that Nihal, our Peni Miris Cinnamon and Kandyan Clove sourcing partner, loves to repeat. Compared to its counterparts cooked across the sea in India, Sri Lankan dal is milder in heat, much creamier, thanks to coconut milk, and far more aromatic—from a combination of lemongrass, pandan, cinnamon, curry leaves, and deeply Sri Lankan Roasted Curry Powder (page 22). While delicate and creamy, the flavors are beautifully layered. Across South Asia, lentils are usually eaten with rice and then a small serving of a brighter, acidic element, like yogurt, achaar, or, in Sri Lanka, sambol. The Carrot Top Sambol (page 41) or Asha's Bitter Melon and Heirloom Tomato Salad (page 74) would be perfect here.

FOR THE DAL

- 1¼ cups (225 g) masoor dal
- 3 tablespoons virgin coconut oil
- 12 fresh curry leaves
- One 3-inch cinnamon stick, broken in half
- 3 large shallots (about ½ pound/227 g), thinly sliced
- 1½ teaspoons fine sea salt, plus more if needed
- 4 garlic cloves, finely chopped
- One 12-inch stalk lemongrass, cut into 4-inch pieces and smashed with the back of a knife
- One 8-inch pandan leaf, tied in a knot, optional
- 1½ tablespoons Sri Lankan Roasted Curry Powder (page 22)
- 1 teaspoon ground turmeric

Place the masoor dal in a bowl and rinse with cold water, swishing it around with your fingers, and rinsing several times until the water runs clear. Cover with cold water and let soak for 30 minutes.

Meanwhile, make the base for the dal. Heat the coconut oil in a large pot over medium heat. Add the curry leaves—be careful, these will crackle and pop!—and cinnamon stick and cook until fragrant, 30 seconds to 1 minute. Add the shallots and ½ teaspoon of the salt and cook, stirring occasionally, until golden around the edges, 5 to 7 minutes. Add the garlic, lemongrass, and pandan, if using, and cook, stirring occasionally, until the garlic softens and starts to turn light golden, 2 to 4 minutes more.

Add the curry powder, turmeric, chilli powder, black pepper, and ¼ cup (60 ml) water and cook, stirring constantly, until most of the water is evaporated and the spices are fragrant, 1 to 3 minutes.

Drain the lentils and add them to the pot along with the coconut milk, the remaining 1 teaspoon salt, and 3 cups (710 ml) water. Bring to a simmer, then reduce the heat to medium-low, cover, and cook, stirring occasionally, until the lentils are soft, 20 to 30 minutes. If the dal is too thick, add a few more splashes of water, and if it is too thin, cook it uncovered until it reduces to the desired consistency. Cover and keep warm.

¾ teaspoon Byadgi chilli powder

¼ teaspoon freshly ground black pepper

One 14-ounce (398 ml) can full-fat coconut milk

Juice of ½ lemon (1 to 2 tablespoons), plus more if needed

FOR THE TADKA

1 tablespoon virgin coconut oil

4 garlic cloves, quartered

1 teaspoon black mustard seeds

12 fresh curry leaves

For the tadka, heat the coconut oil in a small skillet or tadka spoon over medium heat. Add the garlic and mustard seeds and cook until the garlic starts to turn golden around the edges, 1 to 2 minutes. Add the curry leaves—be careful, these will crackle and pop!—and cook until bright green and translucent, 10 to 30 seconds.

To finish, add the tadka to the cooked dal along with the lemon juice and stir to combine. Taste and season with more salt and/or lemon juice, if necessary. Serve hot with rice or Pol Roti (page 203).

Rajasthani Dal

Recipe inspired by Julie Jain | Origin: Udaipur, Rajasthan | Serves 4 to 6

In the arid desert climate of modern-day Udaipur, Rajasthan, dal panchmel is a famously hearty, royal dal made with a blend of five different lentils: toor, urad, chana, matki, and moong. It's best known as one-third of Rajasthan's national dish, dal bati churma, which is a combination of the panchmel dal poured on top of bati (a hard baked wheat ball that is broken up and softened with ghee) and finally topped with churma (a sweet, spiced wheat crumble). According to legend, the dish was made as sustenance for warriors braving intense desert storms on their way to battle.

Given that most of us are not eating to go to war, this version—from our partners Rohit and Julie Jain, who source and process our Jodhana Cumin—is much lighter and fit for everyday cooking. This recipe uses three lentil varieties instead of five and we skip the churma entirely. It's still gloriously creamy, comforting, and nourishing, while also feeling special. High-protein urad gives the dal an indescribable silkiness, the moong is sweet and the easiest of the three to digest, and the chana is nutty and creamy to round it all out.

Make it by itself and eat with hot white rice and a spoonful of the Lahsun Mirchi Chutney (page 42).

FOR THE DAL

- ½ cup (115 g) split urad dal
- ⅓ cup (75 g) whole moong dal
- ⅓ cup (67 g) chana dal
- 2¼ teaspoons fine sea salt, plus more if needed
- 1¼ teaspoons ground turmeric
- 3 tablespoons ghee
- 2 teaspoons coriander seeds
- 1 teaspoon cumin seeds
- ¾ teaspoon black mustard seeds
- One 3-inch cinnamon stick, broken in half
- 5 whole cloves
- Pinch of asafetida, optional

Place the urad dal, moong dal, and chana dal in a bowl and rinse with cold water, swishing it around with your fingers and rinsing several times until the water runs clear. Drain and transfer the dal to an electric pressure cooker (like an Instant Pot) and add 1½ teaspoons of the salt, ¾ teaspoon of the turmeric, and 4 cups (946 ml) water. Cook on high pressure for 18 minutes, then allow to naturally release for 15 minutes. Release the pressure and keep warm.

When the pressure cooker is naturally releasing, start the dal base. Heat the ghee in a Dutch oven or other large, heavy-bottomed pot over medium heat. When the ghee is shimmering, add the coriander seeds, cumin seeds, mustard seeds, cinnamon stick, cloves, and asafetida, if using, and cook, stirring frequently, until the mustard seeds start to pop and the coriander seeds turn a few shades darker, 30 seconds to 2 minutes.

Add the onion and ¼ teaspoon of the remaining salt and sauté, stirring occasionally, until softened and the edges start to turn light golden, 6 to 9 minutes. Stir in the garlic, ginger, and serrano pepper and continue to cook until the garlic turns light golden and the ginger softens, 3 to 4 minutes more. Add the chilli powder and remaining ½ teaspoon turmeric and cook, stirring constantly, for 30 seconds to bloom the spices.

1 white onion, finely diced

4 garlic cloves, minced

1-inch piece ginger, julienned

1 serrano pepper, quartered lengthwise

¾ teaspoon Kashmiri chilli powder

½ cup (25 g) roughly chopped cilantro, leaves and tender stems

Juice of ½ lemon (1 to 2 tablespoons), plus more if needed

FOR THE TADKA

1½ tablespoons mustard seed oil

2 garlic cloves, thinly sliced

½ teaspoon cumin seeds

½ teaspoon black mustard seeds

1 to 2 dried whole Guntur Sannam chillies, torn in half

RECIPE NOTE: If you don't have mustard seed oil, you can use ghee or a neutral oil, like canola or untoasted sesame for the tadka.

Add the cooked dal, the remaining ½ teaspoon salt, and 1 cup (240 ml) water to the onion mixture, stir to combine, and bring to a simmer. Reduce the heat to low, partially cover, and cook, stirring occasionally to make sure the dal doesn't stick to the bottom of the pot, for 20 minutes. If you like your dal a little thinner, you can add a splash or two of water; if you like your dal a little thicker, you can continue to simmer, uncovered, until you reach the desired consistency. Cover and keep warm while preparing the tadka.

To make the tadka, heat the mustard seed oil in a tadka spoon or small saucepan over medium heat. When shimmering, add the garlic, cumin seeds, mustard seeds, and chillies and fry, stirring or swirling frequently, until the garlic is golden and the mustard seeds start sputtering, 1 to 3 minutes.

To finish the dal, pour the tadka into the dal, add the cilantro and lemon juice, and stir to combine. Taste and season with more salt and/or lemon juice, if necessary. Serve with hot rice and ghee.

KADHI, opposite, and KHICHDI, page 187

Kadhi
Yogurt and Turmeric Soup

Recipe by Hetal Sakariya | Origin: Shedubhar, Gujarat | Serves 4

The Sakariya family, who grow our Nandini Coriander and Hariyali Fennel, have trained me to see a tub of yogurt or buttermilk getting a little funky at the back of my fridge and know that it's time to make kadhi! Traditionally a way to extend the life of aging buttermilk, it's made by whisking leftover dairy with chickpea flour and turmeric until it looks like silky smooth sunshine and topping it with a feisty tadka. Kadhi is traditionally served with Khichdi (page 187), but you can also serve it with plain white rice and a side of Bhindi Masala (page 88) for a little extra variety!

1 cup (227 g) plain, full-fat yogurt (not Greek)

1 cup (240 ml) buttermilk

¼ cup (30 g) besan (chickpea flour)

1 teaspoon fine sea salt, plus more if needed

2 tablespoons untoasted sesame oil or other neutral oil

1 serrano pepper, cut in half lengthwise

1 teaspoon finely chopped ginger

1 teaspoon black mustard seeds

½ teaspoon cumin seeds

¼ teaspoon fenugreek seeds

4 whole cloves

1 tejpatta leaf, torn in half

⅛ teaspoon asafetida

¾ teaspoon ground turmeric

1 to 2 dried Byadgi or Guntur Sannam chillies, torn in half

12 fresh curry leaves

½ teaspoon Byadgi chilli powder

Combine the yogurt, buttermilk, besan, and salt in a bowl and whisk for 2 minutes (to help prevent the kadhi from curdling). Whisk in 1½ cups (360 ml) water and set aside.

Heat 1 tablespoon of the sesame oil in a medium saucepan over medium heat. When shimmering, add the serrano pepper, ginger, ¼ teaspoon of the mustard seeds, ¼ teaspoon of the cumin seeds, the fenugreek seeds, cloves, tejpatta leaf, and asafetida and cook, stirring frequently, until the mustard seeds start to sputter and the fenugreek seeds turn a shade darker, 15 to 45 seconds. Stir in the turmeric and continue to cook, stirring frequently, for 15 seconds to let the turmeric bloom.

Give the yogurt mixture another whisk and slowly pour it into the pan, continuing to whisk. Bring the mixture to a gentle boil, whisking constantly, 4 to 7 minutes. Continue to cook, stirring frequently, until the mixture thickens and coats the back of a spoon, 8 to 11 minutes. Taste and season with more salt, if necessary. Turn off the heat, cover, and keep warm.

To make the tadka, heat the remaining 1 tablespoon oil in a tadka spoon or small saucepan. When shimmering, add the chillies and the remaining ¾ teaspoon mustard seeds and ¼ teaspoon cumin seeds and cook, swirling the pan occasionally, until the mustard seeds start to sputter and the chillies turn a couple shades darker, 15 to 45 seconds. Add the curry leaves—be careful, these crackle and pop!—and cook until bright green and translucent, 10 to 30 seconds more. Turn off the heat, add the chilli powder, and swirl to bloom the chilli powder in the fat, 15 to 30 seconds.

Pour the tadka over the kadhi and serve.

Pahadi Rajma
Himalayan Brothy Kidney Beans

Recipe by Gyan Singh Rana | Origin: Kotgaon, Uttarakhand | Serves 6

Rajma may be considered the soul food of the Tons Valley, with most homes cooking it at least a couple times every week. Our version is a little zhuzhed up, but the soul remains the same—beans floating in a light, aromatic broth, with coriander, garlic, and tejpatta. Serve with rice, an extra dollop of ghee—mandatory on the Pahadi table!—yogurt, and Blistered Asparagus with Pisyun Loon (page 76).

½ pound (227 g) dried rajma or red kidney beans

1 white onion, cut into sixths

3 teaspoons coriander seeds

8 garlic cloves

2 teaspoons fine sea salt, plus more if needed

3 tablespoons mustard seed oil

3 dried Sirārakhong Hāthei chillies

1½-inch piece ginger, julienned

½ teaspoon ground turmeric

3 tejpatta leaves

⅓ cup (17 g) roughly chopped cilantro

Juice of ½ to 1 lemon (1 to 4 tablespoons)

2 tablespoons ghee, plus more (optional) for serving

1 teaspoon cumin seeds

Place the dried rajma in a bowl, pick through for stones, then rinse with cold water and drain. Cover with 3 inches of cold water and soak for at least 6 hours, up to overnight.

Place 2 teaspoons of the coriander seeds in a mortar, gently pound to crack open and lightly crush the seeds, and transfer to a small bowl. Roughly chop 5 of the garlic cloves, place in the mortar with 1½ teaspoons of the salt, and pound into a medium-coarse paste. Set all items aside.

Heat 1 tablespoon of the mustard seed oil in a Dutch oven or other large, heavy-bottomed pot over medium-high heat. When shimmering, add the onion wedges, cut-side down, and cook on both cut sides until deeply browned, 2 to 5 minutes per side. Transfer the browned onions to a plate, wipe out the pot, and let cool for 5 minutes.

Return the pot to medium heat and add the remaining 2 tablespoons oil. When shimmering, add 2 of the dried Sirārakhong Hāthei chillies and the crushed coriander seeds and cook until the coriander turns a couple shades darker, 15 to 45 seconds. Add the ginger and the pounded garlic and cook, stirring frequently, until the garlic softens and just starts to turn light golden, 1 to 3 minutes. Add the turmeric and ¼ cup (60 ml) water and cook, stirring frequently, until the water reduces by about half, 1 to 3 minutes.

Drain the soaked rajma, add to the pot along with the tejpatta leaves, the reserved brown onion wedges, the remaining ½ teaspoon salt, and 6 cups (1.4 L) water, stir to combine, and bring to a gentle boil. Cover, reduce the heat to medium-low, and simmer until the beans are tender and just starting to break apart, 2 to 2½ hours. Stir in the cilantro and

RECIPE NOTE: If you can't find mustard seed oil, you can use any neutral oil, like canola or untoasted sesame seed, plus 1 teaspoon Colman's ground mustard, adding the latter when you add the ground turmeric.

the juice of ½ lemon. Taste and season with more salt and/or lemon juice, if necessary.

To make the tadka, thinly slice the remaining 3 garlic cloves. Heat the ghee in a tadka spoon or small saucepan over medium heat. Add the garlic, cumin seeds, the remaining 1 teaspoon coriander seeds, and the remaining 1 Sirārakhong Hāthei chilli, broken in half, and cook, swirling the pan occasionally, until the garlic turns light golden, 1 to 3 minutes. Pour into the rajma and gently stir to combine. Serve with steamed rice and an extra dollop of ghee, if desired.

The Green Heirloom Community
Tools

KOCHI, KERALA

Kaviya Cherian (at right, opposite) is the founder of Green Heirloom, our Kochi-based manufacturing partner for our bronze mortar and pestle sets and hand-painted ceramic Salt Tigers. Our working relationship is both fairly chaotic and wildly productive, meaning that it works brilliantly.

Kaviya comes from a line of fierce Syrian Christian women who are all truly exemplary home cooks. Two of her most precious heirlooms are a notebook full of handwritten family recipes written by her grandmother Anna Thomas and a set of church cookbooks compiled by the Kottayam Ladies Circle No. 48, which has become an incredible resource for her community's cuisine.

On my biannual harvest trip to Kerala, Kaviya makes it a point to always take me to the newest seafood restaurant she's added to her Kochi rotation, knowing that I share her love for eating large quantities of bivalves and crustaceans. On this latest trip, she took us to Karthiyayini, an unassuming family-owned open-air restaurant where you're served on plastic trays lined with banana leaves and there is always a crowd of hungry, knowing local families waiting for the catch of the day. In my many years of traveling the length and breadth of South Asia, I've eaten some truly incredible meals, but our seafood lunch feasts at Karthiyayini remain undefeated. So, we went to great lengths to include renditions of our two favorite menu items—Thenga Aracha Meen Curry (page 144) and Kanthari Chilli Squid (page 146), all thanks to Kaviya, forever Kochi's best ambassador.

Recipes from Kaviya's friends and family

Prawn Head Roast 136

Thenga Aracha Meen Curry 144

Kanthari Chilli Squid 146

Skillet Appams 201

Kappa Puzhukku 206

Beans and Lentils

The Chacko Family
Baraka Cardamom

UDUMBANCHOLA, KERALA

When I first set out to source organically farmed green cardamom, I spent months collecting samples from farmers promising me the moon. But every scientist I got on the phone with was skeptical. One of my most trusted resources, Dr. Vijayan, who works at the Kerala-based Cardamom Research Station, bluntly walked me through the process by which big commercial cardamom growers cheat the organic certification process and to this day get away with selling pesticide-ridden cardamom as organic. Sure enough, every sample from all those promising estates came back from the lab with significant pesticide residue.

When I got a call from Mr. Abraham Chacko, a farmer bang in the middle of the cardamom hills—the region where commercial and corrupt cardamom agriculture is at its worst—I didn't have much faith. But he was persistent, sending me heart-melting sunset selfies with his herd of desi cows and mailing me a very generous sample. And his test came back completely pesticide-free?! I'd seen a couple cardamom labs come back with organic approved pesticides on them before, but I'd NEVER seen a blank lab report. I booked a flight to visit him the next day.

Abraham and his wife, Chachu, started farming on their ancestral land twenty-five years ago. They watched as more and more of their relatives left farming for other industries. Tired of spending more and more money on inputs like pesticides and fertilizers yet seeing lower profits every year, they adopted a zero-budget biodynamic farming model. It's hard to explain how giant that leap of faith was—pulling out fruiting cardamom at its peak productivity in the wild hope that in three to four years their new approach *might* be more sustainable?! Madness. But soon after, they noticed some of their cardamom plants faring much better than others and began selectively breeding these more resilient, healthy plants.

Today, the Chacko estate is unlike any farm I've ever visited—a wild food forest, with cardamom growing tall alongside dripping pepper vines, the occasional coffee bush, and lots of wild greens, butterflies, and bees. Where other farmers obsessively tend to their crops, Abraham and Chachu mostly leave them alone, creating a happy home for all kinds of pollinators. The resulting cardamom seeds are a revelation—fruity, potent, and intoxicatingly fragrant. From day one, I knew that this cardamom would transform people's understanding of the spice and make some of the best chai ever (page 212). For me, the Chackos' cardamom is proof that regenerative farming and agroforestry are inherently linked to better flavor and quality.

In their family home, Chachu's helper Rani has been working with the family for over forty years and, in Chachu's own words, is her closest confidant and support. During our time in their farmhouse kitchen, learning the recipes for this book by the wood-burning stove and heirloom earthen cookware, it was the comradery between Chachu and Rani that was the biggest joy of our visit.

Recipes from the Chacko Family

Pazha Manga Curry 94

Meen Moilee 138

Pepper Pork 154

Thalassery Fish Biryani 183

From the Sea

Kakuluwo Curry 132

Kerala-Style Grilled Prawns 134

Prawn Head Roast 136

Meen Moilee 138

Meen Pollichathu 140

Thenga Aracha Meen Curry 144

Kanthari Chilli Squid 146

Kakuluwo Curry

Jaffna-Style Crab Curry

Recipe inspired by Upali's | Origin: Jaffna, Sri Lanka | Serves 4

It's impossible to discuss the food of Jaffna without discussing Tamil Sri Lankans and all that they have suffered over the past seventy years to stake a right to exist safely and without fear. Preserving Tamil Sri Lankan food culture and recipes has become an act of resistance and perseverance.

My first time trying this dish was at the iconic Palmyrah Hotel in Colombo, run by three generations of the Thambiayah family. The curry is lush, subtly tangy, sweet with coconut milk, and intensely fragrant with roasted curry powder. Skillet Appams (Kerala-Style Lacy Rice Pancakes, page 201) or Sri Lankan Moringa String Hoppers (page 198) are the perfect vessels to soak up all the juicy curry and crab meat.

2¼ pounds (1 kg) stone crab claws, Jonah crab claws, or Dungeness crab clusters (see Recipe Note)

3 tablespoons virgin coconut oil

½ teaspoon black mustard seeds

½ teaspoon coriander seeds

½ teaspoon fenugreek seeds

One 3-inch cinnamon stick, broken in half

4 whole cloves

24 fresh curry leaves

1 red onion, finely diced

1-inch piece ginger, julienned

4 garlic cloves, finely chopped

1¼ teaspoons fine sea salt, plus more if needed

1½ tablespoons Sri Lankan Roasted Curry Powder (page 22)

Prepare the crab. If using claws, take one claw at a time and gently crack with the back of a chef's knife, rolling pin, or meat mallet. If using crab clusters, remove and gently crack the legs, leaving the bodies intact. Set aside.

For the gravy, heat the coconut oil in a Dutch oven or other large, heavy-bottomed pot over medium heat. When shimmering, add the mustard seeds, coriander seeds, fenugreek seeds, cinnamon stick, and cloves and cook, stirring frequently, until the coriander seeds turn a couple shades darker, 15 to 45 seconds. Add 12 of the curry leaves and cook until bright green and starting to turn translucent, 10 to 30 seconds.

Stir in the onion, ginger, garlic, and ½ teaspoon of the salt and cook, stirring occasionally, until the onions soften and start to turn light golden around the edges, 8 to 12 minutes. Add the curry powder, chilli powder, and turmeric and cook, stirring frequently, until fragrant, about 30 seconds. Add the tamarind concentrate, coconut milk, the remaining ¾ teaspoon salt, and 1 cup (240 ml) water, stir to combine, and bring to a gentle boil. Cover, reduce the heat to medium-low, and simmer for 15 minutes.

Add the reserved cracked crab, stirring to coat the crab in the sauce, increase the heat to medium-high, and bring back to a simmer. Cover, reduce the heat to medium-low, and cook until the crab is heated through, 10 to 15 minutes. Rip the remaining 12 curry leaves into the curry. Taste and season with more salt, if necessary.

- 2 to 3 teaspoons Guntur Sannam chilli powder
- ¾ teaspoon ground turmeric
- 2 teaspoons tamarind concentrate
- One 14-ounce (398 ml) can full-fat coconut milk
- 1 lemon

To serve, transfer the crab to a shallow bowl and spoon all the gravy over the top. Cut the lemon into wedges and serve alongside the crab so people can squeeze it over at the table.

RECIPE NOTE: This curry is traditionally made with mud crabs, which are harder to find stateside. The good news is that both American coasts have fantastic crab options, from Dungeness and snow crab to stone and Jonah crab, the latter beloved for their meaty claws. We tried this with cooked Dungeness crab clusters (cleaned bodies with the legs attached) and frozen, thawed stone crab claws to great avail. Choose what is available to you! And, if you're really in a pinch, jumbo, head-on prawns make a great substitution.

Kerala-Style Grilled Prawns

Recipe inspired by Marari Sea Lap Beach Villas | Origin: Marari Beach, Kerala | Serves 4

Between every region on our three-month research trip, we had a few break days to rest and recuperate. On one of these breaks, Asha and Melati, our beloved photographer, spent four glorious sun-and-seafood-filled days on Marari Beach, a seaside village a couple hours from Kochi. On their second day, a photo of plump grilled shrimp made its way into our cookbook WhatsApp group (the FOMO was real, y'all!). Before she left, Asha asked the chef for the recipe, and while he wouldn't share the quantities, he did share the ingredients for his special Kerala masala. Armed with this list and her taste memories, she recreated this glorious plateful, perfectly capturing those oceanside vibes.

1½ tablespoons coriander seeds

1 teaspoon black peppercorns

3 tablespoons Byadgi chilli powder (or sweet or hot paprika in a pinch)

2 teaspoons fine sea salt

1 teaspoon ground turmeric

½ teaspoon ground cinnamon

1 to 1¼ pounds (454 to 567 g) 10/12-count shell-on jumbo shrimp

3 lemons

36 fresh curry leaves

3 tablespoons virgin coconut oil, melted

1 English cucumber, cut on the bias into ¼-inch slices

Combine the coriander seeds and black peppercorns in a spice grinder and grind into a medium-fine powder. Add the chilli powder, salt, turmeric, and cinnamon and pulse to combine. Set aside.

To clean the shrimp, cut down the top of the shrimp, using kitchen shears, from top to tail, and remove and discard the vein. Then, taking one shrimp at a time, butterfly the shrimp by cutting down the middle lengthwise almost all the way through, but leaving both halves connected by about ¼ inch. Repeat with the remaining shrimp.

Transfer the butterflied shrimp to a sheet pan and sprinkle evenly with the reserved spice mixture. Squeeze the juice of 2 lemons (4 to 5 tablespoons) over the shrimp, then, in batches, using your hands, rub the curry leaves between your palms to break them up and release their essential oils and sprinkle over the shrimp. Toss everything together, turning each shrimp so it's coated on both sides with the spice paste. Let the shrimp marinate at room temperature for 30 minutes. (Don't marinate longer than an hour because the amount of lemon juice will start to cook the shrimp.)

Meanwhile, heat a gas or charcoal grill to medium-high heat. Drizzle the coconut oil over the shrimp, turning the shrimp to coat on both sides. Grill the shrimp, flesh-side down, until turning opaque and starting to char in spots, 2 to 3 minutes. Flip and cook until fully cooked through and opaque, 1½ to 3 minutes more. (Alternatively, you can use a grill pan or cast-iron skillet over medium-high heat, using the same timings.)

To serve, transfer the grilled shrimp to a platter and arrange the cucumber around the shrimp. Cut the remaining lemon into wedges, arrange around the platter, and serve immediately.

Prawn Head Roast
Kerala-Style Spicy Fried Shrimp Heads

Recipe inspired by Sheela Michael | Origin: Kochi, Kerala | Serves 4

Sheela Michael is a force—no cooking school, no fancy chef title; just talent and grit have propelled her into the renowned Kochi caterer and cook that she is today. This recipe started out as a way to use the shrimp heads that were left over from the many prawn curries and roasts she was making. It's now become the recipe that everyone asks her for and that she is best known for!

Our version of her famous prawn head roast uses all the classic Kerala spices and aromatics but is extra crunchy from a light batter of rice flour and cornstarch. You want to make sure to eat it right away once the shrimp heads are fully coated in tangy masala, before they lose their addictive crispiness. Squeeze plenty of lemon over each bite. This is honestly perfect drinking food and pairs incredibly well with a couple of cold beers and salty peanuts.

3 tablespoons virgin coconut oil

1½ teaspoons coriander seeds, lightly crushed

½ teaspoon fennel seeds

24 fresh curry leaves

1 large shallot (about 3 ounces/85 g), finely chopped

4 garlic cloves, finely chopped

1-inch piece ginger, finely chopped

1 serrano pepper, quartered lengthwise

1 teaspoon fine sea salt, plus more if needed

3 teaspoons Byadgi chilli powder

1 teaspoon garam masala

¾ teaspoon ground turmeric

½ teaspoon freshly ground black pepper

Heat the coconut oil in a large skillet over medium heat. When shimmering, add the coriander seeds and fennel seeds and cook, stirring frequently, until the coriander seeds are a couple shades darker, 15 to 45 seconds. Add the curry leaves and cook until bright green and translucent, 10 to 30 seconds.

Stir in the shallot, garlic, ginger, serrano pepper, and ½ teaspoon of the salt and cook, stirring occasionally, until the shallots soften and start to turn light golden around the edges, 6 to 9 minutes. Add 1½ teaspoons of the chilli powder, the garam masala, ½ teaspoon of the turmeric, the black pepper, tomatoes, and ½ cup (120 ml) water and cook, stirring occasionally, until the tomatoes become jammy and the oil starts to separate, 6 to 10 minutes. Taste and season with more salt, if necessary. Turn off the heat, cover, and keep warm.

Combine the rice flour, cornstarch, and the remaining 1½ teaspoons chilli powder, ¼ teaspoon turmeric, and ½ teaspoon salt in a bowl. Pat the shrimp heads dry, add them to the bowl, and gently toss to coat.

Heat ½ inch of canola oil in a Dutch oven or other large, heavy-bottomed pot over medium-high heat to 375°F. Fry the seasoned shrimp heads, working in batches, if necessary, until bright pink and crisp, 3 to 6 minutes, flipping halfway through. Drain on a wire rack–lined sheet pan.

- 2 plum tomatoes, finely chopped
- 2 tablespoons rice flour
- 1 tablespoon cornstarch
- 12 jumbo shrimp heads
- Canola oil or other neutral oil, for frying
- 1 to 2 lemons

Return the masala to medium-high heat. Add the fried shrimp heads and quickly toss to coat them in the masala. Transfer to a serving platter, cut the lemons into wedges, arrange around the shrimp heads, and serve immediately.

RECIPE NOTE: Instead of shrimp heads, you can make this with 12 to 16 jumbo, peel-on shrimp.

Meen Moilee

Kerala-Style Coconut Turmeric Fish Curry

Recipe by Chachu Lukose | Origin: Udumbanchola, Kerala | Serves 4

Every Syrian Christian home in Kerala has a Meen Moilee recipe, and the Abraham family, who grow our Baraka Cardamom is no exception. Their famous and wildly aromatic Baraka Cardamom pods are the hero spice in this gentle curry. Use a soft, flaky fish like halibut, cod, or rockfish, that will complement the light, aromatic flavors of the gravy. This dish comes together so quickly, it's my go-to recipe for when I'm cooking to impress but am short on time.

1½ pounds (680 g) skinless firm, flaky white fish fillets

1 tablespoon fresh lemon juice

1¾ teaspoons fine sea salt, plus more if needed

½ teaspoon freshly ground white pepper

¼ teaspoon ground turmeric

3 tablespoons virgin coconut oil

5 green cardamom pods, lightly crushed

4 whole cloves

1 teaspoon black mustard seeds

24 fresh curry leaves

3 large shallots (about ½ pound/227 g), sliced

4 garlic cloves, finely chopped

1-inch piece ginger, julienned

1 to 2 serrano peppers, quartered lengthwise

12 to 15 cherry tomatoes (⅓ pound/151 g), halved

One 14-ounce (398 ml) can full-fat coconut milk

1 teaspoon apple cider vinegar

To prepare the fish, cut into 4-inch pieces and place in a bowl with the lemon juice, 1 teaspoon of the salt, the white pepper, and turmeric and gently toss to coat. Cover and refrigerate while preparing the sauce.

Heat the coconut oil in a Dutch oven or other large, heavy-bottomed pot over medium heat. When shimmering, add the cardamom, cloves, mustard seeds, and 12 of the curry leaves and cook, stirring occasionally, until the spices smell fragrant and the curry leaves turn bright green and translucent, 1 to 3 minutes.

Add the shallots, garlic, ginger, and serrano peppers and cook, stirring occasionally, until the shallots are soft and start to turn translucent but don't take on any color, 4 to 7 minutes. Add the cherry tomatoes, remaining ¾ teaspoon salt, and ¼ cup (60 ml) water, stir, cover, and cook, stirring occasionally, until the tomatoes just start to burst, 5 to 8 minutes.

Stir in the coconut milk, bring to a simmer, cover, and continue to cook until the tomatoes are easily crushed with the back of a spoon. Crush half the tomatoes, then nestle the fish into the sauce, spooning some of the sauce over each piece. Reduce the heat to medium-low, cover, and cook until the fish is cooked through and easily flakes, 5 to 9 minutes. Taste and season with more salt, if necessary.

Turn off the heat, gently stir in the vinegar, then tear the remaining 12 curry leaves and sprinkle them over the top. Serve immediately with steamed short-grain rice or Skillet Appams (Kerala-Style Lacy Rice Pancakes, page 201).

Meen Pollichathu

Kerala-Style Tangy Grilled Fish in Banana Leaves

Recipe inspired by Fusion Bay, Kochi | Origin: Kochi, Kerala | Serves 4

Most of the extremely rural regions that we travel to on our sourcing trips are places where there are no real restaurants to speak of, which means we're exclusively eating delicious homemade farm meals—not that I'm complaining! However, our trips to our cardamom and pepper farm partners in Kerala involve flying in and out of Kochi, a city that is sheer restaurant heaven. Around harvest season, I tend to add on a couple days in Kochi just so I can wander the streets with our team and EAT. Fusion Bay is a fairly touristy restaurant that was highly recommended by Reeshna, our community coordinator, aka the person who thoughtfully answers most of our customer service inquiries.

We ordered this dish on our first day in town, and I loved it so much that I've gone back over ten times in the past couple years. It's one of those dishes that I've now had in many homes, but nobody ever got it quite as tangy, flaky, and aromatic as Fusion Bay—until Asha, of course! The magic of meen pollichathu is the contrast of super-soft flaky white fish and intensely savory, spicy, and tangy masala, all wrapped up and grilled in hella aromatic banana leaves. I hate to play favorites, but if I were to choose from this chapter, this would be it.

1½ pounds (680 g) boneless, skinless flaky white fish fillets, like rockfish, cod, or Dover sole

48 fresh curry leaves (4 to 5 g)

1 tablespoon plus 2 teaspoons Guntur Sannam chilli powder

¾ teaspoon ground turmeric

½ teaspoon freshly ground black pepper

2 teaspoons fine sea salt

1 lemon

¼ cup plus 2 tablespoons (90 ml) virgin coconut oil

1 tablespoon coriander seeds

Place the fish in a bowl (if the fillets are larger, cut them into 6-inch-long pieces) along with 24 of the curry leaves, 1 tablespoon of the chilli powder, the turmeric, black pepper, and 1 teaspoon of the salt. Squeeze the juice of ½ lemon (about 2 tablespoons) over, reserving the other half for serving, and gently toss to coat the fish evenly in the spice mixture, making sure the curry leaves are stuck to the outside of the fillets and not at the bottom of the bowl. Cover and set aside while you prepare the sauce, or if using later, refrigerate up to 4 hours (any longer than that and the lemon juice will start cooking the fish and change its texture).

Heat ¼ cup (60 ml) of the coconut oil in a large skillet over medium heat. When shimmering, add the coriander seeds and fennel seeds and cook, stirring frequently, until the coriander seeds turn a couple shades darker, 15 to 45 seconds. Add the remaining 24 curry leaves—be careful, these will crackle and pop!—and cook until bright green and translucent, 10 to 30 seconds.

Add the shallots, ginger, garlic, serrano peppers, and ½ teaspoon of the remaining salt and cook, stirring occasionally, until the shallots soften and start to turn light golden around the edges, 6 to 9 minutes.

1 teaspoon fennel seeds

3 large shallots (about ½ pound/227 g), diced

¾-inch piece ginger, finely chopped

6 large garlic cloves, roughly chopped

1 to 2 serrano peppers, roughly chopped

3 plum tomatoes, diced

1 teaspoon tamarind concentrate

1 teaspoon powdered jaggery or light brown sugar

Banana leaves, for wrapping

Canola oil or other neutral oil, for oiling the grill

Stir in the tomatoes, tamarind concentrate, jaggery, the remaining 2 teaspoons chilli powder and ½ teaspoon salt, and ¼ cup (60 ml) water. Cover, reduce the heat to medium-low, and cook, stirring occasionally, until the tomatoes become jammy, 7 to 11 minutes. Uncover and continue to cook until the oil starts to separate, 3 to 5 minutes. Transfer to a blender and let cool for 10 minutes. Blend on high speed until smooth. Taste and season with more salt, if necessary.

While the tomato mixture is cooling, heat the remaining 2 tablespoons coconut oil in a large nonstick skillet over medium-high heat. When shimmering, fry the fish in batches, cooking it until it starts to turn opaque but isn't fully cooked through (it will finish cooking when you wrap it in the banana leaves with the sauce), 1 to 2 minutes per side. Transfer the parcooked fish fillets to a plate.

To prepare the fresh banana leaves, cut four 12-inch pieces of banana leaf (the pieces should be about 12 x 10-inch rectangles), rinse under cold water to clean off any dirt, and pat dry. If using frozen, pat the thawed leaves dry with a clean kitchen towel before cutting.

To wrap the fish, if using fresh banana leaves, take one leaf and briefly heat it over medium heat until it turns bright green and becomes pliable, 15 to 30 seconds (you can do this over the open flame or an electric coil on your stove). If using frozen, you can skip this step. Place the leaf diagonally on a flat surface with one of the corners pointed toward you. Spoon ⅓ cup (70 ml) of the blended sauce in the center of the leaf, spreading it into a 6 x 3-inch rectangle. Place one-quarter of the parcooked fish fillets on top of the sauce, then add ¼ cup (60 ml) of the sauce on top of the fish, gently spreading it across so the fish is fully coated. Fold the corner nearest you up and over the fish, then fold in the sides and continue to fold into an envelope-like parcel. Place the finished parcel seam-side down on a sheet pan and repeat with the remaining sauce and three portions of fish.

Meanwhile, prepare your charcoal grill or heat your gas grill to medium-high heat. When hot, oil the grates, place the banana leaf parcels seam-side down, close the lid, and grill for 4 minutes. Using a metal spatula, gently flip the parcels and cook, covered, until they feel firm to the touch, another 3 to 4 minutes.

Remove from the grill and transfer to a serving platter. Cut the remaining ½ lemon into wedges to serve alongside for squeezing. Enjoy with steamed rice or Skillet Appams (Kerala-Style Lacy Rice Pancakes, page 201).

MEEN POLLICHATTHU, page 140

THENGA ARACHA MEEN CURRY, page 144

Thenga Aracha Meen Curry

Kerala-Style Fish and Fresh Coconut Curry

Recipe by Jajina Rajan of Karthiyayini Restaurant | Origin: Kochi, Kerala | Serves 4 to 6

At Karthiyayini—an iconic seafood institution in Kochi, Kerala—the most sought-after dish on the menu is Thenga Aracha Meen Curry, which the owner makes in her own home kitchen using freshly caught thirutha (gray mullet) and then delivers it to Karthiyayini's two locations around noon every day. At the beginning of our time in Kochi, we were lucky enough to score a plate of this tangy, fresh coconut and fish curry the first time we dined there with our manufacturing partner Kaviya. Flavored with coriander, fennel, fenugreek seeds, lots of curry leaves, and Byadgi chillies, the gravy is aromatic to the max with a sour backbone from kudampuli (Kerala's souring agent, akin to kokum or tamarind) and richness from the fresh coconut.

This dish was so epically delicious, we went back to Karthiyayini's second location on our way to the airport and waited for the precious curry to be delivered, hoping it would arrive in time for us to still catch our flight. It was a very good day—we got the fish *and* made our flight.

Serve with Kappa Puzhukku (Kerala-Style Mashed Cassava, page 206).

8 to 10 petals kokum

1½ pounds (680 g) sea bass steaks (about two 1- to 1½-inch-thick pieces)

3½ teaspoons fine sea salt, plus more if needed

5 tablespoons (75 ml) virgin coconut oil

2½ teaspoons coriander seeds

1¼ teaspoons fennel seeds

½ teaspoon fenugreek seeds

48 fresh curry leaves (4 to 5 g)

3 large shallots (about ½ pound/227 g), 2 finely chopped and 1 thinly sliced

1 tablespoon tomato paste

Place the kokum petals in a bowl, cover with 1 cup (240 ml) boiling water, and let steep for at least 30 minutes, up to 4 hours. Season the fish with 1½ teaspoons of the salt, sprinkling it evenly over all sides. Let sit for 30 minutes while you prepare the curry.

Heat 3 tablespoons of the coconut oil in a Dutch oven or other large, heavy-bottomed pot over medium heat. When shimmering, add 1½ teaspoons of the coriander seeds, the fennel seeds, and fenugreek seeds and toast, stirring frequently, until the coriander seeds turn a couple shades darker, 15 to 45 seconds. Add 18 of the curry leaves—be careful, these will crackle and pop!—and cook until bright green and translucent, 10 to 30 seconds.

Stir in the 2 finely chopped shallots and ½ teaspoon of the remaining salt and cook, stirring occasionally, until the shallots soften and start to turn light golden around the edges, 6 to 9 minutes. Add the tomato paste, chilli powder, turmeric, and ½ cup (120 ml) water and continue to cook, stirring frequently, until most of the water has evaporated and the oil starts to separate, 4 to 7 minutes. Turn off the heat, transfer to a blender, and let cool for 10 minutes. Meanwhile, wipe out the pot and reserve it for later use.

1 tablespoon Byadgi chilli powder

½ teaspoon ground turmeric

2 cups (170 g) lightly packed fresh or thawed, frozen grated coconut, lightly packed

1 serrano pepper, quartered lengthwise

Add the coconut and 1 cup (240 ml) water to the blender and start blending on low speed, increasing the speed to high, and blend until the spices and shallots are totally puréed (the mixture will be smooth but retain some texture from the fresh coconut). Set aside.

Heat the remaining 2 tablespoons coconut oil in the reserved Dutch oven over medium heat. When shimmering, add 18 of the remaining curry leaves and cook until bright green and translucent, 10 to 30 seconds. Stir in the serrano pepper, the thinly sliced shallot, and ½ teaspoon of the remaining salt and cook, stirring occasionally, until softened and the shallots start to turn light golden around the edges, 6 to 9 minutes.

Add the reserved blended coconut mixture. Strain the kokum water through a fine-mesh sieve into the blender, swish around to get any last bits of the coconut mixture, and pour into the pot. Discard any of the leftover solids. Stir in the remaining 1 teaspoon salt and 2 cups (480 ml) water and bring to a gentle boil. Cover, reduce the heat to medium-low, and cook, stirring occasionally to make sure the coconut isn't sticking to the bottom of the pot, until some of the oil just begins to separate on the surface, 20 to 25 minutes. Taste and season with more salt, if necessary.

Gently nestle the reserved seasoned fish into the gravy, spooning some over so it is fully submerged. Cover and cook until the fish is cooked through and easily flakes with a fork, 12 to 17 minutes. Rub the remaining 12 curry leaves between your hands to release their essential oils and sprinkle over the fish.

RECIPE NOTES: Since kudampuli is harder to find stateside, we used kokum for this recipe. If you can't find kokum, you can use 1 teaspoon tamarind paste, diluted in 1 cup (240 ml) hot water, instead of the soaked kokum.

The recipe traditionally uses a fatty gray mullet that is found in the southern Arabian Sea—you want a flaky but firm white fish that has a good amount of fat. We tested with sea bass steaks, but it could also be a hit with a whole branzino.

Kanthari Chilli Squid

Kerala-Style Squid with Bird's-Eye Chillies, Cilantro, and Curry Leaves

Recipe by Jajina Rajan of Karthiyayini Restaurant | Origin: Kochi, Kerala | Serves 2 to 4

Kanthari chillies are a small, potent, Indian bird's-eye chilli grown in Kerala and Tamil Nadu, beloved for their verdant heat and citrusy flavor. They're key in fiery kanthari masala, made with chillies and green herbs. Since these chillies are hard to find stateside, we reach for a combo of Thai bird's-eye chillies and Meyer lemon to achieve that zippy, floral taste. It's great with squid but equally tasty slathered over swordfish or sea bass for a fish fry. Serve with rice or Skillet Appams (page 201).

2 teaspoons coriander seeds

1 teaspoon fennel seeds

60 fresh curry leaves (7 g)

1 Meyer lemon (see Recipe Notes)

2 to 3 Thai bird's-eye chillies or 1 to 2 serrano peppers, finely chopped (see Recipe Notes)

4 garlic cloves, finely chopped

½-inch piece ginger, finely chopped

½ teaspoon fine sea salt, plus more if needed

½ teaspoon ground turmeric

¼ teaspoon freshly ground black pepper

⅔ cup (34 g) finely chopped cilantro

1 pound (454 g) cleaned squid tubes and tentacles

2 tablespoons virgin coconut oil

2 medium shallots (about ¼ pound/113 g), thinly sliced

Heat a tadka spoon or small skillet over medium heat. Add the coriander seeds and fennel seeds and toast, swirling the pan frequently, until the coriander turns a couple shades darker, 15 to 45 seconds. Transfer to a mortar and let cool completely.

Meanwhile, chop 45 of the curry leaves and set aside. Zest the lemon, then cut the lemon into wedges and set aside separately.

Add the chillies, garlic, ginger, salt, turmeric, and black pepper to the mortar with the toasted spices. Pound into a medium-fine paste. Add the cilantro and the reserved chopped curry leaves and continue to pound into a medium-coarse paste.

Place the squid between two layers of paper towels and press to dry as much as possible. Discard the paper towels and cut the tubes into ¼-inch rings. Transfer the rings and tentacles to a bowl, add the herb paste, and toss to coat.

Heat the coconut oil in a large cast-iron or other heavy-bottomed skillet over medium-high heat. When shimmering, add the remaining 15 curry leaves and cook until bright green, 10 to 30 seconds. Stir in the shallots and cook until softened and turning light golden, 3 to 6 minutes.

Turn the heat to high and add the squid, plus any leftover paste, stir, spread it into an even layer, and cook undisturbed until starting to turn opaque, 1 to 2 minutes. Continue to cook, stirring frequently, until cooked through and fully opaque, 2 to 3 minutes more. Turn off the heat, stir in the reserved lemon zest, taste, and season with salt, if necessary. To serve, transfer to a serving plate with the reserved lemon wedges.

RECIPE NOTES:
If you can't find Meyer lemons, you can use standard lemons. If you want a milder green chilli flavor, you can remove the seeds and ribs.

See "Wazwan," page 166.

From the Land

Country Chicken Curry 150

Pepper Pork 154

Jammy Egg Curry 156

Sirārakhong Hāthei
Chilli-Lemongrass Chicken
and Rice 158

Hoksa 162

Aab Gosht 165

Tabak Maaz 168

Palak Rista 170

Maaz Rass 174

Country Chicken Curry

Recipe by Asha Loupy | Origin: Daund, Maharashtra | Serves 6

Over the course of our research for this cookbook, we had a bevy of chicken curries, each varying from household to household, and each so delicious in their own ways. So, Asha pulled inspiration from all the curries we ate to create the ultimate Diaspora country chicken curry. The result? An intensely flavored gravy that's fiery—like our fave Sannam chicken of Andhra Pradesh—with a warming, aromatic backbone and thickened by toasted, ground chana dal (a trick we learned from our jaggery farm partners!). Serve with rice or Bajra Na Rotla (page 204), plus plain yogurt or raita.

FOR THE CHICKEN MARINADE

One 3- to 4-pound whole chicken or 3½ pounds (1.4 to 1.8 kg) chicken legs

2 tablespoons Andhra Chilli Powder (page 23)

2 teaspoons fine sea salt

1 teaspoon ground turmeric

1 tablespoon finely grated fresh ginger

2 garlic cloves, finely grated

FOR THE GRAVY AND ASSEMBLY

3 tablespoons untoasted sesame oil or other neutral oil

2 teaspoons coriander seeds

¾ teaspoon cumin seeds

6 green cardamom pods, lightly crushed

6 whole cloves

One 2-inch cinnamon stick

Prepare the chicken. If using a whole chicken—you got this!—place the chicken on a cutting board breast-side up. Using a sharp boning knife, make a slice through the skin connecting the breast to the leg, then flip the chicken over. Cut any skin connecting the thigh to the body of the chicken and pull the leg up, popping it out of the joint, then cut through the joint, removing the leg from the body. To separate the thigh and drumstick, slice down through the joint where they connect. Repeat this process with the other leg.

Flip the chicken on its side and cut between the breast and the wing. Twist the wing to find the joint and cut through the joint to remove the wing. Repeat the process on the other wing. Using kitchen shears, cut through the rib cage to remove the bone-in breasts, saving the backbone for stock or another use. Cut down through the center where the breasts meet and use the kitchen shears to cut through any cartilage or bone to separate the bone-in breasts. Then cut each bone-in breast in half crosswise.

Remove the skin from the thighs, drumsticks, and breast pieces, leaving the skin on the wings (they are hard to take the skin off of!), saving the rest of the skin for another use. Transfer all the chicken pieces to a large bowl. (If using chicken legs, separate the chicken legs into thighs and drumsticks, cutting through the joint connecting them, then remove the skin, saving it for another use, and add them to a large bowl.)

To marinate the chicken, add the chilli powder, salt, turmeric, ginger, and garlic to the chicken and mix well. Cover and refrigerate for at least 2 hours, but preferably overnight.

1 piece stoneflower, optional

36 fresh curry leaves (2 to 3 g)

1 white onion, finely diced

1 teaspoon fine sea salt, plus more if needed

4 garlic cloves, quartered

1-inch piece fresh ginger, julienned

2 to 3 serrano peppers, quartered

2 teaspoons Andhra Chilli Powder (page 23)

½ teaspoon ground turmeric

2 tejpatta leaves

1 teaspoon powdered jaggery or light brown sugar

2 tablespoons chana dal

Juice of ½ lemon (1 to 2 tablespoons), plus more if needed

½ cup (25 g) roughly chopped cilantro, leaves and tender stems

To make the gravy, heat the sesame oil in a Dutch oven or other large, heavy-bottomed pot over medium heat. When shimmering, add the coriander seeds, cumin seeds, cardamom, cloves, cinnamon stick, and stoneflower, if using, and cook, stirring occasionally, until the coriander turns a shade darker, 30 to 45 seconds. Add 18 of the curry leaves—be careful, these will crackle and pop!—and cook until they start to turn bright green and translucent, 10 to 30 seconds. Stir in the onion and ½ teaspoon of the salt and cook, stirring occasionally, until they start to turn translucent and are light golden around the edges, 12 to 16 minutes.

Add the garlic, ginger, serrano peppers, and the marinated chicken, plus any juices that have accumulated, stir to coat in the onion-spice mixture, and cook, stirring frequently, until the chicken starts to lose its raw appearance, 5 to 7 minutes. Stir in the chilli powder, turmeric, tejpatta leaves, jaggery, the remaining ½ teaspoon salt, and 2 cups (480 ml) water, making sure to scrape any stuck-on bits from the bottom of the pan, and bring to a gentle boil. Cover, reduce the heat to medium-low, and cook, stirring occasionally, until the dark meat is tender but not falling off the bone and you have a thin broth, 25 to 30 minutes.

Meanwhile, heat a tadka spoon or small saucepan over medium-low heat. Add the chana dal and toast until light golden, 3 to 6 minutes. Transfer to a spice grinder and allow to cool, then blend into a fine powder and set aside.

Add the ground, toasted chana dal and tear the remaining 18 curry leaves into the curry, gently stir to combine, and cook, partially covered and stirring occasionally to make sure nothing is sticking to the bottom of the pan, until the dark meat easily pulls away from the bone and the gravy has thickened so it lightly coats the back of a spoon, 20 to 25 minutes. (The gravy will be on the looser side of thick, so if you want it thicker, cook the chicken uncovered for the last 10 minutes of cooking.)

To finish, stir in the lemon juice and cilantro. Taste and season with more salt and/or lemon juice, if necessary.

RECIPE NOTE: In India, you're able to buy a chicken cut specifically for curry—aptly called curry-cut—which takes the whole chicken and breaks it down into a big bowl of 1½- to 2-inch pieces, bones, innards, and all. Most butchers stateside don't know that cut, so this recipe calls for you to break down a whole chicken into 10 to 12 pieces. You can also skip the butchering and just use chicken legs.

COUNTRY CHICKEN CURRY, page 150

PEPPER PORK, page 154

Pepper Pork

Recipe inspired by Chachu Lukose and Shirley Parameswaran | Origin: Udumbanchola, Kerala, and Coorg, Karnataka | Serves 6 to 8

The Chacko family, who grow our Baraka Cardamom in central Kerala, and the Parameswaran family, who grow our Aranya Black Pepper in northern Kerala both make iconic pepper pork dishes, but both come from completely different points of reference. Chachu Lukose learned this dish—a Syrian Christian pork ularthiyathu, a traditional Keralan roast—from her mother, while Shirley Parameswaran grew up across the border from Kerala in Coorg, Karnataka, where the famous Kodava-style pork curry was a staple of her childhood.

Given that the Parameswaran family grows truly the most delicious peppercorns in the world, we knew we had to include a pepper-forward pork recipe here. Our final curry is a real best of both worlds situation inspired by two incredible home cooks.

Traditional Kodava pork curry is made with kachampuli, a vinegar made from Malabar tamarind that is able to stand up to the richness of the pork. We braised the pork with tamarind and then finished it with apple cider vinegar to recreate that same luscious, tangy sauce. We've also worked in three main spices—black pepper is the star of the show for floral heat, while fragrant, sweet fennel and citrusy coriander help balance out the warming elements.

2¼ pounds (1 kg) boneless country pork ribs or pork shoulder, cut into 2-inch pieces

2½ teaspoons fine sea salt, plus more if needed

½ teaspoon ground turmeric

2 golf ball–sized pieces (80 g) seedless tamarind pulp

2 cups (480 ml) boiling water

1½ tablespoons black peppercorns

1½ tablespoons fennel seeds

1 tablespoon coriander seeds

1 tablespoon canola oil

36 fresh curry leaves (2 to 3 g)

Put the pork in a bowl, season with 1½ teaspoons of the salt and the turmeric, and toss to coat. Cover and refrigerate for at least 1 hour, up to overnight.

A half hour before starting to brown the meat, rip the tamarind into smaller pieces, place in a bowl, cover with the boiling water, and let soak for 30 minutes, massaging the soaked tamarind with your fingers to release the pulp from the seeds halfway through. Once softened, strain and reserve the tamarind water, discarding any leftover seeds and pulp.

Meanwhile, toast the spices. Heat a tadka spoon or small skillet over medium-low heat, add the black peppercorns, and toast, stirring frequently, until fragrant, 2 to 3 minutes. Transfer to a small bowl and let cool. Return the skillet or tadka spoon to medium heat, add the fennel seeds and coriander seeds, and toast, stirring frequently, until the coriander seeds turn a couple shades darker and the spices smell toasty, 45 to 90 seconds. Transfer to a separate small bowl and let cool completely.

1 red onion, thinly sliced

6 garlic cloves, finely chopped

2 to 3 serrano peppers, quartered lengthwise

1-inch piece ginger, julienned

2 teaspoons apple cider vinegar

Place the toasted peppercorns in a spice grinder and pulse into a very coarse powder, 3 to 6 pulses. Remove 1 teaspoon and reserve for finishing, then add the toasted coriander and fennel seeds and continue to pulse into a medium-coarse powder, another 5 to 10 pulses. Set aside.

Heat the canola oil in a Dutch oven or other large, heavy-bottomed pot over medium-high heat. Working in batches, brown the meat on all sides, 3 to 4 minutes per side. Transfer the browned meat to a plate and set aside.

Reduce the heat to medium and add 12 of the curry leaves—be careful, they will crackle and pop!—and cook until the leaves turn bright green and translucent, 15 to 45 seconds. Add the onion and cook, stirring occasionally, until it starts to soften and turn light golden around the edges, 7 to 9 minutes. Add the garlic, serrano peppers, and ginger and continue to cook, stirring occasionally, until the garlic is light golden and the ginger softens, 3 to 5 minutes.

Add the browned pork back in along with the toasted black pepper, coriander, and fennel mixture, strained tamarind water, 12 of the remaining curry leaves, the remaining 1 teaspoon salt, and 1 cup (240 ml) water, and stir to combine, scraping any bits stuck to the bottom of the pot. Bring to a simmer, cover, reduce the heat to low, and cook, stirring occasionally to prevent the pork from sticking to the bottom of the pot, until the meat is fall-apart tender, 1 hour 45 minutes to 2½ hours. Once the pork is tender, increase the heat to medium and cook uncovered, allowing the sauce to reduce by a third, 9 to 13 minutes.

To finish, turn off the heat, add the vinegar, and gently stir, being careful not to break up the meat too much. Taste and season with more salt, if necessary. Tear the remaining 12 curry leaves over the pork and garnish with the reserved toasted black pepper.

Jammy Egg Curry

Recipe by Shirley Parameswaran | Origin: Thirunelly, Kerala | Serves 4 to 6

Shirley Aunty, the matriarch of the Aranya Pepper farm, is an egg curry queen. Her ingredient list is sparse—just shallots, spices, and coconut milk—but the result is so silky and rich. It's a lesson in simple yet luxurious cooking.

My one request to Asha when we were developing this recipe was that the eggs be jammy but as saturated with the curry and as much flavor as possible. Scoring the sides of a seven-minute egg so that you're effectively braising it in the curry is a game changer. Serve with steamed short-grain rice or Skillet Appams (page 201).

8 large eggs

3 tablespoons virgin coconut oil

2 teaspoons coriander seeds, lightly crushed

4 large shallots (about ⅔ pound/300 g), finely diced

1½ teaspoons fine sea salt, plus more if needed

1 tablespoon Byadgi chilli powder

1 teaspoon ground turmeric

¼ teaspoon freshly ground black pepper

One 14-ounce (398 ml) can full-fat coconut milk

Juice of ½ lemon (1 to 2 tablespoons), plus more if needed

Bring a large pot of water to a boil over high heat. Gently add the eggs and boil for 7 minutes, then, using a slotted spoon, transfer them to an ice bath to cool while you make the sauce.

To prepare the sauce, heat the coconut oil in a large skillet over medium heat. Add the coriander seeds and cook, stirring frequently, until they turn light golden, 30 to 45 seconds. Add the shallots and ½ teaspoon of the salt to the skillet and cook, stirring occasionally, until the shallots soften and turn light golden, 7 to 11 minutes. Stir in the chilli powder, turmeric, black pepper, and ½ cup (120 ml) water and cook until the water evaporates, 4 to 7 minutes.

Stir in the coconut milk and the remaining 1 teaspoon salt. Reduce the heat to medium-low, partially cover, and simmer until the sauce is reduced by a quarter and the oil is starting to separate, 9 to 12 minutes.

Meanwhile, peel the eggs and score the whites of the eggs lengthwise about 5 times around each egg, being careful not to cut too deep and hit the yolk. (This will help the sauce permeate the egg.)

Gently add the scored eggs to the skillet and continue to cook, gently basting and turning the eggs over in the curry until the outsides of the eggs start to take on the color of the sauce and are heated through, 4 to 6 minutes.

To finish, stir in the lemon juice. Taste and season with more salt and/or lemon juice, if necessary.

Sirārakhong Hāthei Chilli-Lemongrass Chicken and Rice

"The World's Most Aromatic Chicken and Rice"

Recipe inspired by Thao Philu | Origin: Sirārakhong, Manipur | Serves 6

One of the last meals we had on our research trip was an intensely savory chicken soup in the home of Thao Philu, in the village of Sirārakhong, Manipur. After spending almost three months on the road across ten states and two countries, this warming bowlful was like the biggest, most comforting hug, wrapping us with fragrant ginger, garlic, smoky Sirārakhong chillies, culantro, and dried Vietnamese lemon balm. The latter gave the broth a super-charged sharp, citrusy aroma that drew Asha and me back for sip after sip. Vietnamese lemon balm isn't easily accessible here, so lemongrass comes in clutch, imbuing the broth with lots of fragrant goodness.

For our Diaspora-ified version, we took that soup as inspiration, combining it with Hainanese chicken rice. The chicken is poached in the broth with all the aromatics, then plunged into an ice bath to preserve the texture of both the meat and skin and keep the chicken nice and juicy. Then, the stock is used to cook the rice, and finally is served alongside for sipping. Like many dishes in Manipur, this dish wouldn't be complete without a fiery chutney—try it with Burst Tomato Chutney (page 48) or Fava Bean Chutney (page 46). Another simple side on many of our Manipuri plates was tender, supple wedges of boiled green cabbage—the bites of cruciferous sweetness calming the mouth between bites of fiery chutney—which would also be a lovely addition here.

Three 12-inch stalks lemongrass

3 green onions

1 to 2 teaspoons Sirārakhong Hāthei chilli powder

2½ teaspoons plus 1 tablespoon fine sea salt, plus more if needed

One 3½- to 4-pound (1.6 to 1.8 kg) whole chicken

2 cups (400 g) short- or medium-grain rice, rinsed

2-inch piece fresh ginger, thinly sliced

continues

Bring 10 cups (2.4 L) water to a boil in a Dutch oven or other large, heavy-bottomed pot over medium-high heat.

While the water is coming to a boil, trim and discard ¼ inch off the bottom of the lemongrass, then peel and discard the dry outer layer. Cut each stalk crosswise into 4-inch pieces and then, using the back of a chef's knife, gently bash the stalks to help release their essential oils and aromas. Cut the green onions crosswise into 4-inch pieces and add the lemongrass and green onions to the boiling water along with the chilli powder and 2 teaspoons of the salt.

Pat the chicken dry, then rub it all over with 1 tablespoon of the remaining salt (this will help with the texture of the skin). When the water is boiling, gently lower the chicken, breast-side up, into the pot. Cover, reduce the heat to low, and simmer until the chicken is cooked through and the internal temperature of the breast reaches 165°F, 40 to 45 minutes. Turn the heat off under the broth.

continues

4 garlic cloves, finely chopped

1 cup (50 g) thinly sliced culantro or ¾ cup (38 g) roughly chopped cilantro leaves and tender stems

During the last 10 minutes of the chicken cooking, prepare an ice bath in a large bowl (big enough to hold the chicken). When the chicken is cooked, carefully remove it using tongs and a large spoon or spatula and plunge it into the ice bath, making sure it is submerged. Let sit in the ice bath for 15 minutes, then transfer to a plate until ready to carve.

Combine the rice, 3½ cups (830 ml) of the aromatic chicken broth, and the remaining ½ teaspoon salt in a medium saucepan. Cover, place over medium-high heat, and bring to a boil. Reduce the heat to medium, cover, and cook until all the liquid has been absorbed and the rice is just cooked through. Turn off the heat and let sit, covered, for 10 minutes.

While the rice is resting, reheat the broth over medium heat. Remove and discard the lemongrass and green onions, add the ginger and garlic, and cook, covered, to allow the ginger and garlic to infuse into the broth (you want them to still retain their freshness), 10 minutes.

Meanwhile, carve the chicken. Place the chicken breast-side up on a cutting board and, using a sharp boning knife, make a shallow cut through the skin connecting the leg to the breast. Flip the chicken

over and pull the leg up and out to pop it out of the joint, then slice through the joint to remove the leg. Cut through the joint connecting the drumstick and thigh, then debone the thigh and cut it crosswise into ½-inch strips. Repeat with the other leg and transfer to a serving plate. Flip the chicken on its side and slice between where the breast meets the wing. Pull the wing up, cut through the joint, and remove the wing. Repeat with the other wing and transfer to the serving platter. Place the chicken breast-side up and cut each one of the breasts off the bone. Slice each breast crosswise into ½-inch pieces and arrange on the serving plate. Save the carcass and bones for stock.

To finish the stock, stir in the culantro, taste, and season with more salt, if necessary. To serve, transfer the rice to a serving bowl and ladle the stock into individual bowls to serve with the chicken, rice, and the chutney of your choice.

RECIPE NOTE: The chicken needs to be cooled in an ice bath, so make sure you have a good amount of ice prepared.

Hoksa

Sirārakhong Hāthei Chilli-Braised Pork

Recipe by Leiyolan Vashum | Origin: Ukhrul, Manipur | Serves 6 to 8

When Leiyolan, one of our Manipuri sourcing partners, first told me about this recipe, both Asha and I were highly skeptical if it would work—only four ingredients?! No way. That turned out to be our ignorance talking. Slow-cooking pork belly until it is perfectly tender is a delicacy for many Northeastern Indian tribes, but the addition of bamboo-smoked Sirārakhong Hāthei Chillies that are indigenous to the hills of Ukhrul makes it a mouthwatering example of true Tangkhul Naga home cooking. While this is traditionally made solely with pork belly, we chose to cut the pork belly in half and add shoulder for a bit more heft and to balance out the fat, but fat is flavor—so, don't skip the belly entirely!

28 to 32 (30 g) whole dried Sirārakhong Hāthei chillies

1 pound (454 g) skin-on, boneless pork belly, cut into 1½-inch cubes

3¼ teaspoons fine sea salt, plus more if needed

2 pounds (908 g) boneless pork shoulder, cut into 1½-inch cubes

To prepare the chillies, remove and discard the stems, then, using scissors or your fingers, cut or rip the chillies into small pieces about twice the size of a standard chilli flake. (If using scissors, cut down the chillies lengthwise and then cut crosswise into ¼-inch pieces.) Set aside.

Place the pork belly into a bowl and season with ¾ teaspoon of the salt. Heat a Dutch oven or other large, heavy-bottomed pot over medium-high heat. Add the seasoned pork belly pieces, reserving the bowl, and brown until deep golden on the four cut sides, 2 to 4 minutes per side. Transfer the browned pieces to a plate.

Add the pork shoulder to the reserved bowl and season with 1½ teaspoons of the remaining salt. Then, in batches, brown until deep golden on all sides, 2 to 4 minutes per side.

Add all the browned pork belly and pork shoulder back into the pot along with 6 cups (1.4 L) water, the torn chillies, and the remaining 1 teaspoon salt, stir, and bring to a boil. Cover, reduce the heat to medium-low, and simmer until the pork is tender and is easily pierced with a knife, 1½ to 2¼ hours. Increase the heat to medium and cook, partially covered, until the meat can be easily pulled apart with a fork and the gravy has reduced by a quarter (this dish is meant to be quite brothy), 20 to 30 minutes more. Taste and season with more salt, if necessary. Serve with steamed rice and Fava Bean Chutney (page 46), Singju (page 80), or Edamame and Cherry Tomato Salad (page 83).

Aab Gosht

Kashmiri Milk-Braised Lamb Shanks

Recipe by Aaliya Mir | Origin: Pampore, Kashmir | Serves 6

Traditionally made with mutton tail braised in milk with a variety of mild, aromatic spices, aab gosht is one of the most loved dishes in wazwan (see page 166). The dairy tames the meat's gamey flavor, while also tenderizing it, resulting in the most sumptuous, supple bite. I've now eaten many aab goshts across the Kashmir Valley, but no one makes it quite as well as Aaliya, our saffron farm partner's wife. It makes sense, since this is her husband, Raqib's, favorite dish of all time—we love a culinary love story.

Instead of mutton tail, Asha reached for lamb shanks, which benefit from a long, slow braise and perfectly complement the gentle spices woven through the cream-based gravy. Don't be fooled by the lack of chillies and beige color—this dish is so big on rich, layered flavor that you'll be fighting for the last drops of sauce. Serve with basmati rice or Kashmiri Pulao (page 178).

2½ to 3 pounds (1.1 to 1.4 kg) lamb shanks

2¾ teaspoons fine sea salt

1 tablespoon canola oil

2 tablespoons ghee

2 large shallots (⅓ pound/151 g), finely diced

6 garlic cloves, peeled

12 green cardamom pods, lightly crushed

8 black cardamom pods, lightly crushed

8 whole cloves

One 3-inch cinnamon stick, broken in half

¼ teaspoon black peppercorns

1½ tablespoons ground fennel seeds

3 tejpatta leaves

¾ cup (180 ml) heavy whipping cream

½ cup thinly sliced fresh coconut, optional

Season the lamb shanks with 1½ teaspoons of the salt.

Heat the canola oil in a Dutch oven or other large, heavy-bottomed pot over medium-high heat. Add the seasoned lamb shanks and brown on all sides, 3 to 5 minutes per side. Remove from the pan and set aside.

Let the pan cool for 5 minutes, wipe it out, and return it to medium heat. Melt the ghee in the pan, add the shallots and ½ teaspoon of the remaining salt, and cook, stirring occasionally, until the shallots are softened and light golden, 9 to 12 minutes. Add the garlic, green cardamom, black cardamom, cloves, cinnamon stick, and black peppercorns and cook, stirring frequently, until fragrant, 1 to 2 minutes.

Stir in the ground fennel seeds, tejpatta leaves, the remaining ¾ teaspoon salt, and 4 cups (960 ml) water. Gently nestle the browned lamb shanks back into the pan, increase the heat to medium-high, and bring to a gentle boil. Cover the pot, reduce the heat to low, and simmer until the lamb is fall-apart tender, 2½ to 3 hours.

Add the cream and coconut, if using, and stir to combine. Increase the heat to medium and cook, uncovered, stirring occasionally and basting the tops of the lamb shanks, until the sauce reduces by a third, 10 to 20 minutes. Taste and add more salt, if necessary.

Wazwan

The first time I experienced wazwan was at our saffron farm partner Raqib's summer wedding, a three-day affair of eating, music, and celebrations. He had thoughtfully paired me with his chattiest cousins, so by the end of the two-hour feast circled around an intricately carved shared platter of food, we were all fast friends. Even now, when Raqib's now wife, Aaliya, is a beloved fixture in my life, I grin every time I think back at those feverish three days of feasting and celebrating at the beginning of their journey together! Wazwan is Kashmiri hospitality at its finest—it is truly extravagant (more than thirty-six courses), but this nose-to-tail communal feast also sends the entire village home well-fed for days.

The multi-course lamb feast is cooked on-site by wazas, chefs for whom this craft has been passed down generationally, beginning as apprentices under their fathers or uncles. The best chefs only cook for weddings, so it really does take a wedding invitation to taste the real deal of this regional feast. The banquet is a testament to their mastery of butchery, spice layering, and slow cooking over fire.

The meal itself is served on a trami, an intricately carved copper platter that is shared by four diners who eat communally. The base is a small mountain of fluffy long-grain rice, but the real ones know that in a banquet this long, the rice is a distraction from the main attraction! The meal usually begins with succulent spicy seekh kebabs—minced meat skewers grilled to perfection—followed by Tabak Maaz (page 168), twice-cooked lamb ribs, crisp on the outside yet meltingly tender within. Then my absolute favorite course—the Palak Rista (page 170), delicately spiced lamb meatballs swimming in a fiery saffron-infused spinach gravy.

As the courses unfolded, my neighbors started taking smaller and smaller bites and packing the majority of the meat into provided takeaway bags, saving precious stomach space for the many dishes to come. Rogan josh, the iconic lamb curry that Kashmir is most famous for, came bathed in a vibrant red gravy, its richness tempered with aromatic fennel and ginger. Aab Gosht (page 165), in contrast, was soothingly mild, tender pieces of lamb tail simmered in a milk-based sauce infused with cardamom and cloves. Toward the end came methi maaz, lamb offal cooked with fenugreek leaves, giving it a savory bitterness that beautifully balanced out the gaminess of the cut—another delicacy I'd never tried before. Finally, came the goshtaba—the literal full stop of the savory courses—a single, giant hand-pounded meatball, made impossibly velvety through beating and aerating the ground meat by hand, served in a silky, gently spiced yogurt-based yakhni gravy (page 102).

Out of the thirty-ish dishes of the meal, choosing which to share with y'all was impossibly hard. While all three of our picks fall into the "project cooking" category best suited for a weekend, they're the three that Asha and I felt were great representatives of Kashmiri cuisine and the spirit of wazwan!

Tabak Maaz
Kashmiri Ghee-Roasted Lamb Ribs

Recipe by Manzoor Ahmed Bhat | Origin: Pampore, Kashmir | Serves 4 to 6

Tabak Maaz is one of the many, many mouthwatering dishes served as part of a wazwan meal, the backbone of all Kashmiri celebrations (see page 166). Traditionally, these ribs are first parboiled in water with garlic and ginger, then boiled again in another water bath flavored with turmeric, salt, and more spices. And, finally, fried in copious amounts of ghee until crisp on the outside while still succulent on the inside.

Asha's version skips the double boiling process, instead seasoning the meat overnight with salt, turmeric, garlic, and ginger powder. The ribs are slowly baked in a warm-spice sauna of fennel, caraway, black and green cardamom, cloves, and Himalayan tejpatta (bay leaves). Then they're finished in a hot oven, basted with ghee, to get that sought-after burnished crust. Serve with basmati rice or Kashmiri Pulao (page 178), or a bright, acid-forward salad like Daikon and Orange Salad (page 78).

4 teaspoons fine sea salt

1 teaspoon garlic powder

1 teaspoon ground turmeric

½ teaspoon ground ginger

2 racks lamb ribs (about 3 pounds/1.4 kg)

1½ tablespoons fennel seeds

2 teaspoons caraway seeds

8 green cardamom pods

6 whole cloves

4 pods black cardamom

3 to 4 tejpatta leaves

¼ cup (60 g) ghee

RECIPE NOTE: The ribs can be baked in advance—just stop before the high roasting step. Refrigerate the baked ribs in the braising liquid for up to 2 days. Bring to room temperature before ghee roasting.

Combine the salt, garlic powder, turmeric, and ginger in a small bowl and mix well. Sprinkle the seasoning over the lamb ribs, evenly seasoning all sides, then wrap each rack of ribs in plastic wrap and refrigerate for at least overnight, up to 48 hours.

Preheat the oven to 300°F.

Place the fennel seeds, caraway seeds, green cardamom, cloves, black cardamom, tejpatta leaves, and 2 cups (480 ml) water in a roasting pan, gently place the ribs on top, seal the pan with aluminum foil, and bake until the meat is tender and can easily be pulled away from the bone, 2 to 2½ hours.

Remove the cooked ribs from the oven and increase the temperature to 475°F. Transfer the ribs, discarding the spices and water, to a rimmed sheet pan. Melt the ghee in the microwave on high in 30-second increments or in a small pan on the stove over medium heat. Brush both sides of the ribs with ghee, place the ribs bone-side down, and pour any of the remaining ghee on top. Roast, basting the top of the ribs with ghee from the pan every 5 minutes, until the fat cap starts to render and the top is deep golden and starting to crisp, 15 to 20 minutes total.

Let the ribs rest for 10 minutes before cutting. Slice the ribs between the rib bones into individual pieces, transfer to a serving platter, and brush with any remaining ghee from the pan.

Palak Rista

Kashmiri Spiced Lamb Meatballs with Spinach

Recipe by Manzoor Ahmed Bhat | Origin: Pampore, Kashmir | Serves 4

Of the three lamb meatball dishes that are in a wazwan (a Kashmiri celebratory feast), palak rista is my fave because it features the smallest meatballs of them all—plush little balls floating in a chilli-hued gravy laced with black and green cardamom, fennel, and tejpatta, plus lots of palak, or spinach.

Traditionally, ground lamb and additional lamb fat is pounded with a mallet until aerated, giving the meatballs a buoyant, bouncy texture (like the ones you might find in Vietnamese pho) and allowing them to soak up whatever gravy they're cooked in. Alas, most home kitchens—ours, at least!—are not equipped with mallets, so stepping in to do the aerating is a stand mixer. To get the right texture, the lamb is mixed with a little extra oil, lamb stock, and spices, then frozen briefly to solidify the fat and liquid so it can emulsify and aerate when whipped.

Palak rista is classically finished with mawal (cockscomb flower) that is steeped in water. This is also used to finish many Kashmiri dishes, like rogan josh, but since it isn't readily available here, a combination of saffron and lemon juice adds the herbaceous brightness and intense color you want.

This is probably the most technical and time-consuming recipe in the book, but it will truly transport you to Kashmir. If you want to save a little bit of time, you can use Asha's ingenious cheat Kashmiri Stock (page 175) instead of starting from scratch with lamb bones. It's also a dish that freezes beautifully and is so cozy to tuck into in the depths of winter, so I highly recommend making a double batch (just note you'll have to make the meatball mixture in two batches due to the size of home stand mixers).

Enjoy with steamed basmati rice and a spoonful of plain yogurt (while this isn't a traditional pairing, we love the acidic foil to the rich, aromatic meatballs and highly spiced gravy).

---

8 black cardamom pods

1 pound (454 g) ground lamb

5 cups (1.2 L) plus 3 tablespoons Kashmiri Lamb Stock (page 174)

1½ tablespoons canola oil or other neutral oil

2 teaspoons plus 1 tablespoon ground fennel seeds

½ teaspoon ground ginger

continues

Place 3 of the black cardamom pods in a mortar, gently pound to break open, and remove the seeds, leaving them in the mortar, and discard the outer husks. Pound the seeds into a fine powder (you should have about ½ teaspoon). Transfer the ground black cardamom to a large bowl along with the ground lamb, 3 tablespoons of the lamb stock, the canola oil, 2 teaspoons of the ground fennel seeds, the ground ginger, and 1½ teaspoons of the salt, and, using your hands, mix until everything is well combined (since this mixture will be whipped later, you don't have to worry about overmixing).

Line a quarter sheet pan with plastic wrap and transfer the meat mixture to the pan. Place another piece of plastic wrap over the top

continues

3¼ teaspoons fine sea salt, plus more if needed

3 tablespoons ghee

4 green cardamom pods, lightly crushed

5 whole cloves

One 3-inch cinnamon stick, broken in half

1 white onion, finely diced

1½ tablespoons Byadgi chilli powder

½ teaspoon ground turmeric

2 to 3 tejpatta leaves

1½ teaspoons powdered jaggery or brown sugar

One 10-ounce package thawed, frozen chopped spinach

Pinch of saffron (15 to 20 threads)

1 ice cube

Juice of ½ lemon (1 to 2 tablespoons)

and press down into a thin, even layer covering the bottom of the pan. Place in the freezer and freeze until almost completely frozen but still pliable, 1 to 1½ hours (if you accidentally over-freeze the meat, you can let it thaw for 5 to 10 minutes at room temperature before breaking it apart in the next step).

About 30 minutes before the meat mixture is frozen, start the sauce. Heat the ghee in a Dutch oven or other large, heavy-bottomed pot over medium heat. Lightly crush the remaining 5 black cardamom pods with the side of a knife and add them to the pot along with the green cardamom, cloves, and cinnamon stick and cook, stirring frequently, until fragrant, 15 to 45 seconds. Stir in the onion and ¾ teaspoon of the remaining salt and cook, stirring occasionally, until the onions soften and turn light golden, 12 to 15 minutes.

Add the chilli powder, turmeric, the remaining 1 tablespoon ground fennel seeds, and ½ cup (120 ml) water and cook, stirring frequently, until most of the water evaporates, 3 to 5 minutes. Add the tejpatta leaves, jaggery, the remaining 5 cups (1.2 L) lamb stock, and remaining 1 teaspoon salt, increase the heat to medium-high, and bring to a gentle boil. Cover, reduce the heat to low, and keep warm while you make the meatballs. (Psst, if you haven't started thawing your frozen spinach, now is the time.)

Break the par-frozen meat mixture into quarter-sized pieces into the bowl of a stand mixer fitted with the paddle attachment. Start beating on low speed until the meat starts to break up, 1 to 3 minutes. Increase the speed to medium and continue to beat until the mixture starts to stick to the sides of the bowl, 2 to 4 minutes more. Scrape down the bowl, then beat on medium-high, scraping down the bowl periodically, until the fat emulsifies and forms a whipped, light pink paste, 3 to 5 minutes more. You should be able to take a piece, put it in ice water, and have it float.

While the meat mixture is whipping, prepare an ice bath in a large bowl. To form the meatballs, dip your hands in the ice water, take a tennis ball–sized piece of the whipped meat mixture, and smooth the top with your wet hands. Hold the piece in your dominant hand and squeeze a walnut-sized ball up between your thumb and forefinger, pinching off the meatball. Cup your hands and gently roll the meatball, making sure to use light pressure (you want them to stay aerated). (This technique takes a few tries to get right, so don't worry if your first few meatballs look a little wonky.) Alternatively, you can break off walnut-sized pieces, gently cup hands and roll, using light pressure to create a ball. Transfer the finished meatballs into the ice bath and repeat with the remaining whipped meat mixture, rewetting your hands between each meatball. (You should have 18 to 22 meatballs.)

Gently lift the formed meatballs out of the ice bath and transfer to the gravy mixture, discarding any leftover ice and water. Increase the heat to medium-high, cover, and bring back to a gentle boil. Reduce the heat to low and cook until the meatballs are cooked through, tender, and puffed in size, 1 to 1½ hours (giving them time to simmer and soak up that spiced broth is what is going to make these plush and buoyant).

Meanwhile, squeeze as much liquid as you can from the thawed spinach and set aside. Pound the saffron in a mortar, add an ice cube, and let melt to bloom the saffron.

When the meatballs are cooked, stir in the drained chopped spinach, increase the heat to medium, and cook, halfway covered, until the gravy has reduced by a third (this is meant to be a pretty brothy sauce), 20 to 30 minutes. Turn off the heat and add the bloomed saffron water and lemon juice. Taste and season with more salt and/or lemon juice, if necessary.

Maaz Rass

Kashmiri Lamb Stock

Recipe by Aliya Mir | Origin: Pampore, Kashmir | Makes 2 quarts

Kashmiri cooking gets its round, soul-hugging depth from a combination of warming and aromatic spices and incredibly luscious lamb bones. The fennel, caraway, peppercorns, tejpatta, cinnamon, and green and black cardamom give this bone broth a fragrant base that becomes a canvas for a variety of Kashmiri dishes like Haakh (braised greens, page 99), Palak Rista (meatballs with spinach in chilli gravy, page 170), and Kashmiri Pulao studded with ghee-fried cashews, coconut, and raisins (page 178). If you want to skip making stock from scratch, try our cheat version (page 175) that takes a helping hand from good-quality, store-bought stock. This recipe makes 8 cups (1.9 L), which is enough for one main, like Palak Rista, and one side, like Haakh or Kashmiri Pulao. You can also freeze the stock for up to 6 months.

1 white onion

2 teaspoons canola oil

2½ to 3 pounds (1.1 to 1.4 kg) lamb neck bones

2½ teaspoons fine sea salt

3 tablespoons fennel seeds

1½ tablespoons caraway seeds

½ teaspoon black peppercorns

10 green cardamom pods

4 black cardamom pods

4 tejpatta leaves

Two 2-inch cinnamon sticks

10 cups (2.4 L) cold water

Preheat the oven to 425°F.

Quarter the onion, leaving the peel and root end intact. Place the quartered onion on a rimmed sheet pan and drizzle with the canola oil, making sure to rub each piece with a thin layer of oil. Add the lamb neck bones and sprinkle the meat and vegetables with 1½ teaspoons of the salt. Roast until the lamb and onions are deeply browned, flipping the onions halfway through, 45 minutes to 1 hour.

Transfer the roasted bones and onions to an electric pressure cooker (like an Instant Pot) and add the fennel seeds, caraway seeds, black peppercorns, green cardamom, black cardamom, tejpatta leaves, cinnamon sticks, cold water, and the remaining 1 teaspoon salt. Cook on high pressure for 1½ hours, then allow to naturally release for 15 minutes before releasing the pressure.

(Alternatively, you can make the stock on the stove: Transfer the browned bones and onions to a Dutch oven or other large, heavy-bottomed pot with the rest of the ingredients and bring to a boil over high heat. Cover, reduce the heat to low, and simmer for 6 to 8 hours.)

Strain the stock through a fine-mesh sieve, discarding the solids, into a large bowl (if the bones are especially meaty, you can remove the meat from the bones, shred it, and add it to haakh, if you'd like!). If not using the stock right away, cool, then transfer to containers and refrigerate for up to 5 days, or freeze for up to 6 months.

Kashmiri Stock (Cheat Version)

Recipe by Asha Loupy | Makes 2 quarts

When roasting bones just isn't in the cards, you can reach for good-quality stock and infuse it with caramelized onions and all those warming, aromatic spices. You don't quite get the collagen-y richness of the original—unless you're buying stock from your local butcher—but the flavor is spot on. This is also a great way to make a meat-free version of Maaz Rass—swapping in your fave veggie or mushroom stock—if you want to make a vegetarian version of the Kashmiri Braised Greens (page 99) or Kashmiri Pulao (page 178).

1 white onion

2 teaspoons canola oil

8 cups good-quality, store-bought lamb, beef, or vegetable stock

3 tablespoons fennel seeds

1½ tablespoons caraway seeds

½ teaspoon black peppercorns

10 green cardamom pods

4 black cardamom pods

4 tejpatta leaves

Two 2-inch cinnamon sticks

1 teaspoon fine sea salt

Quarter the onion, leaving the peel and root end intact. Heat the canola oil in a Dutch oven or other large, heavy-bottomed pot over medium-high heat. When shimmering, add the onions, cut-side down, and sear on both cut sides until deeply browned and starting to char in spots, 3 to 5 minutes per side.

Add the stock and bring to a boil. Stir in the fennel seeds, caraway seeds, black peppercorns, green cardamom, black cardamom, tejpatta leaves, cinnamon stick, and salt. Cover, reduce the heat to low, and simmer until the spices are steeped in the stock and it smells intensely fragrant, 45 minutes to 1 hour.

Strain the stock through a fine-mesh sieve into a large bowl, discarding the solids. If not using the stock right away, transfer to containers and refrigerate for up to 5 days, or freeze for up to 6 months.

Rice, Breads, and Scoopers

Kashmiri Pulao 178

Nimmakaya Pulihora 180

Thalassery Fish Biryani 183

Coconut Lamb Biryani 185

Khichdi 187

Ghee Roast Dosa 192

Idli 195

Sri Lankan Moringa String Hoppers 198

Skillet Appams 201

Pol Roti 203

Bajra Na Rotla 204

Kappa Puzhukku 206

Kashmiri Pulao

Basmati Rice Pilaf with Nuts, Raisins, and Coconut

Recipe by Aaliya Mir | Origin: Pampore, Kashmir | Serves 4 to 6

Rich and comforting, this pulao from Kashmir gets its deep, warming flavor from lamb or mushroom stock steeped with fennel, black and green cardamom, caraway, and cinnamon (if you're short on time, you can use our cheat version on page 175). It's a textural wonderland, packed with golden raisins, nuts, and shaved, ghee-toasted coconut. Serve as part of a Kashmiri meal with Haakh (page 99), Aab Gosht (page 165), or Palak Rista (page 170).

4 tablespoons (60 g) ghee

3 medium shallots (¼ pound/113 g), thinly sliced

1¼ teaspoons fine sea salt, plus more if needed

1½ cups (300 g) basmati rice or other long-grain rice

3 cups (710 ml) Kashmiri Lamb Stock (page 174) or mushroom stock (page 175)

2 tejpatta leaves

¼ cup (40 g) golden raisins

¼ cup (30 g) raw cashews

¼ cup (23 g) sliced almonds

⅓ cup (32 g) shaved, dried unsweetened coconut flakes

RECIPE NOTE: For this recipe, I'd highly recommend sticking to basmati rice. It'll keep each grain fluffy and separate and give you the desired "highly aromatic" effect.

Heat 2 tablespoons of the ghee in a medium saucepan over medium heat. Add the shallots and ½ teaspoon of the salt and cook, stirring occasionally, until the shallots soften, start to caramelize, and turn golden brown around the edges, 9 to 13 minutes.

Meanwhile, place the basmati rice in a bowl and rinse with cold water, swishing it around with your fingers and rinsing several times until the water runs clear. Drain well.

Add the rice to the browned shallots, increase the heat to medium-high, and cook, stirring frequently, until most of the residual moisture from rinsing evaporates and some of the grains start to turn opaque, 3 to 6 minutes. Stir in the lamb stock, tejpatta leaves, and the remaining ¾ teaspoon salt and bring to a gentle boil. Cover, reduce the heat to low, and cook until the rice has absorbed all the liquid and is just cooked through, 15 to 18 minutes.

While the rice is cooking, heat the remaining 2 tablespoons ghee in a large skillet over medium heat. When melted, add the golden raisins, cashews, and almonds and cook, stirring frequently, until the nuts start to turn light golden in spots and the raisins start to puff and turn a shade darker, 2 to 4 minutes. Add the coconut and continue to cook, stirring frequently, until the coconut strips start to toast around the edges and the nuts turn another shade darker, 1 to 3 minutes more. Transfer to a bowl and set aside.

Remove the rice from the heat, pour the nut-fruit mixture and any ghee left at the bottom of the bowl into the par-cooked rice, and gently toss and mix in with a fork. Return the cover and let sit until the rice is fully cooked, 12 to 15 minutes. Taste and season with more salt, if necessary.

Nimmakaya Pulihora

Andhra Lemon Rice

Recipe by Venkata Narasamma Kasaraneni | Origin: Kankipati, Andhra Pradesh | Serves 4 to 6

Lemon rice is a savory confetti of contrasting colors and textures, from the crunch of the toasted lentils and pop of the mustard seeds to the bright yellow rice and flecks of cilantro. It's a party in a bowl! Often rice recipes can be a bit one-note because everything is cooked together, but this becomes a composed rice dish where you're layering in flavor and textures all the way up until you're ready to serve.

1¼ cups (250 g) jeera or samba rice

2 lemons

3 tablespoons untoasted sesame oil or other neutral oil

1-inch piece ginger, finely chopped

¾ teaspoon ground turmeric

1 serrano pepper, quartered lengthwise

1¼ teaspoons fine sea salt, plus more if needed

¼ cup (50 g) raw shelled peanuts

2 tablespoons chana dal

1 tablespoon split urad dal

1½ teaspoons black mustard seeds

24 fresh curry leaves

1 to 2 dried Guntur Sannam chillies, torn in half

⅓ cup (17 g) roughly chopped cilantro, leaves and tender stems

Place the rice in a bowl and rinse with cold water, swishing it around with your fingers and rinsing several times until the water runs clear. Fill the bowl with cold water, making sure the rice is covered by a couple inches, and soak for 30 minutes.

Meanwhile, zest and juice the lemons, keep separate, and set aside.

Heat 1 tablespoon of the sesame oil in a medium saucepan over medium heat. When shimmering, add the ginger and sauté, stirring occasionally, until it begins to soften, 2 to 4 minutes.

Drain the soaked rice and add to the pan, increase the heat to medium-high, and cook, stirring frequently, until the water has evaporated and the grains are opaque, 3 to 6 minutes. Add the turmeric, stir, and continue to cook for another 30 seconds. Add the serrano pepper, salt, reserved lemon zest, and 1¾ cups (420 ml) water, stir, cover, and bring to a boil. Reduce the heat to medium-low and simmer until the rice is just cooked through and all the water is absorbed, 14 to 19 minutes. Add ¼ cup (60 ml) lemon juice, saving any extra juice for another use, fluff with a fork, and cover for another 10 minutes.

While the rice is resting, heat the remaining 2 tablespoons of the sesame oil in a tadka spoon or small saucepan over medium heat. When shimmering, add the peanuts, chana dal, urad dal, and mustard seeds and cook, stirring frequently, until the peanuts start to turn light golden, 2 to 5 minutes. Add 12 of the curry leaves and the chillies and continue to cook until the curry leaves turn bright green and translucent, 10 to 30 seconds. Add the peanut mixture to the rice along with the cilantro, then tear the remaining 12 curry leaves into the rice and gently mix everything together with a fork. Taste and season with more salt, if necessary. Serve warm or at room temperature.

Thalassery Fish Biryani

Recipe by Chachu Lukose | Origin: Udumbanchola, Kerala | Serves 8

Biryani is a love language. This fish biryani—a recipe from Chachu Lukose, our cardamom farm partner's wife and collaborator in all parts of running Baraka Estate—takes time, but the result is deeply fragrant, layered with tender pieces of white fish enrobed in the most luscious, green cardamom-forward gravy, fluffy aromatic grains of samba rice—a short-grain varietal that is used in South India—cilantro, and topped with a tangle of fried onions and cashews.

Yes, this recipe has many steps (though Asha found some ingenious shortcuts, like cooking the raw cashews in the simmering gravy before blending it, nixing a couple hours of soaking time)—so be prepared to spend a nice, leisurely afternoon in the kitchen. If you want to prep some of the components in advance, the masala can be prepared without the fish up to two days in advance. Then, the day of, reheat it with an additional ¼ cup (60 ml) water to thin it back to the right consistency.

FOR THE FISH

2 pounds (907 g) boneless, skinless, firm, flaky white fish fillets, like halibut, sea bass, or black cod, at least 1 inch thick, cut into 2-inch pieces

2 teaspoons Guntur Sannam chilli powder

1½ teaspoons fine sea salt

½ teaspoon ground turmeric

Juice of ½ lemon (1 to 2 tablespoons)

FOR THE RICE

2 tablespoons fine sea salt

5 green cardamom pods, lightly crushed

4 whole cloves

1¾ cups (350 g) samba rice, rinsed

Juice of 1 lemon (2 to 4 tablespoons)

continues

To prepare the fish, place the fish, chilli powder, salt, turmeric, and lemon juice in a large bowl, and gently toss to coat. If cooking the biryani right away, set aside at room temperature, but if preparing later, refrigerate for up to 2 hours (any longer and the lemon juice will start to affect the texture of the fish).

Preheat the oven to 400°F.

To prepare the rice, bring 8 cups (1.8 L) water along with the salt, cardamom, and cloves to a boil in a large pot over high heat. Add the rice and cook, stirring occasionally, until it's just al dente, 6 to 8 minutes. Drain well and rinse with cold water, shaking off any excess water. Transfer to a bowl, mix with the lemon juice, and set aside.

While the water comes to a boil and the rice parcooks, start the masala. Heat the coconut oil in a Dutch oven or other large, heavy-bottomed, oven-safe pot over medium heat. When shimmering, add the cardamom, cloves, cinnamon stick, and fennel seeds and toast, stirring frequently, until the fennel seeds turn a shade darker, 15 to 45 seconds. Stir in the shallots, garlic, ginger, serrano pepper, and ½ teaspoon of the salt and cook, stirring occasionally, until the shallots soften and turn light golden around the edges, 7 to 10 minutes.

Stir in the tomatoes, yogurt, 2 tablespoons of the cashews, 1 teaspoon of the remaining salt, and ½ cup (120 ml) water. Cover, reduce the heat to medium-low, and simmer, stirring occasionally, until the

continues

FOR THE MASALA AND ASSEMBLY

3 tablespoons virgin coconut oil

8 green cardamom pods

4 whole cloves

One 1-inch piece cinnamon stick, broken in half

1 teaspoon fennel seeds

3 large shallots (about ½ pound/227 g), diced

6 garlic cloves, roughly chopped

1-inch piece ginger, roughly chopped

1 serrano pepper, roughly chopped

1¾ teaspoons fine sea salt

2 plum tomatoes, diced

¼ cup (57 g) plain, full-fat yogurt (not Greek)

2 tablespoons plus ½ cup (75 g) raw cashews

1¼ cups (63 g) lightly packed roughly chopped cilantro, leaves and tender stems

½ cup (10 g) lightly packed roughly chopped fresh mint leaves

Canola oil, for frying

1 white onion, thinly sliced

---

tomatoes break down, 11 to 15 minutes. Stir in ½ cup of the cilantro and the mint and let cool for 10 minutes. Then transfer to a blender, reserving the pot, add ½ cup (120 ml) water, and blend, starting on low speed and increasing to high, until smooth.

Transfer the blended masala back to the pot, cover, place over medium heat, and bring back to a simmer. Add the fish and any juices that have accumulated at the bottom of the bowl and gently stir to coat the fish in the gravy. Cover, reduce the heat to medium-low, and cook until the fish just starts to turn opaque (the fish will finish cooking when you bake the biryani), 4 to 6 minutes.

To assemble the biryani, transfer half of the fish and the gravy to a bowl. Sprinkle half of the parboiled rice in an even layer over the fish, followed by ¼ cup of the remaining cilantro. Spoon the remaining half of the fish and gravy over the top, making sure to evenly distribute the pieces of fish around the surface of the rice. Repeat with the remaining rice and another ¼ cup cilantro. Cover and bake until the rice is just cooked through and the fish easily flakes apart, 25 to 30 minutes. Remove from the oven and let sit covered for 15 minutes.

While the biryani is baking, fry the garnish. Heat ½ inch of neutral oil in a high-rimmed skillet over medium heat. When shimmering, place the remaining ½ cup cashews on a slotted spoon, gently lower them into the oil, and fry until light golden, 15 to 45 seconds. Remove with the slotted spoon and transfer to a paper towel–lined sheet pan to drain. Increase the heat to medium-high and, working in two batches, fry the onion, stirring occasionally, until light golden (the onions will continue cooking once you take them out of the oil), 6 to 9 minutes. Transfer the fried onions to the pan with the fried cashews, the remaining ¼ teaspoon salt, and set aside.

To finish the biryani, sprinkle the fried onions and cashews over the top of the biryani and garnish with the remaining ¼ cup cilantro. Alternatively, you can transfer the biryani to a serving platter and garnish with the fried cashews, onions, and cilantro. Serve with Red Onion Raita (page 49) or plain yogurt.

RECIPE NOTE: For the fish, look for a firm, flaky fish, like halibut, sea bass, or black cod. You want the fillets to be at least 1 inch thick, preferably 1½ inches thick, to prevent overcooked fish that falls apart, so avoid thinner fillets like tilapia, flounder, and petrale or Dover sole.

Coconut Lamb Biryani

Recipe by Sulochana Meiyappan | Origin: Pollachi, Tamil Nadu | Serves 6 to 8

Sulochana Meiyappan is the matriarch of Anamalai Estate, a beautiful cacao, nutmeg, and coconut farm that we've been lucky enough to work with for several years. Her entire family was unanimous in declaring this recipe as their most iconic family heirloom. The Meiyappan family's Anamalai Nutmeg is some of the most potent, oil-rich, and aromatic nutmeg in the world—a testament to her son Manoj's regenerative farming practices and deep, holistic care for each plant. I really love how the butteriness of the lamb and the coconut is heightened and complemented by the sweet, strong nutmeg. This is definitely one of the bigger cooking projects in this book, but it is also very high reward, I promise. Serve with Red Onion Raita (page 49).

2¼ pounds (1 kg) boneless lamb shoulder

3½ teaspoons fine sea salt

1½ teaspoons Guntur Sannam chilli powder

½ teaspoon ground turmeric

2½ cups (50 g) fresh mint leaves

1 cup (50 g) roughly chopped cilantro, leaves and tender stems

10 to 12 garlic cloves (50 g), roughly chopped

2 serrano peppers, roughly chopped

2-inch piece fresh ginger, roughly chopped

2 teaspoons coriander seeds

1½ teaspoons fennel seeds

1½ teaspoons freshly grated nutmeg

1 teaspoon black peppercorns

¾ teaspoon cumin seeds

continues

To prepare the lamb, cut it into 1½-inch pieces and place in a bowl with 1½ teaspoons of the salt, the chilli powder, and turmeric. Refrigerate for at least 1 hour, up to overnight.

Place 1¼ cups of the mint, ½ cup of the cilantro, the garlic, serrano peppers, ginger, coriander seeds, fennel seeds, nutmeg, black peppercorns, cumin seeds, cloves, cardamom, cinnamon stick, and ¼ cup (60 ml) water in a high-speed blender and blend until smooth. Set aside.

Heat 1 tablespoon of the ghee in a Dutch oven or other large, heavy-bottomed pot over medium-high heat. When the ghee is shimmering, brown the lamb, working in batches if necessary, until deep golden on all sides, 3 to 5 minutes per side. Transfer the browned lamb to a plate and set aside.

Reduce the heat to medium and add 2 tablespoons of the remaining ghee. When melted, add the curry leaves—be careful, these will crackle and pop!—and cook until bright green and starting to turn translucent, 10 to 30 seconds. Add the shallots and 1 teaspoon of the remaining salt and cook, stirring occasionally, until softened and starting to turn light golden around the edges, 6 to 9 minutes.

Add the reserved paste and fry, stirring frequently, until the paste starts to pull away from the pan and the oil starts to separate, 5 to 8 minutes. Stir in the coconut milk, tomatoes, remaining 1 teaspoon salt, and 1 cup (240 ml) water. Add the browned meat and any juices

continues

Rice, Breads, and Scoopers

- 10 whole cloves
- 8 green cardamom pods
- One 2-inch cinnamon stick, broken into pieces
- 4 tablespoons (60 g) ghee
- 24 fresh curry leaves
- 3 large shallots (about ½ pound/227 g), diced
- One 14-ounce (398 ml) can full-fat coconut milk
- 2 plum tomatoes, diced
- 2 cups (400 g) samba rice
- Juice of ½ lemon (about 2 tablespoons)

that have accumulated to the gravy, making sure the pieces of meat are submerged, and bring to a simmer. Reduce the heat to low, cover, and simmer until the lamb is fall-apart tender, 2 to 2½ hours.

An hour before the lamb is done, rinse the rice, place in a bowl, cover with water, and soak. Drain well.

Preheat the oven to 400°F.

Meanwhile, finely chop the remaining 1¼ cups mint and ½ cup cilantro and set aside. Then, heat the remaining 1 tablespoon ghee in a large skillet. Add the drained rice and toast, stirring frequently, until the water has evaporated from the grains of rice and they start to look opaque, 4 to 7 minutes. (This will help keep each grain separate after cooking.)

Add the toasted rice to the cooked lamb along with the reserved finely chopped herbs and lemon juice. Stir to combine, bring back to a simmer, cover, and bake until the rice has absorbed all the liquid and is just past al dente, 30 to 40 minutes. Remove from the oven and let sit for 30 minutes (this will allow the rice to gently finish cooking).

Khichdi

Rice and Lentil Porridge

Recipe by Nayna Sakariya | Origin: Shedubhar, Gujarat | Serves 4 to 6

The first documented evidence of khichdi can be found in the great Hindu epic the *Mahabharata*, which was written in the third century BCE. So, we South Asians have been turning to this dish for comfort for a casual 2,500 years. As a Gujarati, I can safely say that khichdi is an emotion. Khichdi and chaas (Gujarati spiced buttermilk) were my perfect food combo as a child—made nearly every day specifically for fussy little me who constantly craved gentle, comforting foods. On the Sakariya farm, which grows our Nandini Coriander, Khichdi and Kadhi (Yogurt and Turmeric Soup, page 123) are the backbone of their meal rotation—loved by the kids and elders alike. Living in the hot, flat plains of Saurashtra, the family's cuisine tends to be spicier and more intense than the rest of Gujarat, so I was pleasantly surprised by how simple and light their khichdi is.

Khichdi is infinitely customizable and flexible—this recipe is its most basic form, which is a great starting point. Some days I like to add frozen chopped carrots, cauliflower, and green beans to the pressure cooker. Sometimes I wilt in a whole bag of roughly chopped spinach at the end. When I'm sick, I slice in a couple inches of fresh ginger, or when I'm trying to spruce it up, I make a quick tadka (page 14) of whole chillies, cumin seeds, mustard seeds, and a few curry leaves in untoasted sesame oil and pour it on top.

1 cup (200 g) short-grain rice, such as Calrose

½ cup (113 g) whole moong dal

3 tablespoons toor dal

3 tablespoons ghee, plus more for serving

1½ teaspoons fine sea salt, plus more if needed

¾ teaspoon ground turmeric

A couple grinds black pepper, optional

6 cups (1.4 L) cold water

Place the rice, moong dal, and toor dal in a bowl and rinse with cold water, swishing it around with your fingers, and rinsing several times until the water runs clear. Drain and transfer the lentils to an electric pressure cooker (like an Instant Pot), add the ghee, salt, turmeric, black pepper, if desired, and cold water, and stir to combine.

Cook on high pressure for 5 minutes, then allow to naturally release for 10 minutes. Release the pressure and give it a couple vigorous stirs to release the starches in the rice (this will give you a nice, creamy khichdi!). Taste, and season with more salt, if necessary. If the khichdi is a little too thick for your taste, you can thin with a couple splashes of hot water until you reach the desired consistency. Serve hot with extra melted ghee on top or alongside Kadhi (page 123).

The Parameswaran Family
Aranya Pepper

THIRUNELLY, KERALA

My entire understanding of black peppercorns changed when I met the Parameswaran family, who grow our Aranya Peppercorns. Parameswaran and his son Akash, with the help of the indigenous Adiyar, Kurichiyan, and Kuruma communities, have spent over thirty-five years painstakingly collecting wild and indigenous pepper varieties, grafting them to enhance flavor, and farming in ways that go far beyond organic.

If you've ever been told that Tellicherry or Malabar peppercorns are the fanciest thing you can put in your pepper mill, I'd like to blame my favorite villain, colonialism, for misleading you with stale marketing and good old misinformation.

Tellicherry peppercorns don't actually come from the city of Tellicherry in Kerala, nor are they grown or harvested in any special way—they are simply sorted by size. If a peppercorn is 4.25 mm (about 0.17 inch), it's labeled as Tellicherry and priced higher. But size alone has zero guarantee on quality, aroma, or flavor. Meanwhile, Malabar is the colonial name for the spice-rich coast of Kerala, but in a region so vast, geographic distinction means very little—there is great pepper on the Malabar coast just as there is terrible pepper. Across South Asia, spice farmers and markets are still catering their produce, their processing methods, and their resources to a multi-trillion-dollar industry that was carelessly built on some colonial agents' eighteenth-century disregard for flavor and belief that size is what matters.

The Parameswarans, who are growing their beautiful pepper using a mix of indigenous and self-taught methods, are consciously resisting hundreds of years of being told that their knowledge, culture, and food were inferior.

Unlike the Tellicherry or Malabar pepper, which is usually picked when unripe, blanched for even coloring, and then mechanically flash-dried, Aranya Pepper is an exercise in slowness. The berries are picked only when fully vine-ripened, because it guarantees that they've soaked in the rainforest's nutrients and sunshine to reach their peak flavor potential. They're never blanched, a process that might even out their varied purple-maroon shades into jet-black but strips them of all fruitiness. Instead of being flash-dried, they're gently sun-dried to lock in as many volatile oils as possible. The dried berries are big and bold but also juicy and bright—think ripe figs meet grated nutmeg meets a nice glass of Zinfandel.

Akash's mum, Shirley Aunty, is a doting, generous cook. When she and Akash are in the kitchen together, they are an adorable pair, tag teaming on making appams and assembling dramatic floral arrangements through their home. Meanwhile, Akash and his dad are a proper comic duo, each vying for more braised pepper pork leftovers and the longer stick on their estate walks. May we all aspire to their level of familial tenderness and pepper excellence!

Recipes from the Parameswaran Family

Pepper Pork 154   **Jammy Egg Curry** 156

The Meiyappan Family
Anamalai Cacao, Nutmeg, and Mace

UDUMBANCHOLA, KERALA

I first heard about Anamalai Estate—a lush, picturesque cacao, coconut, and nutmeg farm on the edge of a tiger reserve in Tamil Nadu—in 2016 via a random Instagram post by Meridian Cacao, a Portland-based bean to bar cacao importer. I was a fresh college grad desperately trying to get a job and had reached out to Wynne McAuley, their director of sales at the time. My desire to work with them was only heightened when I saw that they were expanding into sourcing from my homeland! Alas, they did not give me a job at the time, but Wynne very kindly responded to my fervent emails, and we became friends.

Fast-forward eight years and the birth of this lil biz later, we are the proud distributors of Anamalai's cacao, nutmeg, and mace, and that certain Wynne McAuley is the COO of Diaspora Spice Co. and has been my right hand in all parts of this business since 2021—a true multifactorial sourcing love story spanning continents!

Anamalai is run by Karthi and Manoj, two brothers-in-law (Karthi married Manoj's sister Sujini) united by a shared love for delicious food. Over the past seven years, they have gone to great lengths to transform what would've otherwise been any old commodity plantation into a beautiful, sustainable estate.

Cacao is indigenous to Central America and nutmeg and mace to the Banda Islands of Indonesia, so they've come a long way from home to settle in the forests of Tamil Nadu. Nutmeg was first brought to India by the British East India Company and propagated as a way to compete with the Dutch global monopoly over nutmeg in the 1800s, so nutmeg and mace have been grown on plantations across India for two hundred-ish years, but never with the level of care and commitment to the soil regeneration, full tree ripening, and meticulous drying processes that it deserves. Similarly, cacao was introduced to South India by Cadbury using high-yielding, disease-resistant varieties from Malaysia and Indonesia with nary a care for flavor or tasting notes. Seeing the way the Anamalai family has turned these once imported commodity crops into spectacular, high-quality ingredients using innovative farming techniques has been so special. Their luscious cacao powder has triple the cocoa butter content of conventional cacao and their aromatic nutmeg has double the oil content—they clearly like to overachieve.

Over my many visits to the farm over the years, it's become clear that Manoj's mother (also Karthi's mother-in-law), Sulochana Meiyappan, is the true matriarch of the farm. The entire extended family flocks to her home for most meals—and her famous Coconut Lamb Biryani has put an end to many a business discussion because after a farm lunch so good, we simply *must* have a nap.

Recipes from the Meiyappan Family

Palli Chutney 45

Vengaya Thayir Pachadi 49

Coconut Lamb Biryani 185

Idli 195

Spiced Chocolate-Coconut Cookies 233

Ghee Roast Dosa
Fermented Rice and Lentil Crepes

Recipe by Padmavathi Narne | Origin: Vinjanampadu, Andhra Pradesh | Makes 6 to 8

There are thousands of recipes for making dosas that will vary from family to family across the Southern Indian states, but this one is designed to be the perfect crunchy base for the Narne family's Gunpowder Podi (page 26), which is made with their famous Guntur Sannam Chillies. Asha is partial to having her dosa with a side of the gingery Aloo Masala (page 105), whereas I'm a chutney 'n' podi girl all the way. But really, a dosa is nothing if not a vessel for your creativity. Grated cheese! Eggs! Mashed veggies! Kimchi! Whatever filling adventure you choose, it'll be perfect.

½ cup (100 g) idli or sona masoori rice

½ cup (100 g) basmati rice

⅓ cup (67 g) urad gota (whole, skinned urad dal)

2 tablespoons chana dal

2 tablespoons thick poha (flattened rice)

¾ teaspoon fenugreek seeds

1 teaspoon fine sea salt

Canola oil, for greasing

Melted ghee, for cooking

Gunpowder Podi (page 26)

Combine the idli or sona masoori rice and basmati rice in a bowl and rinse with cold water, swishing it around with your fingers, and rinsing several times until the water runs clear. Cover with 3 inches of cold water and set aside. Repeat the rinsing process with the urad gota and chana dal in a separate bowl. Add the poha and fenugreek seeds to the rinsed lentils and cover with 3 inches of cold water. Let the rice and lentils soak for at least 4 hours, up to 8 hours.

Preheat the oven to the lowest setting, 150°F to 170°F.

Meanwhile, make the batter. Place a fine-mesh sieve over a medium bowl and drain the lentil mixture, catching the soaking liquid in the bowl beneath. Transfer the drained lentil mixture into a high-powered blender along with ½ cup (120 ml) of the soaking liquid. Start blending on low speed, increasing the speed to high, and blend until the mixture is thick, smooth (it should feel like lotion when rubbed between your fingers), and slightly warm to the touch, 3 to 5 minutes total. Transfer the mixture to a large bowl, reserving the blender jar.

Discard any leftover lentil soaking liquid, replace the sieve over the bowl, and drain the soaked rice. Transfer the rice along with ½ cup (120 ml) of its soaking liquid to the blender and repeat the blending process until the mixture is smooth. Transfer the blended rice to the bowl with the lentils, add the salt, and mix with your fingertips until well combined, about 3 minutes (this will also help start the fermentation process). Scrape down the sides of the bowl and cover with a clean kitchen towel.

continues

Turn off the oven and turn on the oven light. Place the covered bowl of dosa batter on a baking sheet in the oven, close to the oven light, and let ferment until light, airy, and doubled in size, 10 to 12 hours. (If you live in a colder climate, you can also move the bowl into a sunny spot in the house for the last few hours of fermentation if you are making dosa for breakfast.) If not using right away, transfer to an airtight container and refrigerate for up to 1 week. Bring the batter back to room temperature before using.

To make the dosa, give the batter a gentle stir to make sure everything is evenly distributed. Then add room temperature water, 1 tablespoon at a time, until the batter reaches a thick, pourable consistency somewhere in between pancake and crepe batter. (If you aren't using all the batter at once, you can separate the desired amount of batter, thin it out, and reserve the rest of the batter in the refrigerator for later use. Bring the batter back to room temperature before using.)

Heat a tawa or cast-iron skillet over medium-high heat. Using a paper towel, rub the pan with a thin layer of canola oil. Pour one ladle of batter into the center of the pan, then, using the bottom of the ladle, move it in concentric circles starting from the inside and moving outward, spreading the batter out into a 10-inch circle (the ladle should be hovering over the bottom of the pan, not pressed against it—this will help spread the batter without creating holes).

Drizzle 1 teaspoon melted ghee around the dosa, starting around the edges and moving inward. Sprinkle the dosa with 1 to 2 teaspoons gunpowder podi and cook until golden brown and crisp on the bottom, 2 to 3 minutes. (If it starts to brown too fast, reduce the heat to medium.) Run a spatula along the edges of the dosa to release it from the pan, fold it in half, and transfer to a plate. Repeat with the remaining batter. Enjoy with Seasonal Sambar (page 114), Aloo Masala (page 105), and/or Palli Chutney (page 45).

Idli

Steamed Lentil and Rice Cakes

Recipe by Sulochana Meiyappan | Origin: Pollachi, Tamil Nadu | Makes 16

Idlis will always remind me of Prabhu, our turmeric farmer. During his college days, he used to regularly visit a simple idli stall in the heart of Vijayawada called SSS Idli—an unassuming thatched roof structure with matching black granite countertops and benches and framed photos of Indian freedom fighters on the walls. On my very first harvest visit, Prabhu took me to his old haunt for a little breakfast before we made the drive out to his family's farm. I remember biting into my first idli—softer than anything I've ever experienced, doused in ghee and with a side of umami Gunpowder Podi (page 26) and a dollop of creamy peanut chutney. For 20 rupees per plate (only 25¢), we had the most nourishing—and memorable!—breakfast before heading out to the world's best turmeric fields. Safe to say, I went back every single day of that trip, and on every visit in the seven years since!

This specific idli recipe, however, came to us from Mrs. Meiyappan, the matriarch of Anamalai Estate that grows everyone's favorite nutmeg and cacao in Tamil Nadu and is as close as I've been able to get to SSS Idli's secret recipe. Pillowy soft with generous notes of fenugreek seeds, these are a daily staple across South India, alongside a couple little ladles of ghee and Palli Chutney (page 45).

1 cup (200 g) idli or sona masoori rice

¼ cup (50 g) urad gota (whole, skinned urad dal)

2 tablespoons thick poha (flattened rice)

1¼ teaspoons fenugreek seeds

1 teaspoon fine sea salt

Canola oil, for greasing

EQUIPMENT
Idli steamer

Place the rice in a bowl and rinse with cold water, swishing it around with your fingers, and rinsing several times until the water runs clear. Cover with 3 inches of cold water and set aside. Repeat the rinsing process with the urad gota in a separate bowl. Add the poha and fenugreek seeds to the rinsed lentils and cover with 3 inches of cold water. Let the rice and lentils soak for at least 4 hours, up to 8 hours.

Preheat the oven to the lowest setting, 150°F to 170°F.

Meanwhile, make the batter. Place a fine-mesh sieve over a medium bowl and drain the lentil mixture, catching the soaking liquid in the bowl beneath. Transfer the drained lentil mixture into a high-powered blender along with ½ cup (120 ml) of the soaking liquid. Start blending on low speed, increasing the speed to high, and blend until the mixture is thick, smooth (it should feel like lotion when rubbed between your fingers), and slightly warm to the touch, 3 to 5 minutes total. Transfer the mixture to a large bowl, reserving the blender jar.

Discard any leftover lentil soaking liquid, replace the sieve over the bowl, and drain the soaked rice. Transfer the rice along with ¾ cup (180 ml) of its soaking liquid to the blender and repeat the blending

continues

process until the mixture is smooth. Transfer the blended rice to the bowl with the lentils, add the salt, and mix with your fingertips until well combined, about 3 minutes (this will also help start the fermentation process). Scrape down the sides of the bowl and cover with a clean kitchen towel.

Turn off the oven and turn on the oven light. Place the covered bowl of idli batter on a baking sheet in the oven, close to the oven light, and let ferment until light, airy, and doubled in size, 10 to 12 hours. (If you live in a colder climate, you can also move the bowl into a sunny spot in the house for the last few hours of fermentation if you are making idli for breakfast.) If not using right away, transfer to an airtight container and refrigerate for up to 1 week. Bring the batter back to room temperature before using.

To steam the idli, bring 1 inch of water to a boil in a large pot (big enough to fit an idli steamer) over medium-high heat. Meanwhile, lightly grease each level of the idli steamer with a thin layer of canola oil. Give the fermented batter a gentle stir to make sure everything is evenly distributed—you don't want to knock too much air out of it because it'll result in less fluffy idli—and then ladle ¼ cup (60 ml) into each mold. Place the idli steamer in the pot, cover, reduce the heat to medium, and steam until cooked through, light, and fluffy, 14 to 17 minutes. Partially uncover, let the idli cool for 3 minutes, then use a soft spatula to remove each idli. Serve hot with plenty of ghee and Gunpowder Podi (page 26) or Karivepaku Podi (page 27).

Sri Lankan Moringa String Hoppers

Recipe by Sumithra Attanayake | Origin: Kandy, Sri Lanka | Makes 16

Whoever invented string hoppers was a prodigy of the sauce to starch surface area ratio. Never have I met a scoopable (like bread, pasta, rice, rotis, etc.!) that is so uniquely suited to absorbing and carrying quite as much saucy goodness as possible from plate to bite. Made with finely milled, toasted rice flour, think of these squiggly disks as the bucatini of rice-based noodles. The moringa is, of course, optional, but it does add a craveable, delicately earthy taste. Serve with Jaffna-Style Crab Curry (page 132) or Sri Lankan Cucumber Coconut Milk Curry (page 91).

1½ cups (240 g) string hoppers rice flour

1½ tablespoons (10 g) moringa powder

¾ teaspoon fine sea salt

1 teaspoon canola oil, plus more for greasing

EQUIPMENT

Protective glove, optional

Idli steamer

String hopper press

Combine the flour, moringa powder, and salt in a large bowl. Add the canola oil and rub it into the dry ingredients with your fingertips until it is combined.

Pour 1 cup (240 ml) of boiling water over the dry ingredients and, using a spoon, gently mix to bring into a shaggy dough. (The dough will be hot! You can wear a protective glove if your hands are sensitive.) Once the dough comes together and cools down slightly, switch to your hand and knead it into a smooth, firm dough in the bowl (you're aiming for a texture like Play-Doh). If the dough is too dry, add 1 tablespoon hot water at a time until it reaches the right consistency. Keep the dough covered with a kitchen towel to prevent it from drying out.

To steam the hoppers, bring 1 inch of water to a boil in a large pot (big enough to fit an idli steamer) over medium-high heat. Meanwhile, lightly grease each level of the idli steamer with a thin layer of canola oil.

Break a piece of the dough off, keeping the rest covered, and place it in a string hopper press fitted with the finest extruding plate. Press the dough, moving three times in a circle around each idli mold to create a little string mountain, then cut the dough from the press with a sharp knife. Repeat with the remaining dough. Steam, covered, until cooked through and firm to the touch, 10 to 13 minutes. Remove with a soft spatula. Serve hot.

RECIPE NOTES: You can find string hopper flour at some South Asian supermarkets and online. You can also (1) buy fine milled rice flour from a South Asian market or (2) use regular white rice flour.

Either way, you need to toast it. Heat a skillet over medium-low heat, add the flour, and cook, stirring frequently, until it smells roasty but hasn't taken on any color. For commodity rice flour, grind in a spice grinder or high-powered blender and then sift through a fine-mesh sieve. (You want a total of 1½ cups [240 g], so you may need to start with more rice flour.)

Skillet Appams
Kerala-Style Lacy Rice Pancakes

Recipe inspired by Anna Thomas (Kaviya Cherian's grandmother) | Origin: Kochi, Kerala | Makes 8 to 10

In Kerala, appams—fermented rice pancakes that are a little sweet and perfectly fluffy in the center with lacy crispy edges—are an everyday luxury. They're traditionally made in an appam pan, which has curved edges like a small, shallow wok or kadai, but to make these more accessible to every kitchen, we tweaked the recipe to use a good ol' skillet. The shape isn't as round, but you'll still be able to achieve those signature golden edges and soft, spongy interior, perfect for scooping and sopping up gravies and sauces like Meen Moilee (page 138), Meen Pollichathu (page 140), and Jammy Egg Curry (page 156).

Nailing the swirling of the batter in the hot pan can take a couple tries but is so satisfying once you've got the hang of it! The trick is keeping the pan from getting too hot, which is a much different technique if you're used to making other scoopables like dosas.

In Sri Lanka, appam's coconut milk–based cousins are known as hoppers, and we have scarfed down many, many hopper variations over years of cinnamon and clove harvests. Once you've nailed the plain appam technique, I highly recommend cracking an egg into your appam once it's a little set in the pan but hasn't started browning yet and eating it with a side of Pol Sambol (page 39) as a savory brekkie. My personal favorite is sprinkling jaggery over the appam as it cooks so the sugar caramelizes into the batter—it's truly a lil butterscotchy sweet treat heaven.

1 cup (200 g) idli or sona masoori rice

3 tablespoons thick poha (flattened rice)

1 tablespoon granulated sugar

½ teaspoon active dry yeast

¼ cup (60 ml) lukewarm water

¾ cup (64 g) lightly packed fresh or thawed, frozen grated coconut, lightly packed

1 teaspoon fine sea salt

Place the rice in a bowl and rinse with cold water, swishing it around with your fingers, and rinsing several times until the water runs clear. Cover with 3 inches of cold water, add the poha, and soak for at least 4 hours, up to 8 hours.

Preheat the oven to the lowest setting, 150°F to 170°F.

Meanwhile, make the batter. Combine the sugar, yeast, and lukewarm water in a bowl and let sit until the yeast starts to bloom and the surface starts to look foamy, 5 to 10 minutes. Drain the soaked rice-poha mixture and transfer to a high-speed blender along with the grated coconut, the salt, the bloomed yeast mixture, and an additional ½ cup (120 ml) cold water. Start blending on low speed, increasing the speed to high, until the mixture is thick, smooth (it should feel like lotion when rubbed between your fingers), and slightly warm to the touch, 3 to 5 minutes total. Transfer the mixture to a large bowl and cover with a clean kitchen towel.

continues

Turn off the oven and turn on the oven light. Place the covered appam batter in the oven, close to the oven light, and let ferment until light, airy, and doubled in size, 8 to 10 hours. (If you live in a colder climate, you can also move the bowl into a sunny spot in the house for the last few hours of fermentation if you are making appam for breakfast.) Gently stir in the salt. If not using right away, transfer to an airtight container and refrigerate for up to 3 days. Bring the batter back to room temperature before using.

To make the appam, using a ladle, give the batter a gentle stir to make sure everything is evenly distributed. Then add room temperature water, 1 tablespoon at a time, until the batter reaches a thick, pourable consistency somewhere in between pancake and crepe batter. (If you aren't using all the batter at once, you can separate the desired amount of batter, thin it out, and reserve the rest of the appam batter in the refrigerator for later use for up to 3 days. Bring back to room temperature before using.)

Heat a 6- to 8-inch nonstick skillet over medium heat. When hot but not smoking, add one ladleful of the batter in the center of the pan. Pick up the pan, tilting it slightly, and swirling it one rotation so the batter coats the sides of the pan, and letting any excess batter settle in the bottom of the pan. Return to medium heat, cover, and cook until the edges turn light golden and start to pull away from the sides of the pan, 3 to 6 minutes. Run a spatula under the sides of the appam to remove it from the pan and repeat with the remaining batter. Appam are best made to order and eaten immediately, but you can also keep them warm in the oven set to the lowest setting.

Pol Roti
Sri Lankan Coconut Flatbread

Recipe by Sumithra Attanayake | Origin: Kandy, Sri Lanka | Makes 6

I will admit that my first few attempts at making pol rotis were underwhelming. The rustic little flatbreads, often eaten with spicy coconut-shallot sambol (page 39), are a typical hill country farm breakfast, and I wasn't getting it (fluffy Gujarati chapatis these aren't). Then I learned the key to a truly exemplary pol roti lies in amping up the textural contrast and going heavy on the seasoning.

Thicker than your average roti, they need to be properly seasoned with salt and chilli peppers to cut through the coconutty richness of the dough before being cooked in a hot skillet until they're still soft inside and browned until crispy outside. Use them to scoop up Parippu Curry (page 118).

1½ cups (180 g) all-purpose flour, plus more if needed

1 cup (85 g) lightly packed fresh or thawed, frozen grated coconut, lightly packed

1 serrano pepper, minced

1 teaspoon fine sea salt

1 tablespoon virgin coconut oil, melted, plus more for brushing

4 to 6 tablespoons (60 to 90 ml) cold water

Mix the flour, grated coconut, serrano pepper, and salt in a large bowl, making sure to coat all the coconut in the flour. Drizzle the melted coconut oil over the dry ingredients and rub it in with your fingertips.

Add 4 tablespoons cold water and use your hands to mix, bringing it together into a shaggy dough. If the dough is too dry, add 1 tablespoon of water at a time until it comes together (if you're using fresh coconut, it might take a little more water because frozen has a higher water content). Turn onto the counter and knead a few times into a ball. Wrap the dough in plastic wrap and let rest at room temperature for at least 1 hour, up to 4 hours.

Divide the dough into six equal pieces and roll into balls. Take one ball at a time, leaving the remaining pieces covered to make sure they don't dry out, flatten into a thick disk, and then dip lightly into some flour, shaking off any excess, and roll into a 7-inch circle.

To cook, heat a 10- to 12-inch cast-iron skillet over medium heat. Add the rolled pol roti and cook until it loses its raw look and starts to lightly brown on the underside, 1 to 2 minutes, then flip and cook on the other side. Brush the cooked side with a thin layer of melted coconut oil, flip again, increase the heat to medium-high, and continue to cook, gently pressing down on the top with a spatula, until deep golden in spots, 1 to 2 minutes more per side. (These will puff in some places, but they are not like chapati or other roti that will fully puff.) Place the cooked pol roti in a clean kitchen towel to keep warm, and repeat the rolling and cooking process with the remaining dough.

Bajra Na Rotla
Pearl Millet Flatbread

Recipe by Poonam Rathore and Mohani Devi Bishnoi | Origin: Osian, Rajasthan | Makes 4

Bajra, or pearl millet, is one of the few indigenous food crops of West India that thrive in intense desert and drought-like conditions. Up until the 1960s, it was considered a staple crop, but it has been slowly replaced with the rise of GMO wheat and industrial, monocropped agriculture (higher yield, yes, but lower nutritional value). Today, there are still outliers, like our Nandini Coriander farm partners in Gujarat, Jodhana Cumin partners in Rajasthan, Byadgi Chilli partners in Karnataka, and Madhur Jaggery partners in Maharashtra, who continue to grow bajra, prioritizing heirloom grains and seeds.

While all our farm partners make these with just bajra and hot water, our version uses a blend of millet and all-purpose flours for the heft, nutty flavor, and pliability. Use them to scoop up the Country Chicken Curry (page 150), dip it into your Kadhi (page 123), or eat it with Bhindi Masala (page 88) and a little Rajasthani Garlic-Chilli Chutney (page 42).

1 cup (120 g) all-purpose flour

⅓ cup (40 g) bajra flour (pearl millet flour)

1½ teaspoons powdered jaggery

1 teaspoon fine sea salt, plus more if needed

2 teaspoons melted ghee, plus more for cooking

⅓ to ½ cup (70 to 120 ml) hot water

Combine the all-purpose flour, bajra flour, jaggery, and salt in a large bowl and mix well. Drizzle in the melted ghee and, using your fingertips, rub the ghee into the dry ingredients until it looks like sand. Add ⅓ cup (70 ml) hot water and, using your hand, start to bring together into a shaggy dough, then add 1 tablespoon hot water at a time until a soft, pliable dough comes together. Turn the dough out onto a clean surface and knead a few times to bring the dough together, then wrap in plastic wrap and let rest at room temperature for at least 1 hour, up to 4 hours.

Divide the dough into four equal pieces. Taking one piece at a time, and keeping the rest covered, gently flatten into a disk using the palm of your hand, lightly dip in all-purpose flour, and roll into a 6-inch circle.

Heat a large cast-iron skillet or other heavy-bottomed skillet over medium heat. Add the rotla and cook until it starts to turn opaque and loses its raw appearance, 1 to 1½ minutes. Flip, gently pressing on the edges with a spatula—this encourages it to puff, but don't worry if it doesn't fully puff on the first try! Cook on the other side until light golden in spots, 1 to 2 minutes. Brush the top with ghee, flip, and cook on the first side until light golden in spots, 15 to 30 seconds more.

Transfer the cooked rotla to a kitchen towel–lined plate, brush with more ghee, and keep the rotla wrapped in the towel to keep them warm while you repeat the process with the remaining portions of dough.

Kappa Puzhukku

Kerala-Style Mashed Cassava

Recipe by Anna Thomas | Origin: Kochi, Kerala | Serves 4 to 6

In Kerala, mashed cassava or kappa is paired with tart, spicy red fish curry. You scoop a little kappa with your fingers, mix it with the gravy and some fish, and enjoy the perfectly composed morsel in one bite. There is a time and a place for rice, but kappa with Thenga Aracha Meen Curry (page 144) has become a pretty unbeatable combo for me now.

2 pounds (907 g) yuca or cassava

2 tablespoons plus 1 teaspoon fine sea salt, plus more if needed

3 tablespoons virgin coconut oil

1¼ teaspoons black mustard seeds

36 fresh curry leaves (2 to 3 g)

2 large shallots (about ⅓ pound/151 g), diced

4 garlic cloves, finely chopped

1 to 2 serrano peppers, finely chopped

1 teaspoon ground turmeric

1 cup (85 g) lightly packed fresh or thawed, frozen grated coconut, lightly packed

Slice and discard ¼ inch off the top and bottom of the yuca or cassava. Then, cut crosswise into 3-inch pieces. Place one piece at a time cut-side down and cut the peel off in strips. Cut in half, lengthwise, then cut each half in half lengthwise, so you're left with 4 spears. There is a fibrous root that runs down the center; to remove, diagonally cut ¼ inch off lengthwise from the center of each spear and discard. Then, cut each spear crosswise into ½-inch pieces.

Transfer the cleaned yuca to a large pot, cover with cold water by 3 inches, and add 2 tablespoons of the salt. Place over medium-high heat and bring to a boil. Cover, reduce the heat to medium, and cook at a gentle boil, until cooked through, slightly translucent, and easily mashed, 55 minutes to 1 hour 30 minutes. Drain, add back to the hot pot, and cover to keep warm.

Heat the coconut oil in a Dutch oven or other large, heavy-bottomed pot over medium heat. When shimmering, add the mustard seeds and cook, stirring frequently, until the seeds start to sputter, 15 to 45 seconds. Add the curry leaves and cook until bright green, 10 to 30 seconds. Stir in the shallots, garlic, serrano peppers, and ½ teaspoon of the remaining salt. Cook, stirring occasionally, until the shallots soften and start to turn light golden, 6 to 9 minutes. Add the turmeric and ¼ cup (60 ml) water and cook, stirring frequently, until most of the water has evaporated, 2 to 4 minutes.

Stir in the coconut, the reserved cooked yuca, ¾ cup (180 ml) water, and the remaining ½ teaspoon salt. Using a potato masher, mash into a medium-coarse paste, leaving some bigger chunks. Cook, stirring occasionally, until most of the liquid has evaporated and the yuca starts to pull away from the pan, 8 to 12 minutes. Taste and season with salt, if necessary. Let cool until warm to the touch before serving.

Drinks

Kadak Masala Chai 212
Jaggery Chai 213
Noon Chai 214
Methi Latte 216
Kehwa 218

Haldi Doodh 219
Fennel Soda 220
Fennel Tom Collins 221
Heimang Soda 224
Hyun Mezcalita 225

The History of Chai

Every sip of chai is a symbol of over two hundred years of South Asian resilience. From the tea to the spices that flavor it, chai is a beverage that carries both the weight of colonial exploitation and the defiance of desi ingenuity and resilience.

Tea's Colonial Beginnings

Wild tea plants grew in the hills of Assam and Arunachal Pradesh and were consumed as medicinal brews by local tribes as early as the twelfth century, but South Asia lacked widespread tea culture prior to colonization. Meanwhile, the Chinese had refined tea cultivation for millennia. By the eighteenth century, the British had developed an insatiable thirst for tea and were importing millions of pounds annually from China, paying for it first with silver and then opium.

Following the infamous Opium Wars, the East India Company wanted to circumvent Chinese dominance by cultivating tea in India. British botanists smuggled tea plants and knowledge out of China, and in 1837, they established the first tea gardens in Assam. These plantations were modeled after the exploitative systems of American cotton farms and Jamaican sugar estates. The labor was supplied by indentured workers tricked into servitude from regions like Odisha, Bihar, and Bengal. Working conditions were brutal, with mortality rates soaring as high as 40 percent.

The Birth of Indian Chai

For decades, Indians themselves were not avid tea drinkers. Tea consumption was largely limited to the British elite. Desperate to increase domestic consumption, the Indian Tea Association launched aggressive campaigns in the early twentieth century. They distributed free tea at railway stations and festivals, even mandating tea breaks for industrial workers. This tea was bitter and strong, often brewed with the lowest quality leaves.

Starting in the 1920s, to boost flagging sales, chaiwallahs began adding spices like ginger, cardamom, cinnamon, and cloves to their tea, inspired by Ayurvedic brewing traditions. This both masked the bitterness of the low-grade tea and gave their customers a drink more suited to their palates.

A Symbol of Resistance

British tea purists viewed the addition of spices as adulteration, a move that could reduce tea consumption and thus profits. Inspections and crackdowns ensued, but masala chai persisted.

For South Asians, it has become a staple, especially for women and workers who rely on its energizing properties during long hours of domestic and physical labor. The symbolic power of chai extends beyond its ingredients—it represents our postcolonial reality—as something forced upon a population and then reshaped into something uniquely ours.

Kadak Masala Chai

Recipe by Sana Javeri Kadri | Origin: Mumbai, Maharashtra | Makes 2 cups

This chai is a love letter to the roadside cutting chai of my Bombay childhood (freshly brewed, very spicy, very sweet, drunk in teeny tiny cups), with a couple very California twists (substitutes for literally every dietary restriction—oat vs. cow milk, iced vs. hot, strong vs. weak caffeine, refined vs. unrefined sweetener, lol). My goal was a really stiff cup with just the right balance of cardamom richness, sweet notes of cinnamon and fennel, and a lasting kick of pepper and clove. This blend is one I personally adore, but everyone is different! So, please feel free to play with the spice proportions until you find the blend that works perfectly for you!

CTC tea—named after a processing method known as crush, tear, curl—yields a stiff, medium-strength cup because the tea leaves are broken up during processing so there's more surface area for it to quickly diffuse into milk or water. This means that it holds up beautifully to milk and spices, making it the tea of choice for the millions of cups of chai made every day on the subcontinent.

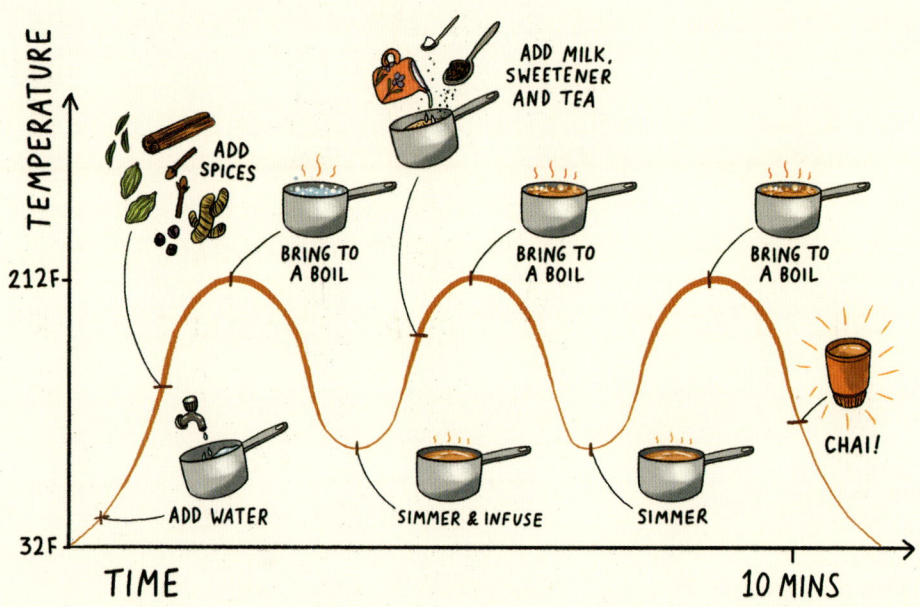

- 1 cup (240 ml) water
- 12 green cardamom pods, lightly crushed
- 1 teaspoon black peppercorns
- 1 teaspoon finely grated fresh ginger or ½ teaspoon ground ginger
- ½ teaspoon fennel seeds
- ½ teaspoon ground cinnamon
- 4 to 5 whole cloves
- 1 cup (240 ml) cow's or plant-based milk
- 1 to 2 tablespoons sweetener, such as jaggery or date syrup
- 1½ teaspoons CTC black tea leaves or 1 to 2 black tea bags

Bring the water to a boil in a medium saucepan over medium-high heat. Add the cardamom pods, peppercorns, ginger, fennel seeds, cinnamon, and cloves, stir well to make sure the ground spices dissolve into the water, reduce the heat to medium-low, and simmer to infuse the spices in the water, 3 to 4 minutes.

Stir in the milk, sweetener, and tea. Bring the mixture back to a boil, then reduce the heat to medium-low and simmer for 1 minute. Repeat this boiling and simmering process until you reach the desired consistency (imagine this process as a sine curve). For a thinner chai, repeat 2 or 3 times, 3 to 5 minutes total. For a thicker consistency, repeat 4 or 5 times, 6 to 8 minutes total.

Strain the finished chai through a fine-mesh strainer into 2 cups and enjoy immediately.

NOTES: Want iced chai? Use 2 cups milk instead of the water/milk combo, and boil and simmer the chai 4 or 5 times for a thicker, more concentrated tea (keep in mind the ice will dilute it!). Cool in the fridge, pour over ice, and enjoy!

Jaggery Chai

Recipe by Poonam Swapnil Shelke | Origin: Daund, Maharashtra | Serves 2

On the jaggery farm—and many of the farms we visited—this is their simple, everyday chai.

- 2 cups (480 ml) cow's or plant-based milk
- 1-inch piece ginger
- 2 to 4 teaspoons powdered jaggery
- 1 to 2 teaspoons CTC black tea leaves or broken black tea

Bring the milk to a gentle boil in a medium saucepan over medium-high heat.

Grate the ginger on the large side of a box grater, then add to the boiling milk along with the jaggery and tea. Bring the mixture back to a boil, then reduce the heat to medium-low and simmer for 1 minute. Repeat this boiling and simmering process until you reach the desired consistency. For a thinner chai, repeat 2 or 3 times, 3 to 5 minutes total. For a thicker consistency, repeat 4 or 5 times, 6 to 8 minutes total.

Strain the finished chai through a fine-mesh strainer into 2 cups and enjoy immediately.

Noon Chai

Kashmiri Savory Green Milk Tea

Recipe by Aaliya Mir | Origin: Pampore, Kashmir | Makes 1 cup

I first had noon chai—also known as gulabi chai, namkeen chai, or sheer chai—at the iconic Chai Jaai in Srinagar. It was unlike any chai I've ever had. Made with green tea and a pinch of salt instead of sugar, it's warming, savory, fruity, and a little tannic. But why is it pink? A small spoonful of baking soda reacts with the tannins in the green tea.

In order to keep folks high up in the mountains hydrated in the cold, noon chai is part of a long tradition of Himalayan salt teas that are drunk across Mongolia, Bhutan, Tibet, Nepal, and, of course, Kashmir. It is perfect sipped on a cold winter's morning with a piece of toast slathered in salted butter and drizzled with honey.

½ cup (120 ml) cow's or plant-based milk

⅓ cup (120 ml) Noon Chai Concentrate (recipe follows)

Pinch of fine sea salt

Combine all the ingredients in a small saucepan and bring to a boil over medium-high heat. Pour into a mug and enjoy.

Noon Chai Concentrate

Makes 3 cups concentrate, enough for 9 cups of noon chai

6 cups (1.4 L) water

½ cup (20 g) green tea leaves

¼ teaspoon baking soda

Bring the water to a boil in a medium saucepan over medium-high heat. Add the tea leaves and boil, uncovered, for 5 minutes. Stir in the baking soda, cover, reduce the heat to medium-low, and simmer covered until deep reddish brown, 30 to 40 minutes.

Uncover, increase the heat to medium, and simmer, uncovered, until reduced by about one-third and the color deepens a couple shades. Strain into a container, cool to room temperature—you'll notice that the color will change from red to a deeper pink hue as it cools—and then transfer to the refrigerator. The concentrate will keep in an airtight container in the refrigerator for up to 2 weeks.

Methi Latte
Fenugreek Milk "Coffee"

Recipe by Nayna Sakariya | Origin: Shedubhar, Gujarat | Serves 2 to 4

While "coffee" may be in the title, this recipe doesn't actually call for coffee beans. Instead of roasting coffee beans, which don't grow in the climate and terroir of Shedubhar, Nayna ingeniously toasts fenugreek seeds until deeply roasty-toasty, turning fenugreek's sweet maple flavor caramelized with a hint of pleasing, chicory-like bitterness (think: Nescafé). This is a great caffeine-free coffee alternative for people trying to cut back or if you want an afternoon pick-me-up that won't keep you up all night! Enjoy hot or iced. And for all you dessert lovers out there, this makes a great base for custard, ice cream, or dairy-based sweets.

3 tablespoons fenugreek seeds

3 cups (710 ml) cow's or plant-based milk

1 to 2 tablespoons sweetener of your choice, like jaggery, or date syrup, to taste

Place the fenugreek seeds in a medium saucepan over medium-low heat. Toast the seeds, stirring frequently, until they turn a couple shades darker, 2 to 3 minutes, then increase the heat to medium and continue to toast, stirring constantly, until they are deep brown and smell roasty, 3 to 5 minutes more. Add the milk and sweetener, increase the heat to medium-high, and bring to a boil, reduce back to medium-low, and simmer until it reaches your desired strength, 4 to 6 minutes for a lighter taste, 7 to 10 minutes for a bolder cup.

If serving hot, strain directly into cups and enjoy immediately. If serving iced, strain into a container and chill in the refrigerator, then pour over ice into individual glasses.

Kehwa
Kashmiri Spiced Saffron Tea

Recipe by Aliya Mir | Origin: Pampore, Kashmir | Makes 2 cups

This tea is really the story of the Silk Route and the many migrations it spurred distilled into one golden cup. The saffron came to Kashmir via Iran, almonds from Afghanistan, the samovar that it is brewed in from Russia via Iranian and Turkish traders, and the green tea from China—all now distinctly Kashmiri ingredients and part of the region's rich culture.

When I think of kehwa, I always think of my first snowy February visit to the Mir family home. Raqib, our now beloved Kashmiri Saffron farm partner, sweetly poured me a cup of his mother's famous drink and garnished it with a few fresh strands of the highest grade of saffron his family processes—a trumpet-shaped long dark strand. The almond-laced, marigold-hued tea was the soothing potion I needed to conduct business in such bitter cold, and it was also the perfect closing move on a long-term business relationship and now dear friendship.

Kehwa is usually served with Sheermal, a crumbly milk bread said to have originated in Persia. Kehwa and Noon Chai (page 214) alike are best drunk with a little bread alongside. A buttery shortbread, a yolk-enriched mooncake, or simply buttered toast have all done the trick for me.

3 cups (710 ml) water

10 green cardamom pods, lightly crushed

One 3-inch cinnamon stick, broken in half

One 1½-inch piece dried licorice root, broken into big pieces

1 to 2 teaspoons granulated sugar, plus more if needed

Pinch of saffron (12 to 15 strands), plus more for garnishing

1 tablespoon roughly chopped blanched almonds

Bring the water to a boil in a medium saucepan over medium-high heat. Add the cardamom, cinnamon stick, licorice root, and sugar. Reduce the heat to medium, keep at a gentle boil, and boil until reduced by about one-third (you don't need to be super strict about this, just eyeball it), about 10 minutes. Add the saffron and boil for another 5 minutes to allow the saffron to steep. Taste, and sweeten with more sugar, if desired.

To serve, divide the almonds between 2 mugs and add 2 or 3 saffron strands to each mug. Strain the kehwa between the two mugs and enjoy hot.

RECIPE NOTE: Dried licorice root can be quite tough and come in long sticks. We've found the best way to get a 1½-inch piece (you can really be approximate here!) is to place it on a cutting board and smash the root with a heavy pestle, a rolling pin, or the back of a sturdy chef's knife.

Haldi Doodh
Golden Turmeric Milk

Recipe inspired by Siva Nagendramma Kasaraneni | Origin: Kankipadu, Andhra Pradesh | Serves 2 to 4

Silky, luxurious, and packed with healing, pure sunshine-y taste, our Diaspora version of Haldi Doodh (or, golden milk) is very different from (read: much yummier than) the medicinal drink so many of us grew up drinking.

Here, the turmeric is layered with ground ginger for warmth, cinnamon for sweetness, and green cardamom for richness. And don't forget a couple good cracks of black pepper—the piperine in the freshly milled pepper will make the curcumin in the turmeric more bioavailable to your body! In the Kasaraneni family home—who grow our Pragati Turmeric—they like to double down on the fat, which also aids in the absorption of turmeric's anti-inflammatory properties, by adding a small dollop of ghee to every cupful of haldi doodh.

3 cups (710 ml) cow's or plant-based milk

1 tablespoon plus ½ teaspoon ground turmeric

6 to 8 green cardamom pods, lightly crushed

¾ teaspoon ground cinnamon

¼ teaspoon freshly ground black pepper

2 teaspoons minced fresh ginger or 1 teaspoon ground ginger

Sweetener of your choice, such as jaggery, honey, or date syrup, to taste

Ghee, optional

Combine the milk, turmeric, cardamom, cinnamon, and black pepper in a medium saucepan and bring to a gentle boil over medium heat, whisking to dissolve the spices.

When boiling, add the ginger (if you add it before the milk is boiling, the enzymes in the ginger will curdle the milk!) and sweetener. Stir, bring back to a boil, then reduce the heat to medium-low and simmer to infuse the ginger in the haldi doodh, 1 to 3 minutes, depending on how pronounced you want the ginger taste.

For hot haldi doodh, strain into the desired number of glasses and finish with a small spoonful of ghee (about ½ teaspoon per cup), if desired. Enjoy immediately.

For iced haldi doodh, let the mixture cool to room temperature, strain in a large container, seal, and chill in the refrigerator for up to 5 days. To serve, pour or shake with ice and enjoy.

Fennel Soda

Recipe by Nayna Sakariya | Origin: Shedubhar, Gujarat | Makes 1 soda

The Hariyali Fennel harvest at the Sakariya family farm is usually in March. The nights are still cool, but the days can get *really* hot. To cool themselves down during the long sun-filled hours of harvest, Nayna makes a fennel sharbat for the whole family. It's ground fresh fennel seeds, sugar, and cold water mixed together for a very refreshing afternoon drink.

We knew we wanted to keep the cooling, fennel-forward properties but balance out its sweetness. Asha made a shrub and then topped it with sparkling water to make the perfect bubbly bevvy or base for a truly spectacular gin-based cocktail (see page 221).

1 ounce (30 ml) Fennel Shrub (recipe follows)

8 ounces (240 ml) club soda

Ice

Fennel seeds, for garnishing

Combine the fennel shrub and club soda in a Collins or other tall glass and gently stir. Add enough ice to fill the glass, garnish with a tiny pinch of fennel seeds, and enjoy immediately.

Fennel Shrub

Makes ¾ cup

2 tablespoons fennel seeds

1 cup (192 g) granulated sugar

⅔ cup (160 ml) white balsamic or apple cider vinegar

⅛ teaspoon fine sea salt

Place the fennel seeds in a mortar and pound until about half the seeds are broken apart (don't worry too much about crushing all of them—this is just to release their essential oils into the syrup). Transfer the crushed fennel seeds to a medium saucepan along with the sugar, vinegar, ⅓ cup (80 ml) water, and the salt and bring to a boil over medium-high heat. Reduce the heat to medium, keeping it at a gentle boil, and simmer until reduced by a quarter, 5 to 8 minutes. Remove from the heat, let cool completely, and strain. Store in an airtight container in the refrigerator for up to 3 months.

Fennel Tom Collins

Recipe by Asha Loupy | Makes 1 cocktail

After developing our fennel shrub—starring the Hariyali Fennel, grown by the Sakariya family farm—we knew we wanted to create a bright, lively fennel-forward cocktail. The herbaceous nature of gin enhances the fresh, herbal notes of the fennel, making for a highly sippable libation. The shrub brings some acidity, but lemon juice really rounds things out, and the cucumber garnish is not only pretty, but also infuses the cocktail with a subtle cool crispness.

Ice

2 ounces (60 ml) gin

1 ounce (30 ml) Fennel Shrub (page 220)

¾ ounce (22 ml) fresh lemon juice

Cucumber ribbon, for garnish

Club soda

Fill a cocktail shaker two-thirds of the way with ice. Add the gin, fennel shrub, and lemon juice. Shake vigorously until the outside of the shaker is icy, 30 to 45 seconds. Place a cucumber ribbon around the inside of a Collins or highball glass, fill with ice, then strain the gin mixture into the glass. Top with club soda, gently stir, and enjoy immediately.

KEHWA, page 218   HALDI DOODH, page 219

FENNEL SODA, page 220

FENNEL TOM COLLINS, page 221

Heimang Soda
Manipuri Sumac Soda

Recipe by Zeinorin Angkang | Origin: Ukhrul, Manipur | Makes 1 soda

This tart lil soda—starring wild Heimang (sumac), grown in the hills of Manipur—reminds me so much of my favorite fizzy drink of all time: Jarritos Tamarind Soda. It's perfect to wash down the fiery, ghost pepper–packed foods of the region (or any spicy foods, really!). The sumac is cooked down with lemon juice, sugar, and a whisper of salt to create a deep, layered sour concentrate that when combined with sparkling water transforms into a bright, zippy bevvy.

Plus, this concentrate is excellent in cocktails—it's particularly brilliant in margaritas and mezcalitas. While we use our Manipuri Wild Heimang Sumac in this recipe, which is a bit more tannic and intense than other varieties of sumac, you can get away with using whichever sumac you have on hand.

1 tablespoon Heimang Concentrate (recipe follows)

Ice

6 ounces (180 ml) club soda

Lemon wheel, for garnishing

Pour the Heimang Concentrate into a glass filled with ice, top with the club soda, and gently stir to combine. Garnish with a lemon wheel and enjoy.

Heimang Concentrate

Makes ½ cup

2 cups (480 ml) water

½ cup (96 g) granulated sugar

¼ cup (25 g) ground sumac

½ cup (120 ml) lemon juice

¼ teaspoon fine sea salt

Combine the water, sugar, sumac, lemon juice, and salt in a small saucepan. Place over medium-high heat and bring to a boil. Reduce the heat to medium and keep at a gentle boil, stirring occasionally, until the mixture reduces by three-quarters, turns deep mahogany brown, and is thick enough to just barely cling to the back of a spoon, 35 to 45 minutes. Strain into a container, cover, and refrigerate until chilled. The concentrate can be stored in an airtight container in the refrigerator for up to 1 month.

Hyun Mezcalita
Tangy Apricot Mezcalita

Recipe by Asha Loupy | Origin: Kotgaon, Uttarakhand | Makes 2 cocktails

In the Tons Valley, Hyun is a giddy event as much as it is a recipe. Villagers speculate madly about when the first snow is likely to fall, and even if it's just a first sprinkling, it'll be *just* enough to make hyun! Pahadi village children run around collecting fresh snow while their mothers get to work over the silbatta (stone mortar and pestle) grinding a wet paste—chulond, a paste of sun-dried apricots, super-sour amloch (concentrated sea buckthorn extract), cumin, jaggery, green garlic, cilantro, and chilli powder—to pour over the fresh snow, making for the most delicious tart-sweet-spicy-savory shaved ice.

Living in urban Northern California, fresh snow and seabuckthorn aren't particularly accessible to us, so Asha transformed our memories of Hyun into an icy, tangy apricot cocktail. Serrano peppers, cumin, cilantro, white balsamic vinegar, and sugar join the party to create an incredibly sour-savory shrub. And, while the shrub is great on its own with some bubbly water as a cooling drink, it's even better shaken up with some smoky mezcal, tequila, and citrus juices. This cocktail is delightful over cubed ice, but if you have crushed or shaved ice, go with that for the ultimate Hyun vibes.

FOR THE RIM

½ teaspoon fine sea salt

½ teaspoon Guntur Sannam chilli powder

½ teaspoon ground sumac

1 ounce (30 ml) lime juice

FOR THE COCKTAIL

Ice

2 ounces (60 ml) silver tequila

1 ounce (30 ml) mezcal

2½ ounces (75 ml) Apricot-Tamarind Shrub (page 226)

1 ounce (30 ml) freshly squeezed orange juice

2½ ounces (75 ml) fresh lime juice

Club soda

Lime wheel

To make the rim, combine the salt, chilli powder, and sumac in a shallow bowl and mix well.

Place the lime juice in a shallow bowl, dip the rim of a lowball glass in the lime juice, and then dip in the spicy salt mixture. Repeat with the remaining glass.

Fill each glass with ice. To make the cocktail, combine the tequila, mezcal, shrub, orange juice, and lime juice. Shake vigorously until the outside of the shaker is icy, 30 to 45 seconds. Strain into the two prepared glasses, top with a splash of club soda, and garnish with a lime wheel.

Apricot-Tamarind Shrub

½ pound (227 g) apricots

1 serrano pepper, roughly chopped

⅓ cup (64 g) granulated sugar

¼ teaspoon fine sea salt

¼ teaspoon cumin seeds

⅓ cup (79 ml) white balsamic or apple cider vinegar

2 teaspoons tamarind concentrate

4 sprigs cilantro

Halve, pit, and dice the apricots and transfer to a bowl along with the serrano pepper, sugar, and salt. Put the cumin seeds in a mortar, lightly crush into a coarse powder, and transfer to the bowl with the apricots. Gently toss to coat the fruit in the sugar, cover, and let sit at room temperature for 4 hours, or in the refrigerator overnight.

Transfer the fruit-sugar mixture and any juices that have accumulated to a medium saucepan, add the vinegar and tamarind concentrate, and bring to a boil over medium-high heat. Cover, reduce the heat to medium-low, and cook until the fruit is tender and starting to fall apart, 10 to 12 minutes. Taste and season with more sugar, if necessary.

Place a fine-mesh sieve over a medium bowl and strain the fruit mixture, gently pressing on the solids to extract as much liquid as possible. Add the cilantro and let cool to room temperature (the residual heat of the shrub will gently steep the cilantro). Remove the cilantro, transfer the cooled shrub into a container, cover, and refrigerate for up to 3 months.

Desserts

Turmeric-Banana Snacking Cake 230

Spiced Chocolate-Coconut Cookies 233

Apricot-Saffron Frangipane Galette 234

Spiced Date Cake with Coconut Caramel 237

Puran Poli 240

Watalappam-ish Crème Caramel 244

Turmeric-Banana Snacking Cake

Recipe by Asha Loupy | Serves 8 to 10

This golden, spice-forward cake is an ode to Prabhu Kasaraneni, our Pragati Turmeric farmer, who inspired this entire business (see page 30). In addition to turmeric, the family farm grows an indigenous variety of peanuts, coconut palms, and multiple banana varieties to provide supplementary income when the turmeric season is done. Inspired by a banana cake made by Prabhu's mum, Siva Nagendramma Kasaraneni, Asha's version adds orange zest and a toasty coconut-peanut topping.

2¼ cups (270 g) all-purpose flour

1 teaspoon baking powder

½ teaspoon baking soda

1¼ teaspoons ground turmeric

¾ cup (144 g) granulated sugar

¼ cup (48 g) light or dark brown sugar

Zest of 1 large orange

2 very ripe bananas, mashed well (about 1 cup/225 g)

⅔ cup (160 ml) neutral oil, such as canola

⅓ cup (80 ml) fresh orange juice (from the zested orange)

½ cup (120 g) full-fat sour cream

2 large eggs, at room temperature

1½ teaspoons vanilla extract

¾ teaspoon fine sea salt

⅔ cup (85 g) roasted, salted peanuts

1 cup (96 g) shaved, dried, unsweetened coconut strips

2 tablespoons demerara sugar

Preheat the oven to 350°F. Line a 9-inch round cake pan with parchment paper and set aside.

Combine the flour, baking powder, baking soda, and turmeric in a bowl, mix well, and set aside.

Place the granulated sugar, brown sugar, and orange zest in a large bowl and rub the zest into the sugar with your fingertips until it looks like wet sand, 1 to 3 minutes. Add the bananas, neutral oil, orange juice, sour cream, eggs, vanilla, and salt and whisk until smooth and most of the sugar has dissolved, 1 to 4 minutes. Add the dry ingredients and gently fold in until incorporated, being careful not to overmix.

Scoop half of the batter into the prepared pan and spread into an even layer. Sprinkle with half of the peanuts, half of the coconut strips, and half of the demerara sugar, then dollop the remaining batter on top, gently spreading it into an even layer. Sprinkle the top with the remaining half of the peanuts, coconut, and demerara sugar. Bake until deeply golden on top and a toothpick comes out clean when inserted into the center of the cake, 50 to 60 minutes.

Cool for 1 hour in the pan. To remove from the pan, run a paring knife around the edge of the pan, place a plate over the top, and flip. Remove the parchment paper, place a serving plate on the bottom of the cake, and flip it to be right-side up. Serve slightly warm (it'll still be warm after an hour) or at room temperature. Store any leftovers in an airtight container at room temperature for up to 3 days.

RECIPE NOTES: If you are avoiding peanuts, you can swap in cashews, walnuts, pecans, or even almonds.

To amp up the coconut taste, swap in melted virgin coconut oil for the neutral oil.

Spiced Chocolate-Coconut Cookies

Recipe by Asha Loupy | Makes 32 cookies

In Tamil Nadu on the Anamalai Estate, cacao trees are intercropped with nutmeg trees and coconut palms. These crinkle cookies are an ode to that estate, made with nutmeg, cinnamon, and green cardamom, and rolled in desiccated coconut. Enjoy with coffee or Jaggery Chai (page 213).

8 tablespoons (1 stick/113 g) unsalted butter

¾ cup (60 g) natural cocoa powder, sifted

¾ cup (90 g) all-purpose flour

1 teaspoon baking powder

1½ teaspoons freshly grated nutmeg

1¼ teaspoons ground cinnamon

⅛ teaspoon ground green cardamom

½ cup (96 g) granulated sugar

½ cup (85 g) powdered jaggery or light brown sugar

2 large eggs, straight from the refrigerator

1½ teaspoons instant espresso powder

1 teaspoon vanilla extract

½ teaspoon fine sea salt

6 ounces (170 g) bittersweet chocolate, roughly chopped

1 cup (85 g) desiccated coconut

Place the butter in a medium saucepan and melt over medium heat. Cook the butter, stirring often, until it foams and then browns, 4 to 6 minutes. Transfer to a large bowl and let cool for 20 minutes.

In a large bowl, combine the cocoa powder, flour, baking powder, nutmeg, cinnamon, and cardamom. Mix well.

Add the granulated sugar, jaggery, eggs, espresso powder, vanilla, and salt to the cooled brown butter. Whisk vigorously until thick, lighter in color, and ribbony, 2 to 4 minutes. Add the dry ingredients to the wet mixture and, using a spatula, fold them in. When the dry ingredients are almost completely incorporated, add the chopped chocolate and gently fold until all the dry ingredients are combined. Chill the dough for at least 2 hours, up to 48 hours.

Preheat the oven to 375°F. Line two baking sheets with parchment paper and set aside.

Place the desiccated coconut on a plate in an even layer. Roll 1 tablespoon (about 22 g) chilled dough into a ball, roll in the coconut so it is evenly coated, and transfer it to one of the parchment-lined baking sheets. Repeat with the remaining dough, spacing the cookies 1 inch from each other, until one sheet is full.

Bake the cookies one sheet at a time, rotating halfway through until puffed and cooked through, 9 to 12 minutes (if you like a fudgier cookie, bake for 9 minutes; for a cakier cookie, bake for 11 to 12 minutes). While the first batch is baking, roll and coat the remaining cookies. Refrigerate the tray until ready to bake. Let the cookies cool on the tray for 30 minutes before transferring to a wire rack to cool completely. (The chocolate chunks need time to cool so they don't fall apart.) Store in an airtight container for up to 5 days.

RECIPE NOTE: The unbaked cookie dough balls can be frozen after being rolled in the coconut and kept in an airtight container in the freezer for up to 3 months. Bake from frozen, adding a couple minutes to the baking time.

Apricot-Saffron Frangipane Galette

Recipe by Asha Loupy | Serves 8 to 10

On a magical October afternoon, as the final hours of the sunlight trickled through the trees, our Kashmiri Saffron farmer Raqib and his wife, Aaliya, took us to visit the saffron fields that were now speckled with purple flowers ready to be harvested. What caught Asha's eye was the apricot trees growing among the saffron flowers. From that moment, she knew there *must* be a dessert with apricots and saffron in this book.

This galette starts with a buttery crust, which encases a fragrant, saffron-tinged almond frangipane—almonds being another prized crop in Kashmir—and is topped with sweet, jammy apricots. Serve with lightly sweetened whipped cream or vanilla ice cream. It's also pretty damn dreamy with a cup of coffee in the morning!

FOR THE CRUST

1⅔ cups (200 g) all-purpose flour, plus more for rolling

2 tablespoons (24 g) granulated sugar

¾ teaspoon fine sea salt

8 tablespoons (1 stick/113 g) cold unsalted butter, cut into cubes

4 to 5 tablespoons ice water

FOR THE FILLING, FRANGIPANE, AND ASSEMBLY

1½ pounds (680 g) apricots

3 to 4 tablespoons jaggery or light brown sugar

2 tablespoons (16 g) cornstarch

1 tablespoon fresh lemon juice

¾ teaspoon fine sea salt

continues

To make the dough, combine the flour, sugar, and salt in a medium bowl. Cut the cold butter into cubes and add it to the flour mixture. Using your fingers, rub the cubes of butter into the flour until the butter is the size of chickpeas.

Add 4 tablespoons ice water to the flour-butter mixture and gently stir until a very shaggy dough starts to form. (It's okay if it looks dry—it'll come together! But if it's looking too dry, you can add another 1 tablespoon water.) Turn the dough out onto a clean surface, gathering all the shaggy pieces, and press it together with your hands—it will still look dry now—then roll the dough into a long rectangle. Pile any floury bits on top of the dough, then fold the top third of the dough down, followed by the bottom third up. Rotate the dough 90 degrees and then repeat the rolling process until the dough comes together (this will make sure you're not overhydrating the dough, plus it's creating all those layers in the crust!), 3 to 5 times. Form the dough into a disk, wrap in plastic wrap, and roll it over the plastic wrap to create an even thickness. Chill in the refrigerator for at least 1 hour, up to overnight.

Meanwhile, pit and quarter the apricots. Combine the quartered apricots with the jaggery, cornstarch, lemon juice, and ¼ teaspoon of the salt in a large bowl. Using a paring knife, split the vanilla bean in half lengthwise. Using the tip of the knife, scrape out the vanilla beans, add to the apricot mixture, saving the scraped vanilla pod for another

continues

1 vanilla bean

2 pinches (30 to 40 threads) Kashmiri saffron

1½ teaspoons hot water

8 tablespoons (1 stick/113 g) unsalted butter, softened

½ cup (96 g) plus 1 tablespoon granulated sugar

2 large eggs

1 cup (112 g) almond flour

2 tablespoons (15 g) all-purpose flour

⅛ teaspoon almond extract

⅓ cup (30 g) sliced almonds

RECIPE NOTE: Don't skip the almond extract—it really makes a difference, lifting the almond taste, while also complementing the aromatic saffron flavor. If you can't find almond extract, ½ teaspoon vanilla extract will work in a pinch.

use like vanilla sugar or extract, and gently toss to combine. Let the fruit macerate for at least 30 minutes, up to 2 hours.

To make the frangipane, place the saffron in a mortar and grind into a medium-fine powder. Add the hot water, gently swirl, and let steep for 15 minutes.

Combine the softened butter, sugar, and remaining ½ teaspoon salt in the bowl of a stand mixer fitted with the paddle attachment. Beat on medium-high speed until light and fluffy, scraping down the bowl as needed, 2 to 4 minutes. Add 1 egg, the almond flour, all-purpose flour, almond extract, and the steeped saffron water and beat on medium speed until combined, about 1 minute. Scrape down the bowl with a spatula, making sure everything is well combined, transfer to a bowl, and refrigerate the frangipane until using, no more than 30 minutes, otherwise it will become too firm to spread. (If you are making the frangipane in advance, refrigerate until about 30 minutes before using, then let it sit at room temperature to become spreadable again.)

To roll and assemble the galette, place the chilled dough on a lightly floured surface, roll into a 15-inch round (if the dough chilled for more than an hour and starts to crack because it is too cold, let it sit for 5 minutes before rolling), and transfer to a parchment-lined baking sheet. Dollop the frangipane around the center of the dough and spread in a circle, leaving a 2½-inch border all the way around. (The frangipane will puff when baked, so I like to make the layer a little thicker in the center and taper it to a thinner layer on the outer 1 inch.)

Give the apricots a gentle stir, and then, taking one piece of fruit at a time, arrange in concentric circles, cut-side down with the peel facing outward. Drizzle any of the remaining cornstarch-apricot juice mixture over the top. Working around the edges, fold the dough up over the apricots and frangipane, pleating as needed. Transfer the pan to the freezer and chill for 15 to 20 minutes.

While the galette is chilling, preheat the oven to 400°F.

Whisk together the remaining 1 egg in a small bowl until smooth. Remove the chilled galette from the freezer, brush the dough liberally with egg wash, and sprinkle with the sliced almonds and the remaining 1 tablespoon sugar. Bake until the crust is deep golden and the frangipane is puffed and starting to brown on top in spots, 45 to 52 minutes. Allow to cool for 15 minutes before serving. Serve warm or at room temperature on its own, or with a dollop of lightly sweetened whipped cream or a scoop of vanilla ice cream.

Spiced Date Cake with Coconut Caramel

Recipe by Asha Loupy | Serves 8 to 10

I've talked about Perera & Sons before (see Sri Lankan Fish Puffs, page 61), the iconic bakery chain that has been churning out nostalgic treats for the island since 1902. This dessert is inspired by a spiced date muffin that was on the P&S menu that was warm and cozy without being too sweet.

Our take is a deeply spiced loaf cake, chock-full of cinnamon, nutmeg, cloves, molasses, and chopped Medjool dates. To top everything off, it's drizzled with the most luscious coconut caramel, which is so good I asked Asha to double the amount so there's plenty for both glazing the cake and pouring over every bite. And, if you have extra coconut caramel left, it makes a damn good addition to your morning latte, too. This cake is great on its own with a cup of coffee or Jaggery Chai (page 213), or zhuzh it up with big dollops of lightly sweetened whipped cream or scoops of vanilla ice cream.

FOR THE CAKE

- ¼ cup (30 g) plus 1¾ cups (210 g) all-purpose flour
- 8 to 10 (155 g) Medjool dates, pitted
- 1½ teaspoons baking powder
- ½ teaspoon baking soda
- 2 teaspoons ground cinnamon
- 1 teaspoon freshly grated nutmeg
- ¼ teaspoon ground cloves
- ¾ cup (180 ml) buttermilk
- 2 tablespoons molasses
- 1 teaspoon vanilla extract
- 8 tablespoons (1 stick/113 g) unsalted butter, softened
- ½ cup (96 g) granulated sugar

continues

Preheat the oven to 375°F. Cut a piece of parchment paper the width of a 9-inch loaf pan and line the pan with the parchment so there is at least 2 inches of overhang on each side (this will make it easier to lift the cake out of the pan once it's baked), and set aside.

To prepare the dates, place ¼ cup (30 g) of the flour in a medium bowl. Tear each date in half, then, taking one half at a time, cut it into ¼-inch strips lengthwise and then cut crosswise in ¼-inch cubes (they should be about the size of a chocolate chip). Transfer the diced dates into the bowl of flour and toss with the flour so each piece is coated (doing this gradually will help prevent them from creating one big sticky clump). Repeat with the remaining dates, making sure to toss the chopped dates in the flour after each addition. Set aside.

To make the cake batter, combine the remaining 1¾ cups (210 g) flour, the baking powder, baking soda, cinnamon, nutmeg, and cloves in a bowl, whisk to mix well, and set aside.

Measure the buttermilk into a 2- to 4-cup (480 to 960 ml) glass measuring cup, then add the molasses and vanilla and whisk until smooth. Set aside.

Combine the softened butter, granulated sugar, brown sugar, and salt in the bowl of a stand mixer. Whip on medium-high speed until light and fluffy, scraping halfway through, 2 to 4 minutes. Add the eggs,

continues

½ cup (96 g) lightly packed light or dark brown sugar

1 teaspoon fine sea salt

2 large eggs, at room temperature

2 tablespoons virgin coconut oil, melted

FOR THE CARAMEL

1½ cups (288 g) granulated sugar

1 cup (240 ml) coconut cream

2 tablespoons unsalted butter

1 teaspoon vanilla extract

½ teaspoon fine sea salt

Flaky sea salt, optional

one at a time, beating on medium-high until each is incorporated and scraping down the bowl between each one.

Add a third of the dry ingredients and mix on medium-low speed until just incorporated, then add half the wet ingredients and mix until well combined, followed by a third of the dry ingredients and the last half of the wet ingredients and the coconut oil, mixing to incorporate between each addition (don't worry if it looks a little curdled). After mixing in the last of the wet ingredients, remove the bowl from the mixer, add the last third of the dry ingredients and the floured chopped dates, including any excess flour with the dates, and, using a spatula, fold in until all the dry ingredients are incorporated. Transfer the batter to the prepared loaf pan, spreading the top into an even layer. Bake until deep golden on top and a toothpick comes out clean when inserted into the center of the cake, 55 to 65 minutes.

While the cake is baking, make the caramel. Combine the granulated sugar and ⅓ cup (70 ml) water in a medium saucepan and place over medium heat. Heat, undisturbed, until the sugar is fully melted, 4 to 5 minutes. Continue to cook, gently swirling the pan every so often, until the sugar starts to caramelize and turns a deep amber color, 6 to 9 minutes.

Add the coconut cream—be careful, this will bubble and seize, but don't worry!—and continue to cook, stirring constantly, until the sugar dissolves again, 1 to 2 minutes. Turn off the heat, add the butter, vanilla, and sea salt, and stir until the butter has melted and is fully incorporated into the sauce. Transfer to a container and refrigerate until completely chilled.

Remove the cake from the oven and let cool in the pan for 30 minutes. Carefully lift the cake out of the pan using the parchment, transfer to a wire rack, and let cool to room temperature. To finish, give the chilled caramel a stir and spoon half of it over the center of the cake, letting it drip down the sides of the cake. Garnish with a sprinkle of flaky sea salt, if desired.

To serve, slice with a serrated knife and serve with the rest of the coconut caramel on the side for drizzling on at the table. Top with lightly sweetened whipped cream or vanilla ice cream, if desired, or serve with a piping hot cup of Jaggery Chai (page 213).

Puran Poli
Jaggery and Lentil-Filled Flatbread

Recipe by Poonam Swapnil Shelke | Origin: Daund, Maharashtra | Makes 6

A delicacy in Maharashtra, where some of the most delicious indigenous varieties of purple sugarcane are grown, puran poli is a wheat roti that is stuffed with a jaggery-sweetened chana dal mixture. Puran poli is quintessential celebratory food for jaggery farmers and other locals alike and is made for just about every auspicious day. I honestly can't think of a sweet treat that better represents the cultural context and deliciousness of jaggery better than this one! Poonam is our jaggery sourcing partner's wife, and we were lucky to stop by her house for a sweet, filling breakfast before a long day in the fields for the sugarcane harvest.

My perfect puran poli is heavy on the jaggery—giving all those molten, sumptuous caramel, maple-y feels—with a generous amount of filling tucked between crisp whole wheat layers, and finished with a slick of ghee. Green cardamom is a classic flavoring, but on our farm partner's jaggery farm they added a touch of ground ginger, which was absolutely revolutionary, bringing a bit of extra spicy warmth and sweetness to the lentil-based filling. Serve these with a cup of Jaggery Chai (page 213) or Fenugreek Milk "Coffee" (page 216). See photo on page 229.

FOR THE FILLING

¾ cup (143 g) chana dal, rinsed

6 pods green cardamom or ¼ teaspoon ground green cardamom

1½ cups (288 g) powdered jaggery

½ teaspoon ground ginger

⅛ teaspoon fine sea salt

For the filling, place the chana dal in a bowl and rinse with cold water, swishing it around with your fingers, and rinsing several times until the water runs clear. Drain and transfer the lentils to an electric pressure cooker (like an Instant Pot) and add 3 cups (710 ml) water. Cook on high pressure for 22 minutes, then allow to naturally release for 15 minutes.

Meanwhile, if using whole cardamom, place the cardamom pods in a mortar and gently pound to release the seeds. Discard the husks and pound the seeds into a fine powder. Set aside.

Release the pressure on the pressure cooker, place a fine-mesh sieve over a large bowl, and drain the cooked lentils, catching their cooking liquid in the bowl. Transfer the cooked lentils to a medium saucepan and add the jaggery, ground ginger, salt, and the reserved ground cardamom. Mash with a potato masher or the back of a soft spatula to break up all the lentils, and then stir in ¾ cup (180 ml) of the lentil cooking liquid.

Place over medium-high and bring to a boil, stirring occasionally. Cook, stirring frequently and continuing to mash with the back of a spatula, until most of the liquid evaporates and the mixture pulls away

FOR THE DOUGH AND ASSEMBLY

2 cups (240 g) atta flour, plus more for dusting

½ teaspoon fine sea salt

1 tablespoon ghee, softened

½ cup plus 4 tablespoons (177 ml) room temperature water

Neutral oil, such as canola, for cooking

Melted ghee, for cooking and finishing

from the sides of the pan and leaves a thin film, 16 to 22 minutes. Transfer the sweetened mashed lentils to a bowl and cool completely, at least 1 hour, up to 4 hours. (The mixture will continue to thicken and should resemble the consistency of mashed potatoes, which will make it easier to fill and roll.)

While the filling is cooling, make the dough. Combine the atta flour and salt in a large bowl and mix well. Add the softened ghee and rub it into the flour with your fingertips until incorporated and the mixture looks like fine sand. Add ½ cup (120 ml) of the room temperature water and mix with your hands until a soft dough forms, adding 1 tablespoon of water at a time until you get the right consistency (you might not need all 4 remaining tablespoons of water). Give the dough a few kneads in the bowl, then wrap the dough in plastic wrap and let rest at room temperature for at least 45 minutes, up to 4 hours.

To fill, divide the dough into six equal pieces. Take one piece at a time, keeping the rest covered so they don't dry out, roll it into a ball, then press it out into a 4½-inch round with the outer ½ inch a little thinner than the center. Take 3 tablespoons of the filling, roll it into a ball, place it in the center of the dough round, bring the edges tightly around the filling ball, and pinch the dough together at the top so it's fully enclosed. Repeat with the remaining dough and filling, keeping the filled rounds covered as you go.

To form, take one filled dough ball, place it on a lightly floured surface, gently press down to create a thick disk, and turn in the flour so both sides are coated. Using the palm of your hand, gently press down, working in circular motions around the dough and flouring as needed, until you have a thin 6-inch disk. You should be able to see the filling through the dough in spots. (Alternatively, you can use a rolling pin, but using your hands helps prevent the dough from sticking or ripping, keeping all that filling inside.)

To cook, heat a medium skillet over medium heat. Brush with a thin layer of neutral oil, heat for 15 seconds, and then place the formed puran poli on the pan. Cook until opaque and starting to lightly brown in spots, 1 to 2 minutes. Flip, and cook on the other side, 45 seconds to 1½ minutes. Brush the top parcooked side with a thin layer of melted ghee, flip, and cook until it is starting to crisp and is dappled with brown spots, about 30 seconds. Brush the top with ghee, flip, and cook on the other side, 15 to 30 seconds. Transfer to a plate.

While the first puran poli is cooking, press out the next one, and repeat the cooking process with the rest of the filled dough balls.

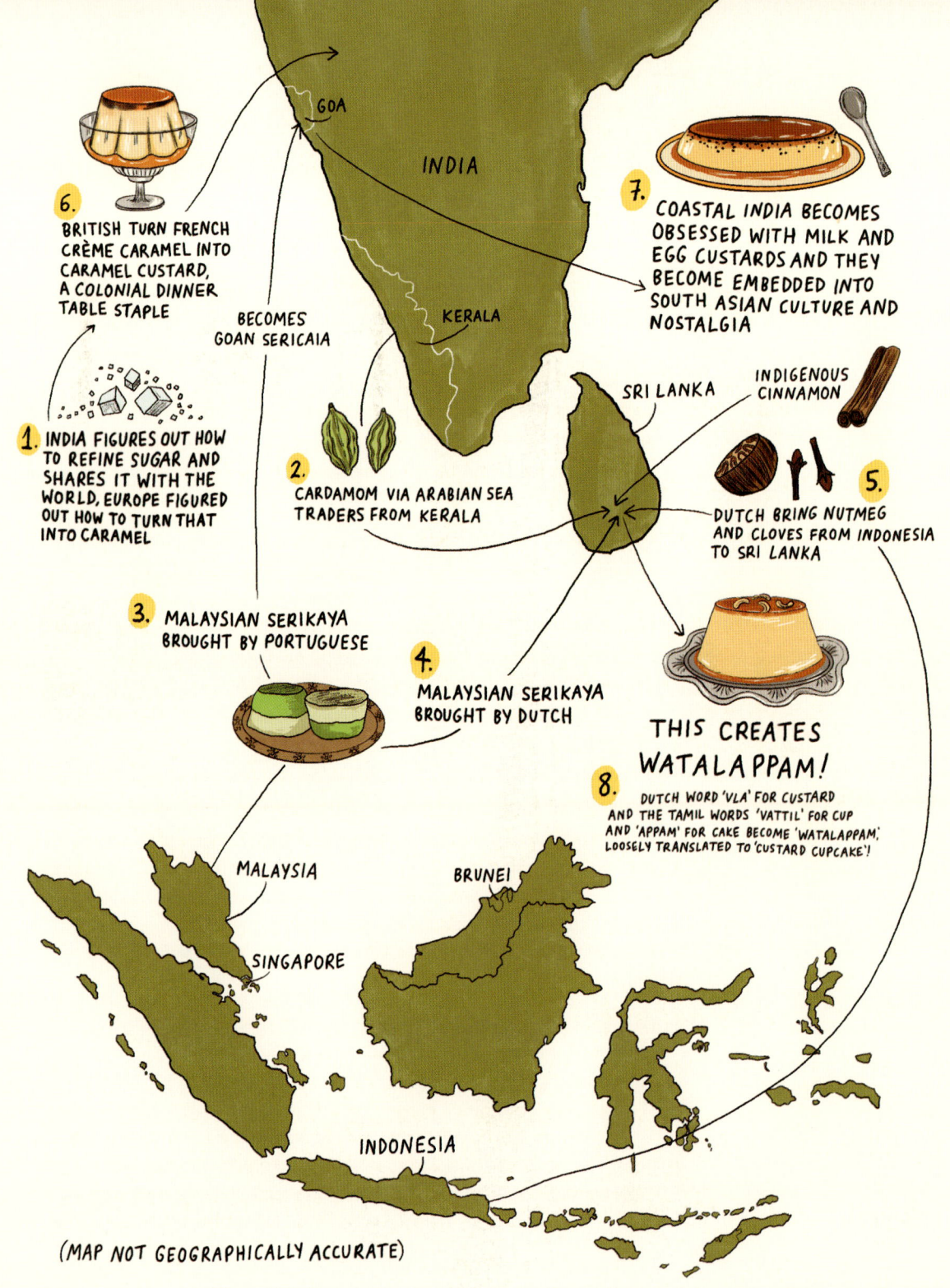

One Dessert, Global Spice Trade

WATALAPPAM-ISH CRÈME CARAMEL, page 244

Watalappam-ish Crème Caramel
Sri Lankan Spiced Caramelized Custard

Recipe by Asha Loupy | Origin: Colombo, Sri Lanka | Serves 6 to 8

At a roadside lunch on the way to Kandy, where our cinnamon and clove farm partners are, I ate a 140 rupee (48¢) packaged watalappam—a super eggy, coconut milk–based custard flavored with green cardamom, nutmeg, and kithul (Sri Lankan jaggery)—and I couldn't stop thinking about it. Every stop we made, I had to have one! Luckily, as always, Asha couldn't stop thinking about it either.

After we left Sri Lanka and traveled to more of our farm partners across the west coast of India, many of them would bring out a crème caramel or caramel custard at the end of a meal—each rich, jiggly, lush, and drenched in a caramelized sugar sauce. So, we combined the flavors of watalappam with a larger format crème caramel into a show-stopping dessert that is sure to wow. It's topped with cashews and shaved coconut that have been toasted in coconut oil, providing a crunchy textural foil to the silken custard.

FOR THE CRÈME CARAMEL

2½ cups (590 ml) whole milk

One 14-ounce (398 ml) can full-fat coconut milk

1 cup (192 g) powdered jaggery or light brown sugar

2 teaspoons freshly grated nutmeg

One 4-inch cinnamon stick, broken into pieces

10 green cardamom pods, lightly crushed

8 whole cloves

½ teaspoon fine sea salt

¾ cup (144 g) granulated sugar

5 large eggs

5 large egg yolks

To make the base, combine the whole milk, coconut milk, jaggery, nutmeg, cinnamon stick, cardamom, cloves, and salt in a medium saucepan. Place over medium heat and bring to a gentle boil, stirring occasionally. Turn off the heat, cover, and let steep for at least 1 hour, up to 3 hours, at room temperature.

To make the caramel, combine the granulated sugar and 2 tablespoons water in a small saucepan over medium heat. Cook, undisturbed, until the sugar has dissolved, 3 to 5 minutes. Continue to cook, gently swirling the pan occasionally, until the sugar caramelizes and turns amber, but not burnt caramel territory, 3 to 6 minutes more. Carefully pour into a 9-inch round baking pan and gently tilt the pan so the caramelized sugar coats the bottom of the pan evenly. Allow to cool completely.

Preheat the oven to 300°F. Fill a roasting pan big enough to hold a 9-inch cake pan with 1 inch of water and place in the oven while it is preheating. (Make sure the water is hot before adding the sealed watalappam to the water bath.)

Return the steeped milk mixture to medium heat and bring back to a simmer. Whisk the eggs and egg yolks in a large bowl until smooth. While continuing to whisk, slowly pour the hot milk mixture into the

FOR THE TOPPING

1 tablespoon virgin coconut oil

⅓ cup (40 g) raw cashews

½ cup (48 g) shaved, dried, unsweetened coconut strips

⅛ teaspoon fine sea salt

eggs in a slow, steady stream until fully incorporated. Strain the egg-milk mixture through a fine-mesh sieve into the prepared cake pan. Seal tightly with aluminum foil.

Carefully place the sealed cake pan in the water bath and bake until the center of the crème caramel is just set but still jiggly, 40 to 50 minutes. Remove the water bath with the crème caramel in it and allow to cool in the hot water for 30 minutes. Remove from the water bath, transfer to the refrigerator, and cool completely, at least 4 hours, up to overnight.

To make the topping, heat the coconut oil in a small skillet over medium heat. When melted, add the cashews, stirring to coat the nuts in the oil. Cook, stirring occasionally, until the cashews start to turn light golden in spots, 2 to 4 minutes. Add the coconut strips and salt and continue to cook until the cashews are golden and the coconut strips start to toast and turn brown around the edges, 1 to 3 minutes more. Transfer to a shallow bowl and let cool completely.

To serve, run a paring knife around the edge of the cooled crème caramel, then place a lipped serving plate over the pan. Muster your confidence, hold the plate tightly against the pan, and flip so the plate is on the bottom. Gently tap the pan to release the custard and then remove the pan. Garnish with cooled toasted cashews and coconut and serve immediately.

Acknowledgments

Sana

The biggest thank-you will always be to my parents, Rahul and Shimul Javeri Kadri—I am grateful every day to be yours. Neither Diaspora Spice Co. nor this story would exist without your relentless belief in your baby hunterwali and your support of my wildest dreams every step of the way. Thank you for the tofu sandwiches, for the commitment to being a feminist family despite our patriarchal surroundings, and for letting me go away when it was most scary—that trust changed my life.

To my nani, for teaching me to read and write so early that my teachers (very, very briefly) thought I was a prodigy. All the best childhood memories involve being curled up with a book at Nani's house.

To my abbu, whose library was my after-school sanctuary and whose love for and patronage of South Asian literature, art, and culture I'm so proud to have inherited and am committed to always carrying forward.

To my baby brother, Aman, who taught me to be tolerant of his very loud breathing, and always picks up his frantic, frazzled big sister's calls. Forever my favorite roommate and traveling bud.

To Chase, who I fell in love with midway through this process. I can't believe we get to build the most tender, queer family of our dreams together. To my stepdaughters, Ella and Lucy, who I met just days before this manuscript was due. I spent many nights (very slowly) editing this cookbook while Daddy bathed and sang y'all to sleep. It took me a full seventy-two hours to fall in love with your dad, but I can safely say that I've loved you both from the very first day we met and am so honored to be your bonus parent and private chef.

To Prabhu and the entire Kasaraneni family, for believing in the twenty-three-year-old girl in the orange jumpsuit who showed up at your doorstep. For working so hard to share your beautiful Pragati Turmeric with the world. I could never have done this without your family's trust and relentless commitment to excellence.

To our 140-plus regenerative spice farm partners whose labor, resilience, and precious harvests are the center of everything we do. To the nearly forty women who welcomed us into their homes, showed us the warmth of South Asian hospitality, and ultimately make up the heart of this book.

To Sayed, our operations manager extraordinaire, without whom I never could've exported that first shipment of turmeric, nor this latest one. Thank you for taking the chance to build this with me.

To Wynne, the organized, hella on-top-of-it-all, highly meticulous powerhouse COO to my constant creative chaos CEO. Without your leadership, the space and resources for this book simply would not have been possible and I am so, so grateful.

To Will, for being my first business coach when I was a wee budding entrepreneur to becoming Diaspora's absolutely favorite board member—we are so lucky to have your steady, firm counsel as we grow this biz.

To Saqib, Norma, and Stephen, this journey of building businesses with our values and hearts on our sleeves would have been so much more difficult and lonelier without each other. Growing into our best selves and growing our companies alongside each other has been such a gift. Thank you for holding me accountable, picking up every WhatsApp call, and always sharing the good goss.

To my UWCAd community, I came to Duino as a broken, very sad little girl and I left brimming with a hope and an idealism that guides me every single day. I will never take for granted the transformative power of a UWC education.

To Pooja, my most serendipitous hire and Diaspora's best ambassador. Having your Swiss Army knife of nerdy, punny brilliance in our corner has been the best darn thing.

To Eve, for three formative, tremendous years of growing together. For taking such tender, radical care of me and of the heart of this biz.

To Nina, who joined us the week we began eighty-four days of travel (very much in the deep end!) and has kept me and this wild undertaking of a book afloat in more ways than one ever since.

To my eleventh-hour editors, Wynne, Pooja, Arundhati, Aileen, Neha, and Aria. Thank you for your time, narrative muscle, and willingness to overlook my grammar for the bigger picture.

To the legendary cookbook authors who came before us for taking the time to give me pep talks, being candid about money, and responding to all my earnest, urgent email summons—Priya, Samin, Sonoko, Hetty, Nik, Padma, Shamil, and Yasmin.

To our beloved Diaspora team past and present—Namita, Swasti, Kumud, Shrishti, Riya, Saachi, Ajit, Rahul, Kartik, Dena, Mike, Jon, Bobby, Dani, Kristen, Shruti, Prajakta, Neha, Amaya, Lianne, Kinshuk, Miriam, Aashna, Helena, Reeshna, Saachi, Riya, Nicole, Blake, Emel, David, and Paola—we are so much better for each of your contributions. Thank you, thank you!

To Shilpa and Sonia at Breakaway Travels, for getting the three of us across the length and breadth of India and Sri Lanka over eighty-four days!

To Shubhra, for the invaluable and tremendous dossiers of research and historical context that allowed us to write this book from a highly informed point of view, rather than a remotely half-baked one.

To Jillian and Cyn, ten days on set were made far more beautiful, more delicious, and a lot more humorous with your talent and energy in our corner.

To Michele, for believing in this book back when it was just a kernel of an idea and sticking with us for the five long years it took to bring it to life!

To Sarah, for editing this book down to its most accessible, relevant self and patiently getting us to the finish line!

To Kinshuk, for making this book as beautiful as possible, despite the wild process. Your talent and ambition burn so bright, we're lucky to have you!

And finally, to Asha and Melati! I greatly underestimated the amount of work this would be, the sheer intensity of what we were setting out to do, and just how tough it would be to do it right. Y'all rose to the task on every occasion. I'm so grateful that if this is my first and last cookbook, I got to do it with absolute pros like y'all for whom this is absolutely just the beginning!

Asha

First and foremost, thank you to my mom, Chris Loupy. I wouldn't be here without your constant support throughout my life—which you did as a single parent!—from getting up early on Saturday mornings to help me write down recipes from PBS cooking shows and driving me to cooking classes at California Culinary Academy when I was twelve to cheerleading me when I quit my full-time job to go freelance and always being the first one to cook my recipes. There are no words in the human language that encapsulate how much I love you.

To Summer, Daryah, Eve, Parisa, and Wendy, the bestest friends and hype people a girl could ask for—thank you for constantly rooting for me and keeping me running toward that ever-moving finish line.

To Megan, Christine, Sonni, Monika, Jessie, Sara, and Jaimie. You women inspire me every day—I am so happy to call you my soulmates. And, of course, to Abba. Best friend doesn't describe how much I love you—and, also, thank you for always letting me take over the fridge and kitchen!

All my gratitude and love to those who provided community, support, laughter, and levity during this entire cookbook journey—sometimes from half a world away!—Kumud, Aleesha, Pooja, Dena, Nathaniel, and Isaac.

To Melati, the most amazing travel buddy (eighty-four days, baby!), friend, photographer, and lighting wizard. And a huge thank-you to our studio shoot team: Jillian, Cyn, and Nina. Y'all are magic.

To Sana, it was such a joy to write this book with you. Thank you for taking a chance on me back in 2020. It's been a pleasure to grow alongside Diaspora Spice Co. and get to go on this wild adventure with you—from being hunched over your dining room table mapping out our proposal during the pandemic, boarding more than eighteen flights over three months, and you carrying my backpack when I hurt my wrist during our trip to laughing over crispy dosas, taste testing rajma after rajma after rajma, and getting giddy when we hit that perfect final recipe time and time again. I am so proud of what we made together.

And, finally, thank you to all the women across ten states and two countries who welcomed us into their kitchens and taught us with kindness and patience. Those home-cooked meals will be some of the most delicious, special meals of my lifetime.

Melati

Thank you to the many families who shared their time, wisdom, and kitchens so generously, without pause. Thank you to the Diaspora team for trusting me. Thank you to Peter for embracing the many ways this book changed me. Thank you to the land for continuing to love us despite it all.

Universal Conversion Chart

Oven Temperature Equivalents

250°F = 120°C
275°F = 135°C
300°F = 150°C
325°F = 160°C
350°F = 180°C
375°F = 190°C
400°F = 200°C
425°F = 220°C
450°F = 230°C
475°F = 240°C
500°F = 260°C

Measurement Equivalents

Measurements should always be level unless directed otherwise.

⅛ teaspoon = 0.5 mL
¼ teaspoon = 1 mL
½ teaspoon = 2 mL
1 teaspoon = 5 mL
1 tablespoon = 3 teaspoons = ½ fluid ounce = 15 mL
2 tablespoons = ⅛ cup = 1 fluid ounce = 30 mL
4 tablespoons = ¼ cup = 2 fluid ounces = 60 mL
5⅓ tablespoons = ⅓ cup = 3 fluid ounces = 80 mL
8 tablespoons = ½ cup = 4 fluid ounces = 120 mL
10⅔ tablespoons = ⅔ cup = 5 fluid ounces = 160 mL
12 tablespoons = ¾ cup = 6 fluid ounces = 180 mL
16 tablespoons = 1 cup = 8 fluid ounces = 240 mL

Index

NOTE: Page references in *italics* refer to photos of recipes.

A

Aab Gosht (Kashmiri Milk-Braised Lamb Shanks), *164*, 165
Aloo Masala (Spiced Potatoes), 105
amchur, 12
Andhra Chilli Powder, 23, *24*
apricot
    Apricot-Saffron Frangipane Galette, 234–236, *235*
    Apricot-Tamarind Shrub, 226
    Hyun Mezcalita (Tangy Apricot Mezcalita), 225–226, *227*
Aranya peppercorns, 188–189
asafetida, 5
Asparagus with Pisyun Loon, Blistered, 76, *77*

B

Bajra Na Rotla (Pearl Millet Flatbread), 204
banana and banana leaves
    Meen Pollichathu (Kerala-Style Tangy Grilled Fish in Banana Leaves), 140–141, *142*
    Turmeric-Banana Snacking Cake, 230, *231*
basmati rice, 18
beans and lentils, 107–129. *See also* lentils
    Chaaru (Andhra-Style Spicy Lentil Soup), *111*, 112–113
    dal (lentils, pulses, and beans), about, 15–18
    Fava Bean Chutney, 46, *47*
    Gongura Pappu (Andhra-Style Dal with Sorrel), 108–109, *110*
    Kadhi (Yogurt and Turmeric Soup), *122*, 123
    Pahadi Rajma (Himalayan Brothy Kidney Beans), 124–125, *125*
    Parippu Curry (Sri Lankan Lentils with Coconut and Lemongrass), *117*, 118–119
    Rajasthani Dal, 120–121, *121*
    Seasonal Sambar (South Indian Lentil Soup), 114–115, *116*
Bhindi Masala (Stir-Fried Spiced Okra), 88, *89*
Bitter Melon and Heirloom Tomato Salad, 74, *75*
black pepper, 1, 188–189. *See also* chillies and peppers
Blistered Asparagus with Pisyun Loon, 76, *77*
Burst Tomato Chutney, *47*, 48
byadgi chilli powder, 7

C

Cabbage Salad, Manipuri (Singju), 80, *81*
cacao, 190–191
Cake, Spiced Date, with Coconut Caramel, 237–239, *238*
Cake, Turmeric-Banana Snacking, 230, *231*
cardamom, 1, 128–129
Carrots, Spiced Maple-Roasted, with Carrot Top Sambol, 92, *93*
Carrot Top Sambol, *40*, 41
Cassava, Kerala-Style Mashed (Kappa Puzhukku), *205*, 205–206, *207*
Chaaru (Andhra-Style Spicy Lentil Soup), *111*, 112–113
chai
    Jaggery Chai, 213, *215*
    Kadak Masala Chai, *211*, 212–213
    Noon Chai Concentrate, 214
    Noon Chai (Kashmiri Savory Green Milk Tea), 214, *215*
chana dal, 15
Chicken and Rice, Sirārakhong Hāthei Chilli–Lemongrass, 158–161, *159–161*
Chicken Curry, Country, 150–151, *152*
chillies and peppers
    about, 7–10 (*see also* pepper(s); *individual names of chillies*)
    Andhra Chilli Powder, 23, *24*
    Hoksa (Sirārakhong Hāthei Chilli–Braised Pork), 162, *163*
    Kanthari Chilli Squid (Kerala-Style Squid with Bird's-Eye Chillies, Cilantro, and Curry Leaves), 146–147, *147*
    Karam Podi, aka Gunpowder Podi (Chilli Coconut Spice Blend), *25*, 26
    Lahsun Mirchi Chutney (Rajasthani Garlic-Chilli Chutney), 42, *43*
    Pepper Pork, *153*, 154–155
    Sirārakhong Hāthei Chilli–Lemongrass Chicken and Rice, 158–161, *159–161*
Chocolate-Coconut Cookies, Spiced, *232*, 233
chutneys and pickles, 35–55
    Burst Tomato Chutney, *47*, 48
    Carrot Top Sambol, *40*, 41

chutneys and pickles (*cont.*)
  Fava Bean Chutney, 46, *47*
  Green Chutney, 36–38, *37*
  Lahsun Mirchi Chutney (Rajasthani Garlic-Chilli Chutney), 42, *43*
  Palli Chutney (Peanut Chutney), *44,* 45
  Pol Sambol (Sri Lankan Coconut and Shallot Chutney), 39, *40*
  Tomato Pachadi (Andhra-Style Tomato Pickle), 50, *51*
  Vengaya Thayir Pachadi (Red Onion Raita), 49, *49*
cilantro, 13
cinnamon, 3, 32–33
cloves, whole, 3
coconut
  about coconut oil, 6
  about fresh, dried, milk, cream, 12
  Coconut Lamb Biryani, 185–186, *186*
  Karam Podi, aka Gunpowder Podi (Chilli Coconut Spice Blend), *25,* 26
  Kashmiri Pulao (Basmati Rice Pilaf with Nuts, Raisins, and Coconut), 178, *179*
  Meen Moilee (Kerala-Style Coconut Turmeric Fish Curry), 138, *139*
  Parippu Curry (Sri Lankan Lentils with Coconut and Lemongrass), *117,* 118–119
  Pipinna Kiri Hodi (Sri Lankan Cucumber Coconut Milk Curry), *90,* 91
  Pol Roti (Sri Lankan Coconut Flatbread), 203
  Pol Sambol (Sri Lankan Coconut and Shallot Chutney), 39, *40*
  Spiced Chocolate-Coconut Cookies, *232,* 233
  Spiced Date Cake with Coconut Caramel, 237–239, *238*
  Thenga Aracha Meen Curry (Kerala-Style Fish and Fresh Coconut Curry), 144–145
Cookies, Spiced Chocolate-Coconut, *232,* 233
coriander seeds, 1, 55
Country Chicken Curry, 150–151, *152*
Crab Curry, Jaffna-Style (Kakuluwo Curry), 132–133, *133*
Crepes, Fermented Rice and Lentil (Ghee Roast Dosa), 192–197, *193, 197*
Cucumber Coconut Milk Curry, Sri Lankan (Pipinna Kiri Hodi), *90,* 91
culantro, 13
cumin seeds, 1, 84–85
curry dishes
  Country Chicken Curry, 150–151, *152*

  Jammy Egg Curry, 156, *157*
  Kakuluwo Curry (Jaffna-Style Crab Curry), 132–133, *133*
  Meen Moilee (Kerala-Style Coconut Turmeric Fish Curry), 138, *139*
  Nadru Yakhni (Kashmiri Lotus Root Yogurt Curry), 102–104, *103*
  Parippu Curry (Sri Lankan Lentils with Coconut and Lemongrass), *117,* 118–119
  Pazha Manga Curry (Kerala-Style Ripe Mango Curry), 94–95, *95*
  Pipinna Kiri Hodi (Sri Lankan Cucumber Coconut Milk Curry), *90,* 91
  Thenga Aracha Meen Curry (Kerala-Style Fish and Fresh Coconut Curry), 144–145
curry leaves
  curry leaves, 13
  in Kanthari Chilli Squid (Kerala-Style Squid with Bird's-Eye Chillies, Cilantro, and Curry Leaves), 146–147, *147*
  Karivepaku Podi (Curry Leaf Spice Blend), *25,* 27
Curry Powder, Sri Lankan Roasted (Kalu Kudu), 22, 24
Custard, Sri Lankan Spiced Caramelized (Watalappam-ish Crème Caramel), *243,* 244–245

D
Daikon and Orange Salad with Sesame-Cumin Dressing, 78–79, *79*
dal. *See also* beans and lentils
  Gongura Pappu (Andhra-Style Dal with Sorrel), 108–109, *110*
  lentils, pulses, and beans, 15–18
  Rajasthani Dal, 120–121, *121*
desserts, 229–245
  Apricot-Saffron Frangipane Galette, 234–236, *235*
  Puran Poli (Jaggery and Lentil-Filled Flatbread), 240–241
  Spiced Chocolate-Coconut Cookies, *232,* 233
  Spiced Date Cake with Coconut Caramel, 237–239, *238*
  Turmeric-Banana Snacking Cake, 230, *231*
  Watalappam-ish Crème Caramel (Sri Lankan Spiced Caramelized Custard), *243,* 244–245
Diaspora Spice Co.
  Bishnoi family and, 84–85, *85*
  Chacko family and, *128,* 128–129
  Eko Land Community and, *32,* 32–33, *33*
  ethical business model of, viii–x
  Green Heirloom community and, *126,* 126–127, *127*

252   **Index**

harvest season and, vii–viii
Hill Wild Community and, *70,* 70–71
Kasaraneni family and, *30,* 30–31, *31*
Meiyappan family and, *190,* 190–191, *191*
Mir family and, *86,* 86–87, *87*
Narne family and, *52,* 53
Parameswaran family and, 188, *188*
Sakariya family and, *54,* 55
timeline of, xi–xiii
Dip, Roasted Squash and Labneh (Doud Alle Dip), *58,* 59–60
Dosa, Ghee Roast (Fermented Rice and Lentil Crepes), 192–197, *193, 197*
Doud Alle Dip (Roasted Squash and Labneh Dip), *58,* 59–60
drinks, 209–227
    chai, about, 210
    Fennel Soda, 220, *223*
    Fennel Tom Collins, 221, *223*
    Haldi Doodh (Golden Turmeric Milk), 219, *222*
    Heimang Soda (Manipuri Sumac Soda), 224
    Hyun Mezcalita (Tangy Apricot Mezcalita), 225–226, *227*
    Jaggery Chai, 213
    Kadak Masala Chai, *211,* 212–213
    Kehwa (Kashmiri Spiced Saffron Tea), 218, *222*
    Methi Latte (Fenugreek Milk "Coffee"), 216, *217*
    Noon Chai (Kashmiri Savory Green Milk Tea), 214, *215*

E

Edamame and Cherry Tomato Salad, *82,* 83
Egg Curry, Jammy, 156, *157*
Eggplant, Gujarati Charred (Ringan no Oro), 96–98, *97*
extra virgin olive oil, 6

F

fats, 6, 14
Fava Bean Chutney, 46, *47*
fennel
    about fennel seeds, 1, 55
    Fennel Shrub, 220
    Fennel Soda, 220, *223*
    Fennel Tom Collins, 221, *223*
fenugreek leaves, dried, 15
Fenugreek Milk "Coffee" (Methi Latte), 216, *217*
fenugreek seeds, 5
fish, salted, 10
fish dishes. *See* seafood

flatbread
    Bajra Na Rotla (Pearl Millet Flatbread), 204
    Pol Roti (Sri Lankan Coconut Flatbread), 203
    Puran Poli (Jaggery and Lentil-Filled Flatbread), 240–241
Fritters, Mixed Herb and Onion (Sakariya Fam Pakora), 66
fruit. *See individual names of fruit*

G

Galette, Apricot-Saffron Frangipane, 234–236, *235*
ghee, 6
Ghee Roast Dosa (Fermented Rice and Lentil Crepes), 192–197, *193, 197*
Ghee-Roasted Lamb Ribs, Kashmiri (Tabak Maaz), 168, *169*
Gongura Pappu (Andhra-Style Dal with Sorrel), 108–109, *110*
Green Chutney, 36–38
    Gujarati Green Chutney, *37,* 38
    Rajasthani Green Chutney, 36, *37*
Greens, Kashmiri Braised (Haakh), 99–101, *100*
Guntur Sannam chillies, 7, 53

H

Haakh (Kashmiri Braised Greens), 99–101, *100*
Haldi Doodh (Golden Turmeric Milk), 219, *222*
hands, eating with, 17
Heimang Concentrate, 224
Heimang Soda (Manipuri Sumac Soda), 224
herbs and aromatics, about, 13–15. *See also* curry leaves
Hoksa (Sirārakhong Hāthei Chilli–Braised Pork), 162, *163*
Hyun Mezcalita (Tangy Apricot Mezcalita), 225–226, *227*

I

idli rice, about, 18
Idli (Steamed Lentil and Rice Cakes), 195–197, *196, 197*

J

jaggery
    about, 12–13
    Jaggery and Lentil-Filled Flatbread (Puran Poli), 240–241
    Jaggery Chai, 213

Jammy Egg Curry, 156, *157*
jeera samba rice, 18

K

Kadak Masala Chai, *211,* 212–213
Kadhi (Yogurt and Turmeric Soup), *122,* 123
Kakuluwo Curry (Jaffna-Style Crab Curry), 132–133, *133*
Kalu Kudu (Sri Lankan Roasted Curry Powder), 22, 24
Kanthari Chilli Squid (Kerala-Style Squid with Bird's-Eye Chillies, Cilantro, and Curry Leaves), 146–147, *147*
Kappa Puzhukku (Kerala-Style Mashed Cassava), *205,* 205–206, *207*
Karam Podi, aka Gunpowder Podi (Chilli Coconut Spice Blend), *25,* 26
Karivepaku Podi (Curry Leaf Spice Blend), *25,* 27
Kashmiri Pulao (Basmati Rice Pilaf with Nuts, Raisins, and Coconut), 178, *179*
Kehwa (Kashmiri Spiced Saffron Tea), 218, *222*
Kerala-Style Grilled Prawns, 134, *135*
Khichdi (Rice and Lentil Porridge), 187
kokum, 12

L

Labneh Dip, Roasted Squash and (Doud Alle Dip), *58,* 59–60
Lahsun Mirchi Chutney (Rajasthani Garlic-Chilli Chutney), 42, *43*
lamb
    Aab Gosht (Kashmiri Milk-Braised Lamb Shanks), *164,* 165
    Coconut Lamb Biryani, 185–186, *186*
    Maaz Rass (Kashmiri Lamb Stock), 174–175
    Palak Rista (Kashmiri Spiced Lamb Meatballs with Spinach), 170–173, *171*
    Tabak Maaz (Kashmiri Ghee-Roasted Lamb Ribs), 168, *169*
land, food from the, 149–175. *See also* lamb
    Country Chicken Curry, 150–151, *152*
    Hoksa (Sirārakhong Hāthei Chilli–Braised Pork), 162, *163*
    Jammy Egg Curry, 156, *157*
    Pepper Pork, *153,* 154–155
    Sirārakhong Hāthei Chilli–Lemongrass Chicken and Rice, 158–161, *159–161*
lemon, 10
lemongrass
    about, 15
    Parippu Curry (Sri Lankan Lentils with Coconut and Lemongrass), *117,* 118–119
    Sirārakhong Hāthei Chilli–Lemongrass Chicken and Rice, 158–161, *159–161*
Lemon Rice, Andhra (Nimmakaya Pulihora), 180, *181*
lentils
    Ghee Roast Dosa (Fermented Rice and Lentil Crepes), 192–197, *193, 197*
    Idli (Steamed Lentil and Rice Cakes), 195–197, *196, 197*
    Khichdi (Rice and Lentil Porridge), 187
    Puran Poli (Jaggery and Lentil-Filled Flatbread), 240–241
Lotus Root Yogurt Curry, Kashmiri (Nadru Yakhni), 102–104, *103*

M

mace, 190–191
Mango Curry, Kerala-Style Ripe (Pazha Manga Curry), 94–95, *95*
Maple-Roasted Carrots, Spiced, with Carrot Top Sambol, 92, *93*
masala dabba, 4
matta rice, 18
meats. *See* lamb; land, food from the
Meen Moilee (Kerala-Style Coconut Turmeric Fish Curry), 138, *139*
Meen Pollichathu (Kerala-Style Tangy Grilled Fish in Banana Leaves), 140–141, *142*
Melon and Heirloom Tomato Salad, Bitter, 74, *75*
Methi Latte (Fenugreek Milk "Coffee"), 216, *217*
Mezcalita, Tangy Apricot (Hyun Mezcalita), 225–226, *227*
moong dal, whole, 17
mustard seed oil, 6
mustard seeds, 1

N

Nadru Yakhni (Kashmiri Lotus Root Yogurt Curry), 102–104, *103*
Nimmakaya Pulihora (Andhra Lemon Rice), 180, *181*
Noon Chai Concentrate, 214
Noon Chai (Kashmiri Savory Green Milk Tea), 214, *215*
nutmeg, 5, 190–191

O

Okra, Stir-Fried Spiced (Bhindi Masala), 88, *89*
onion
    Sakariya Fam Pakora (Mixed Herb and Onion Fritters), 66

Vengaya Thayir Pachadi (Red Onion Raita), 49, *49*
Orange Salad with Sesame-Cumin Dressing, Daikon and, 78–79, *79*

P

Pahadi Rajma (Himalayan Brothy Kidney Beans), 124–125, *125*
Pakora Party (Diaspora's Pakora), 64–65, *65*
Palli Chutney (Peanut Chutney), 44, 45
Pancakes, Kerala-Style Lacy Rice (Skillet Appams), *200*, 201–202, *202*
pandan leaves, 15
pantry
    about, xiv
    chillies and peppers, 7–10
    coconut, 12
    dal (lentils, pulses, and beans), 15–18
    fats, 6
    herbs and aromatics, 13–15
    recipe key and building blocks of, 19
    rice, 18
    salty foods, 10
    sour foods, 10–12
    spices, 1–5 (*see also individual spice names*)
    sweetener (jaggery), 12–13
    tadka technique and, 14
Parippu Curry (Sri Lankan Lentils with Coconut and Lemongrass), *117*, 118–119
Pazha Manga Curry (Kerala-Style Ripe Mango Curry), 94–95, *95*
pepper(s)
    Aranya peppercorns, 188–189
    black pepper, 1
    fresh peppers, 10 (*see also* chillies and peppers)
    Pepper Pork, *153,* 154–155
    Tellicherry peppercorns, 188–189
Pickle, Andhra-Style Tomato (Tomato Pachadi), 50, *51*
Pipinna Kiri Hodi (Sri Lankan Cucumber Coconut Milk Curry), *90,* 91
Pisyun Loon (Herb Spiced Salt), 28
podis, about, 26
poha rice, thick vs. thin, 18
Pol Roti (Sri Lankan Coconut Flatbread), 203
Pol Sambol (Sri Lankan Coconut and Shallot Chutney), 39, *40*
pork
    Hoksa (Sirārakhong Hāthei Chilli–Braised Pork), 162, *163*
    Pepper Pork, *153,* 154–155
Porridge, Rice and Lentil (Khichdi), 187
Potatoes, Spiced (Aloo Masala), 105
Prawn Head Roast (Kerala-Style Spicy Fried Shrimp Heads), 136–137, *138*
Prawns, Kerala-Style Grilled, 134, *135*
Puran Poli (Jaggery and Lentil-Filled Flatbread), 240–241

R

Raita, Red Onion (Vengaya Thayir Pachadi), 49, *49*
Rajasthani Dal, 120–121, *121*
Rajasthani Green Chutney, 36, *37*
rajma, 18
recipes, where to begin, 19
rice, breads, and scoopers, 177–207
    about rice, 18
    Bajra Na Rotla (Pearl Millet Flatbread), 204
    Coconut Lamb Biryani, 185–186, *186*
    Ghee Roast Dosa (Fermented Rice and Lentil Crepes), 192–197, *193, 197*
    Idli (Steamed Lentil and Rice Cakes), 195–197, *196, 197*
    Kappa Puzhukku (Kerala-Style Mashed Cassava), *205,* 205–206, *207*
    Kashmiri Pulao (Basmati Rice Pilaf with Nuts, Raisins, and Coconut), 178, *179*
    Khichdi (Rice and Lentil Porridge), 187
    Nimmakaya Pulihora (Andhra Lemon Rice), 180, *181*
    Pol Roti (Sri Lankan Coconut Flatbread), 203
    Skillet Appams (Kerala-Style Lacy Rice Pancakes), *200,* 201–202, *202*
    Sri Lankan Moringa String Hoppers, 198–199, *199*
    Thalassery Fish Biryani, *182,* 183–184
Ringan no Oro (Gujarati Charred Eggplant), 96–98, *97*

S

saffron
    about, 5, 86–87
    Apricot-Saffron Frangipane Galette, 234–236, *235*
    Kehwa (Kashmiri Spiced Saffron Tea), 218, *222*
Sakariya Fam Pakora (Mixed Herb and Onion Fritters), 66
salads
    Bitter Melon and Heirloom Tomato Salad, 74, *75*
    Daikon and Orange Salad with Sesame-Cumin Dressing, 78–79, *79*
    Edamame and Cherry Tomato Salad, *82,* 83
    Singju (Manipuri Cabbage Salad), 80, *81*
salts and salty foods, about, 10

Savory Pan-Fried Zucchini Cakes (Zucchini Na Muthiya), 67–69, *68*
seafood, 131–147
    about salted fish, 10
    Kakuluwo Curry (Jaffna-Style Crab Curry), 132–133, *133*
    Kanthari Chilli Squid (Kerala-Style Squid with Bird's-Eye Chillies, Cilantro, and Curry Leaves), 146–147, *147*
    Kerala-Style Grilled Prawns, 134, *135*
    Meen Moilee (Kerala-Style Coconut Turmeric Fish Curry), 138, *139*
    Meen Pollichathu (Kerala-Style Tangy Grilled Fish in Banana Leaves), 140–141, *142*
    Prawn Head Roast (Kerala-Style Spicy Fried Shrimp Heads), 136–137, *138*
    Sri Lankan Fish Puffs, 61–63, *62*
    Thalassery Fish Biryani, *182,* 183–184
    Thenga Aracha Meen Curry (Kerala-Style Fish and Fresh Coconut Curry), 144–145
Seasonal Sambar (South Indian Lentil Soup), 114–115, *116*
Sesame-Cumin Dressing, Daikon and Orange Salad with, 78–79, *79*
sesame oil, untoasted, 6
shrimp. *See individual prawn dishes*
Shrub, Apricot-Tamarind, 226
Shrub, Fennel, 220
Singju (Manipuri Cabbage Salad), 80, *81*
Sirārakhong Hāthei chillies
    about, 7, 70–71
    Hoksa (Sirārakhong Hāthei Chilli–Braised Pork), 162, *163*
    Sirārakhong Hāthei Chilli–Lemongrass Chicken and Rice, 158–161, *159–161*
Sivathei chillies, 7
Skillet Appams (Kerala-Style Lacy Rice Pancakes), *200,* 201–202, *202*
snacks, 57–71
    Doud Alle Dip (Roasted Squash and Labneh Dip), *58,* 59–60
    Pakora Party (Diaspora's Pakora), 64–65, *65*
    Sakariya Fam Pakora (Mixed Herb and Onion Fritters), 66
    Sri Lankan Fish Puffs, 61–63, *62*
    Zucchini Na Muthiya (Savory Pan-Fried Zucchini Cakes), 67–69, *68*
sona masoori rice, 18
Sorrel, Andhra-Style Dal with (Gongura Pappu), 108–109, *110*

soup and stock
    Chaaru (Andhra-Style Spicy Lentil Soup), *111,* 112–113
    Kadhi (Yogurt and Turmeric Soup), *122,* 123
    Kashmiri Stock (Cheat Version), 175
    Maaz Rass (Kashmiri Lamb Stock), 174–175
    Seasonal Sambar (South Indian Lentil Soup), 114–115, *116*
sour foods, 10–12
Spiced Chocolate-Coconut Cookies, *232,* 233
Spiced Date Cake with Coconut Caramel, 237–239, *238*
Spiced Maple-Roasted Carrots with Carrot Top Sambol, 92, *93*
spices and spice blends, 1–5, 21–33. *See also* Diaspora Spice Co.
    about spice trade history, vii
    about using, 2
    Andhra Chilli Powder, 23, *24*
    asafetida, 5
    black pepper, 1, 188–189
    cardamom, 1, 128–129
    cinnamon, 3, 32–33
    coriander seeds, 1, 55
    cumin seeds, 1, 84–85
    fennel seeds, 1, 55
    fenugreek seeds, 5
    Kalu Kudu (Sri Lankan Roasted Curry Powder), 22, *24*
    Karam Podi, aka Gunpowder Podi (Chilli Coconut Spice Blend), *25,* 26
    Karivepaku Podi (Curry Leaf Spice Blend), *25,* 27
    masala dabba for, 4
    mustard seeds, 1
    Pisyun Loon (Herb Spiced Salt), 28
    podis, about, 26
    saffron, 5, 86–87
    tadka technique and, 14
    tejpatta leaves, 3–5
    Tellicherry peppercorns, 188–189
    whole cloves, 3
split masoor dal, 15
split toor dal, 17–18
split white urad dal, 17
Squash, Roasted, and Labneh Dip (Doud Alle Dip), *58,* 59–60
Squid, Kerala-Style, with Bird's-Eye Chillies, Cilantro, and Curry Leaves (Kanthari Chilli Squid), 146–147, *147*
Sri Lankan Fish Puffs, 61–63, *62*

Sri Lankan Moringa String Hoppers, 198–199, *199*
String Hoppers, Sri Lankan Moringa, 198–199, *199*
sumac, 11–12
Sumac Soda, Manipuri (Heimang Soda), 224
sweetener (jaggery), 12–13

T

tadka technique, 14. *See also individual recipes*
tamarind, 11
Tamarind Shrub, Apricot, 226
tea. *See* drinks
tejpatta leaves, 3–5
Thalassery Fish Biryani, *182,* 183–184
Thenga Aracha Meen Curry (Kerala-Style Fish and Fresh Coconut Curry), 144–145
thick poha rice, 18
tomatoes
    Bitter Melon and Heirloom Tomato Salad, 74, *75*
    Burst Tomato Chutney, *47,* 48
    Edamame and Cherry Tomato Salad, *82,* 83
    Tomato Pachadi (Andhra-Style Tomato Pickle), 50, *51*
tools, source for, 126–127
toor dal, split, 17–18
turmeric
    about, 1, 30–31
    Haldi Doodh (Golden Turmeric Milk), 219, *222*
    Kadhi (Yogurt and Turmeric Soup), *122,* 123
    Meen Moilee (Kerala-Style Coconut Turmeric Fish Curry), 138, *139*
    Turmeric-Banana Snacking Cake, 230, *231*

U

untoasted sesame oil, 6
urad dal, 17

V

veggies, 73–105
    Aloo Masala (Spiced Potatoes), 105
    Bhindi Masala (Stir-Fried Spiced Okra), 88, *89*
    Bitter Melon and Heirloom Tomato Salad, 74, *75*
    Blistered Asparagus with Pisyun Loon, 76, *77*
    Daikon and Orange Salad with Sesame-Cumin Dressing, 78–79, *79*
    Edamame and Cherry Tomato Salad, *82,* 83
    Haakh (Kashmiri Braised Greens), 99–101, *100*
    Nadru Yakhni (Kashmiri Lotus Root Yogurt Curry), 102–104, *103*
    Pazha Manga Curry (Kerala-Style Ripe Mango Curry), 94–95, *95*
    Pipinna Kiri Hodi (Sri Lankan Cucumber Coconut Milk Curry), *90,* 91
    Ringan no Oro (Gujarati Charred Eggplant), 96–98, *97*
    Singju (Manipuri Cabbage Salad), 80, *81*
    Spiced Maple-Roasted Carrots with Carrot Top Sambol, 92, *93*
Vengaya Thayir Pachadi (Red Onion Raita), 49, *49*

W

Watalappam-ish Crème Caramel (Sri Lankan Spiced Caramelized Custard), *243,* 244–245
wazwan, 166, *167*
    Maaz Rass (Kashmiri Lamb Stock), 174–175
    Palak Rista (Kashmiri Spiced Lamb Meatballs with Spinach), 170–173, *171*
    Tabak Maaz (Kashmiri Ghee-Roasted Lamb Ribs), 168, *169*
white urad dal, split, 17
whole cloves, 3
whole moong dal, 17

Y

Yogurt and Turmeric Soup (Kadhi), *122,* 123
Yogurt Curry, Kashmiri Lotus Root (Nadru Yakhni), 102–104, *103*

Z

Zucchini Na Muthiya (Savory Pan-Fried Zucchini Cakes), 67–69, *68*

Without limiting the exclusive rights of any author, contributor or the publisher of this publication, any unauthorized use of this publication to train generative artificial intelligence (AI) technologies is expressly prohibited. HarperCollins also exercise their rights under Article 4(3) of the Digital Single Market Directive 2019/790 and expressly reserve this publication from the text and data mining exception.

THE DIASPORA SPICE CO. COOKBOOK. Copyright © 2026 by Diaspora Spice Co. All rights reserved. Printed in Malaysia. No part of this book may be used or reproduced in any manner whatsoever without written permission except in the case of brief quotations embodied in critical articles and reviews. For information, address HarperCollins Publishers, 195 Broadway, New York, NY 10007. In Europe, HarperCollins Publishers, Macken House, 39/40 Mayor Street Upper, Dublin 1, D01 C9W8, Ireland.

HarperCollins books may be purchased for educational, business, or sales promotional use. For information, please email the Special Markets Department at SPsales@harpercollins.com.

hc.com

FIRST EDITION

*Photographs by Melati Citrawireja
except for page vi by Gentl and Hyers
Illustrations by Aleesha Nandhra
Culinary assistant: Cyn Hollingshead
Food and prop styling by Jillian Knox*

Library of Congress Cataloging-in-Publication Data has been applied for.

ISBN 978-0-06-327782-3

26 27 28 29 30 PCA 10 9 8 7 6 5 4 3 2 1